Karl Mannheim's

Sociology of Knowledge

Karl Mannheim's Sociology of Knowledge

A. P. SIMONDS

Clarendon Press · Oxford
1978

Oxford University Press, Walton Street, Oxford OX2 6DP

OXFORD LONDON GLASGOW NEW YORK
TORONTO MELBOURNE WELLINGTON CAPE TOWN
IBADAN NAIROBI DAR ES SALAAM LUSAKA
KUALA LUMPUR SINGAPORE JAKARTA HONG KONG TOKYO
DELHI BOMBAY CALCUTTA MADRAS KARACHI

© *A. P. Simonds 1978*

British Library Cataloguing in Publication Data

Simonds, A P
  Karl Mannheim's sociology of knowledge.
  1. Mannheim, Karl   2. Knowledge, Sociology of
  I. Title
  301.2'1   BD175.M323   77–30733

ISBN 0–19–827238–3

Typesetting by Burgess & Son (Abingdon) Ltd.
and printed in Great Britain by
Richard Clay & Co Ltd, Bungay.

For
Ruth Simonds and Robert Simonds,
my teachers of longest standing,
with respect, appreciation, and thanks

Preface

THIS BOOK is intended to provide an introduction to the work of Karl Mannheim and also an introduction to the sociology of knowledge. To a considerable extent, of course, these objectives overlap but the reader should notice that they are not identical and indeed that each interferes to some extent with the accomplishment of the other. This is neither a systematic theoretical account of the sociology of knowledge nor an intellectual biography of Mannheim but a certain sort of compromise between the two. Because I wanted to call attention to a particular achievement, I have excluded (beyond an occasional passing reference) consideration of the work of others such as Vilfredo Pareto, Émile Durkheim, Max Scheler, or George Herbert Mead who conceived the problem of a sociology of knowledge quite differently. Similarly, consideration of a tradition of ideological analysis which runs from Marx to such diverse contemporary figures as Jürgen Habermas, Louis Althusser, Karel Kosík, and E. P. Thompson, has been left for another occasion—though here I believe that substantial and important connections need to be made. On the other hand, because my interest in Mannheim's work has been a constructive as well as an expositive one, I have not hesitated to select, reformulate, and develop from his arguments in order to reappraise certain of the unresolved issues of contemporary social theory. Thus much on the following pages concerns the work of writers who might not be expected to make an appearance in a discussion of the sociology of knowledge: for instance, H. P. Grice, Stuart Hampshire, E. D. Hirsch, Peter Winch, Quentin Skinner, Charles Taylor, and Stephen Toulmin. This double reference to a collection of essays written more than fifty years ago and to the debates of recent philosophers of social inquiry is, I think, entirely consistent with the approach which Mannheim himself always invited. Mannheim sought in his reader a participant rather than an observer. Understanding in social studies, as in life itself, requires (he believed) an act of attention which is both outward, using every available resource to grasp authentically the message of the other, and also inward, taking advantage of this new perspective to question and rethink the most familiar and accepted propositions of our own universe of thought. In recommending that contemporary readers reacquaint themselves with Mannheim's early writings, I would like to encourage both of these activities of the intellect.

During the years in which I have been occupied with this book, I have enjoyed the help, encouragement, friendship, and support of a great many persons, among whom I especially wish to thank Maria H. M. Alves, Christopher Brewin, Juan Corradi, Louis Hartz, Leonard Kirsch, Alasdair MacIntyre, Jeremy J. Shapiro, Daisy Tagliacozzo, and Kurt H. Wolff.

Quotations from *Ideology and Utopia* (Harcourt Brace Jovanovich and Routledge and Kegan Paul) and *From Karl Mannheim* (Oxford University Press, New York), are reprinted here by kind permission of their publishers.

University of Massachusetts at Boston   A. P. S.
Department of Political Science
June 1977

Contents

Abbreviations used in referring to Mannheim's writings

DT   *Diagnosis of Our Time: Essays of a Sociologist* (Routledge & Kegan Paul, London, 1943)

ESC   *Essays on the Sociology of Culture*, ed. and trans. Ernest Manheim and Paul Kecskemeti (Routledge & Kegan Paul, London, 1956)

ESK   *Essays on the Sociology of Knowledge*, ed. Paul Kecskemeti (Routledge & Kegan Paul, London, 1952)

ESSP   *Essays on Sociology and Social Psychology*, ed. Paul Kecskemeti (Routledge & Kegan Paul, 1953)

FKM   *From Karl Mannheim*, ed. Kurt H. Wolff (Oxford University Press, New York, 1971)

FR   'The Function of the Refugee: A Rejoinder', *The New English Weekly*, 27 (19 Apr. 1945): 5–6

IAU   *Ideology and Utopia*, trans. Louis Wirth and Edward Shils (Harvest Books, New York, n.d.)

IUU   *Ideologie and Utopie*, Fünfte Auflage (Verlag G. Schulte-Bulmke, Frankfurt/Main, 1969)

WAW   *Wissenssoziologie: Auswahl aus dem Werk*, ed. Kurt H. Wolff (Hermann Luchterhand Verlag, Neuwied/Rhein and Berlin, 1964)

1.

Introduction: Mannheim in Retrospect

SHORTLY BEFORE the final defeat of Hitler's armies in 1945, a review in *The New English Weekly* warned of a 'Germanization of Britain' which threatened the health and vigour of English Reason with exposure to the 'infection' of German speculative thought. The sounder of this alarm, Montgomery Belgion, traced the threat to a diverse collection of sources (including Goethe, Marx, Schopenhauer, and Nietzsche) but devoted most of his attention to two contemporary 'illustrations': H. A. Hodges's recently published *Wilhelm Dilthey: An Introduction,* and the work of the immigrant sociologist Karl Mannheim. Belgion's complaints were essentially confused and grievously lacking in substance, but they stimulated a lively exchange in subsequent issues which included Herbert Read's rather deflating observation that Mannheim was not German after all but Hungarian, and T. S. Eliot's avowal of the importance of having German thought available to disagree with: 'No contemporary thinker', the latter concluded, 'has more enriched my mental life in this way than Dr. Mannheim, to whom I feel I owe a considerable debt.'[1]

The crudity of Belgion's attack made easy Mannheim's own rejoinder, which proved to be one of the last of his writings to appear before his death in January 1947. Although quite brief in keeping with the immediate journalistic occasion, Mannheim's comments expressed many of the most pervasive and deep-seated themes of his entire life work. Methods appropriate to the study of the physical world, he argued, cannot be simply transferred to social phenomena; a 'wooden type of empiricism' relying entirely upon 'measurement and the description of external relations' is necessarily excluded from comprehension of 'the most important

---

[1] Belgion, 1945, pp. 137–8. The letters from Read and Eliot may be found in the issues of 1 and 29 Mar. 1945.

factors in human life'. Unless methods of interpretation (the development of which must be credited to some of the thinkers most abhorred by Belgion) are admitted to the social sciences, 'you blind yourself to the understanding of motivation and purpose—in a word, to the understanding of the share the human mind has in social affairs'. But more significant than the strength or weakness of his argument, Mannheim suggested in closing, was Belgion's fear of an 'invasion' of foreign thought and the attitude toward the refugee which this entailed.

Mannheim's views of 'the function of the refugee' were not, of course, detached: he wrote as a man whose life had been carved into three parts by political exile. The establishment of the counter-revolutionary Horthy regime in his native Budapest had made him a refugee in Weimar Germany in 1920; the triumph of Nazism made him a refugee for a second time in London in 1933. And among the many political nomads of modern European history, none was more attentive to the intellectual, the cultural, and the moral significance of his situation than Mannheim. The refugee, he claimed against Belgion, should consider his background neither a source of infection nor an embarrassing memory in his new environment. His responsibility, rather, is to bring his novel 'perspective' to bear upon his adopted society, and in so doing to facilitate an 'interpenetration of ideas' that, Mannheim insisted, is not only desirable but essential to the prospects for a decent human order.[2] Mannheim's own life expressed a continuous effort to discharge this responsibility.

I

A full account of this life has yet to be written; even the briefest biographical sketch, however, reveals the the variety of influences and associations that touched upon his intellectual career. Mannheim was born of a Hungarian father and a German mother in Budapest in 1893, and he received his early training in the distinctive cultural environment, at once intimate and cosmopolitan, of that central European capital.[3] The Budapest intellectual community in this period was animated by a vigorous and highly conscious sense of mission: to open the country to the influence of western ideas and by so doing to stimulate national reform and

[2] FR, pp. 5, 6.
[3] By far the most valuable source for Mannheim's Hungarian period is Kettler, 1971; see also, Tôkés, 1967, and the brief note of Gabel, 1975.

cultural renewal. Measured by the number of individuals involved, the significance of this movement was modest, confined for the most part to circles and societies outside of the established institutional framework of the universities, in a capital city that was itself almost entirely isolated from the rest of the country. Yet its influence, as so often is the case when a traditional social order is sharply challenged from the outside, bore little relation to the size of its ranks. The reformist intellectuals comprised, as the leading historian of the period has put it, 'a handful of people, who—talking to one another, writing for one another—made one another believe (and perhaps also believed) that an army stood behind them. And they actually managed it so that power did not merely argue with them in a theoretical way, but also had to include them into its calculations.'[4]

Mannheim was involved in the activities of a number of these groups while a student at the University of Budapest between 1912 and 1918. He attended meetings of the Social-Scientific Society, a group of vaguely socialist orientation somewhat similar to the English Fabians, and was a member of a radical lodge of freemasons which was associated both in membership and in programme with that society. Most important, however, was his participation in a small group, founded and dominated by the already celebrated critic Georg Lukács, which engaged in extended discussions every Sunday afternoon and evening during the war years. Although a number of its members were to follow Lukács's example in joining the Hungarian Communist Party at the end of 1918, the concern of the circle was not with politics (at least directly) but with philosophy, literature, and religion. Its members were preoccupied with what they judged to be a major 'crisis of culture' and they devoted their attention to the problem of making spiritual (in the sense of the German *geistliche*) renewal possible. This programme of cultural renovation, advanced in conscious opposition to the positivizing and 'scientistic' programme of the Social-Scientific Society, was the subject of a series of public lectures which the group's 'Free School for Studies of the Human Spirit' sponsored in the Autumn of 1917. In his introductory lecture on 'Soul and Culture', Mannheim described the orientation of the group, summarized its main principles and concerns, gave voice to its (rather extravagant) hopes for a 'renewal of culture', and concluded with a description of the

[1] Zoltán Horvárth, quoted by Kettler, 1971, p. 40.

programme of lecturers to come—an illustrious list that included
the poet Béla Balázs, the art historian Arnold Hauser, composers
Zoltán Kodály and Béla Bartók, as well as Lukács and
Mannheim.[5]

Mannheim was not among those of Lukács's circle who joined
the Communist Party, but he retained his ties to the group and
indeed attempted (unsuccessfully) to keep it alive after Lukács
took up his active political role in the establishment of the
Hungarian Soviet Republic in March 1919. In the following
month, Lukács, serving as deputy Commissar for Culture in the
new government, appointed Mannheim professor of philosophy at
the University. But with the collapse of the Commune and the
inauguration of the White Terror shortly thereafter, all experi-
ments with cultural revolution came to an abrupt end; Mannheim
and some hundred thousand others avoided death or imprison-
ment at home by taking up an exile's residence abroad.

Like most Hungarian intellectuals, Mannheim was no stranger
to German academic life. He had interrupted his residence at the
University of Budapest to study in Berlin (where he had taken
courses with Georg Simmel) as well as Heidelberg, Freiburg, and
Paris in 1912–14. He returned to Heidelberg in 1920 and worked
there for ten years, habilitating as a *Privatdozent* in 1926. Toward
the end of his life, Mannheim was to look back on the Weimar
period as 'a new Periclean age',[6] and unquestionably these were
years in which the exchange of intellectual positions showed a
special intensity and creative vigour. The debates of the period
addressed issues that have proved to be of perennial concern to
twentieth-century social thought: the relationship of the sciences
of man to the sciences of nature, of values to facts, of claims for the
historicity of truth to the anti-metaphysical programme of
positivism. And the debate was charged by the general assumption
that the resolution of such philosophical and methodological
questions directly implicated one's moral and political position.[7]
Mannheim's investigations in this decade issued in a series of
papers which include his most significant work: an essay 'On the
Interpretation of *Weltanschauung*' (published in 1921–2), an essay
on 'Historicism' (1924), a discussion of 'The Problem of a

[5] WAW, pp. 66–84.
[6] In a conversation with Hannah Arendt, reported in Gay, 1970, p. xiv.
[7] Hughes, 1961, Gay, 1970, Ringer, 1969, and Struve, 1973, provide helpful
introductions to this chapter of intellectual history.

Sociology of Knowledge' (1925), an investigation of nineteenth-century German 'Conservative Thought' (1927), a paper on 'Competition as a Cultural Phenomenon' (first presented in 1928), and his most famous work, *Ideology and Utopia* (1929), itself composed of two essays ('Is Politics Possible as a Science?' and 'The Utopian Consciousness') tied together with an introduction bearing the title of the book. (The 1936 English edition, of which more will be said below, added a 1931 Encyclopedia article on 'The Sociology of Knowledge' and a further introduction written especially for the translation.) In these essays, which will be the primary subject matter of the present study, Mannheim presented an evolving, many-sided, but also (as I shall argue) ultimately coherent view of the nature of social knowledge and the means by which it is acquired—a view which he came to identify by the not altogether precise rubric 'sociology of knowledge'. The influences on Mannheim's work in this period were as manifold as the movements which made him find Weimar intellectual life so stimulating: the Heidelberg neo-Kantianism of Lask and Weber, the phenomenology of Husserl and Scheler, the historicism of Dilthey and Troeltsch, the Marxism of Lukács.

But the image of a 'new Periclean age' fails to capture the other, more ominous side of the Weimar environment to which a foreign Jew of leftist sympathies must have been particularly vulnerable. The German academic establishment remained firmly anti-democratic and anti-modernist; the dominant climate of opinion, both among faculty and students, was hostile to the Republic, to socialism, to Jewishness, to pacifism, indeed to any kind of critical stance toward the extravagant and uncompromising mythology of German nationalism. Fritz Ringer, who gives a chilling account of the effects of this 'mandarin tradition' in Weimar academic life, reports that other than Mannheim and his friend Emil Lederer, he could identify only four Social Democrats teaching at the universities of Berlin, Freiburg, Heidelberg, or Munich. The most comfortable environment for academics of socialist or republican sympathies in this period was to be found at Frankfurt, and the publication of *Ideology and Utopia* brought Mannheim an invitation to succeed Franz Oppenheimer to the chair which was, at the time, the only full professorship in sociology in Germany. At Frankfurt Mannheim shared office space with the Marxist Institute of Social Research, and while his relationship with its members seems to have been a cool one, he shared with its director Max Horkheimer the unhappy honour of being in the first group of faculty to be dismissed by the Nazis on 13 April 1943. (The wife of another member of this group, Mannheim's friend Paul Tillich, recalls in her memoirs: 'Karl had been called by the president of the university, who urged him and the others to resign from the unversity, to help the endangered institution. His answer had been just short of contempt, "You must throw us out".'[8])

Mannheim's second journey into exile took him to England where, in Autumn 1933, he became a lecturer in sociology at the London School of Economics. Mannheim was acutely aware of being an outsider to the Anglo-American tradition of social science, but equally he was concerned with exploiting the opportunity (which he felt this position afforded him) for establishing productive contact across traditions. His last writings in Germany as well as his first in England addressed this theme[9] and, as we have seen in his response to Belgion, it remained of special concern to him until his death. This effort to make a successful crossing from German to English sociology can also be viewed, somewhat less charitably, in terms of Mannheim's desire to find academic acceptance in his new environment. Certainly we observe a decided change of emphasis in his published work after 1933; the concerns of the German writings on the sociology of knowledge recede into the background (though they do not entirely disappear), and the problems of social planning and reform in the context of the liberal state come into prominence. This shift of interest was coupled with a search for a wider audience: Mannheim's English contributions appear increasingly in the form of articles for a non-specialist public, addresses to educators and administrators, B.B.C. lectures, etc. In the last decade of his life he participated in a small group (composed, in addition to his friend Adolf Löwe, of a number of influential Christian thinkers including Joseph Oldham, J. Middleton Murray, and T. S. Eliot) that met three or four times a year to discuss 'recent changes in society and their relevance for Christianity'.[10] His growing preoccupation with the reconstruction of public education eventuated in his acceptance of a position at the Institute of Education at the University of London in 1946.

[8] Ringer, 1969, p. 497n. and *passim;* Salomon, 1947, p. 354; Jay, 1973, pp. 29, 63; Tillich, 1973, p. 153.
[9] See especially the 1932 review 'American Sociology' and the 1934 essay on 'German Sociology (1919–1933)' in ESSP, pp. 185–208.
[10] See the concluding essay, 'Towards a New Social Philosophy: A Challenge to Christian Thinkers by a Sociologist' in DT, pp. 100–65.

He was offered the post of director of the European UNESCO just prior to his death in the following January.

With the exception of a few glances backward and forward, this book confines its attention entirely to the writings of Mannheim's German period. It is thus concerned with his contribution to the clarification of a particular set of problems, and makes no pretence of offering an account of his intellectual biography as a whole. This approach is dictated by the belief, not only that Mannheim's main achievement is to be found in this early work, but that renewed acquaintance with these writings may persuade a new generation of readers of the pertinence and vitality of his sociology of knowledge.

II

One way of characterizing a field of study is by listing its classics, which is to say those texts that have come to be accepted as standard points of reference in the literature of the field and which reappear on the reading lists of its courses of instruction year after year. *Ideology and Utopia* has enjoyed such a reputation among English-speaking social scientists ever since the appearance of the 1936 translation. The volume has undergone repeated printings, has been regarded as important by generations of sociologists and political scientists, and is routinely included among the 'major works' surveyed in textbooks of twentieth-century thought. And yet the contents of the book, its arguments, its method, its *point*, have remained oddly problematic and out of focus. Again and again, for instance, one finds this collection of essays referred to as a 'systematic treatise' on the sociology of knowledge—a description which is scarcely appropriate and which seems to be founded less on the evidence of the text itself than on a kind of tacit supposition that a book which has established itself as a classic of modern social thought must be a systematic treatise of some sort or another. Considering its long-standing popularity, the demonstrable impact of *Ideology and Utopia* has been surprisingly modest: the kind of investigation which Mannheim hoped to stimulate and the methods of inquiry which he sought to develop and recommend have not been paid much explicit attention, much less carried forward and elaborated, by the mainstream of twentieth-century social science, and those individual scholars who might be said to share something of his approach and his concerns have rarely related their own work to his. Although Mannheim's general reputation seems secure, the *basis* of this reputation (in the content of his writings) has remained remarkably vague.

Closer inspection of the secondary literature that has been devoted to *Ideology and Utopia* and Mannheim's sociology of knowledge strengthens this impression, for it is extremely difficult to reconcile the picture which emerges from such discussion with the reputation that would seem appropriate even to a minor classic. One notices, first of all, that while the body of writing on various conceptions of 'the sociology of knowledge' is large and sprawling, critical analysis concerned specifically with Mannheim is sparse. Mannheim has been a rare subject for book-length treatment, and while brief discussions of his work may be found in practically any survey of the period or the discipline, these rarely develop an interpretation or critique in any depth.[11] Most of the commentary which does exist, moreover, is decidedly unsympathetic. Discussions typically begin with some kind of acknowledgement of Mannheim's importance as a 'major figure' of the field, and proceed quickly to reject or discount precisely those parts of his work which Mannheim himself considered the most essential and significant. A more forthright brand of criticism dispenses even with the prefatory gestures of respect; the sociology of knowledge has been charged with providing the 'philosophical foundation of totalitarian ideology', Mannheim's claims dismissed as 'sheer bluff', and his work characterized as possessing a 'particular *naiveté*' composed of 'ancient and banal ideas'.[12] When a recent writer makes the very unusual claim that Mannheim 'was *the* inventor of contemporary sociology', it is not to praise Mannheim but to condemn contemporary sociology.[13] Whether patronized or repudiated, Mannheim's contribution rarely receives more than a perfunctory hearing.

The problem with this literature is that Mannheim's work is not only dismissed, it is rendered unintelligible. Mannheim's critics come from very diverse camps, both philosophically and politically, but they are remarkably consistent—one might even say monotonous—about their choice of arguments to 'refute' him. The most important critiques were published in the early thirties

---

[11] Book-length or near book-length sources in English include Maquet, 1951; Rempel, 1965; Connolly, 1967; Remmling, 1975; and the papers of Wolff, 1974. The periodical literature, much of which has been reprinted in book form, is a bit larger: see Curtis and Petras, 1970; Remmling, 1973.

[12] See Crick, 1964, p. 46; Watkins, 1956, p. 258; Aron, 1964, pp. 57, 61.

[13] Sahay, 1971, p. 78.

by Ernst Grünwald and Alexander von Schelting.[14] Since that time, one writer after another has been content to recapitulate their arguments, often without acknowledgement and typically without the subtlety of the original formulation. As a result, what passes for Mannheim criticism is rarely more than a thoroughly standardized itemization of his 'blunders': failure to avoid the self-destructive consequences of relativism, commission of the genetic fallacy, illegitimate reduction of the cultural 'superstructure' to a material 'base', hypostatization of a collective 'mind', etc.

Now charges such as these raise a great number of serious difficulties, and it may seem churlish to complain of the continued repetition of a standard critique if that critique happens to be sound. (My own reasons for concluding that it must be rejected will only be developed later on.) The problem here, however, is that the effect of the critique is not so much to undermine Mannheim's answers as to distort and obscure his questions. The blunders charged to his sociology of knowledge are, after all, rather obvious ones; Mannheim would have had to have been both naive and obtuse to have failed to notice them. Yet we discover from his writings that not only was he aware of such arguments, they are in almost every case identical to arguments which had been proposed and discussed by Mannheim himself in his earliest work. The papers of the mid-twenties are significant not merely because they represent the first steps in the development of his sociology of knowledge but also because (and this is but another way of expressing the same thing) they express a reasoned and deliberate decision to part company with the framework of assumptions that governed previous discussion (including some of his own) about the nature of the relation between social and cultural phenomena and the consequences of this relation for socio-historical investigation. Mannheim's reflections led him to the conculsion that the problem itself had been improperly construed, and that the effect of the standard arguments about relativism and reductionism was to pose false (or at least thoroughly misleading) alternatives—alternatives which serve to obstruct rather than to advance inquiry. Mannheim may, of course, have been quite unsuccessful in his attempts to fashion a more satisfactory approach to the problem, but criticism is pointless if it fails to grasp the nature of his enterprise. Those who have been quick to repeat the standard

---

[14] Grünwald, 1934, *passim;* Schelting, 1934, pt. 3. The essence of Schelting's critique appeared in English in his 1936 review of *Ideology and Utopia.*

criticisms of his sociology of knowledge have too often been entirely uncritical about the very presuppositions which this work had endeavoured to call into question. In supposing that his position can be refuted so simply, these critics ignore or obscure the process of thought which led Mannheim to the sociology of knowledge and which makes his defence of it intelligible.

A critic who is content merely to identify the blunders of a serious thinker always runs a considerable risk of misunderstanding him. Unless there are very good reasons for supposing that the writer in question was unaware of or indifferent to the trap into which he is alleged to have fallen, it behoves the critic to ask some further questions. Why did the writer, who must have given considerable thought to this objection, nevertheless decide that it was misplaced? What reasons could have convinced him that so great and obvious a danger could be accepted? Did he judge the danger to be illusory or uncompelling, or was he persuaded that the only alternative to it was other, still more serious, consequences for the argument? In either case, what were the grounds of his belief? Above all, what was the theoretical objective that he regarded as so important that it justified such risks? Inquiry of this type is especially important to the evaluation of Mannheim's sociology of knowledge, for there exists quite unambiguous textual evidence that he was from the outset acutely conscious of and attentive to the type of argument that was later to be brought against him.

The issue of relativism may serve as an example. Mannheim's claim for the existentiality of thought, it is suggested, impugns itself just as surely as did that of Epimenides the Cretan who maintained that all Cretans are liars. Few of his critics fail to point to this paradox of self-reference, often with an air of having made an extraordinary discovery.[15] Mannheim's arguments in support of what he calls a 'relationist' position are dismissed as a purely defensive move in which, having been made aware of his blunder, he attempts to protect his position by confusing the issue. Treated in this way, Mannheim's claim becomes nothing more than a

---

[15] Some examples: Grünwald, 1934, pp. 228–32; Schelting, 1934, pp. 666–7; Dahlke, 1940, p. 87; Kecskemeti, 1952, pp. 28–9; Hartung, 1970, pp. 698, 704; Bottomore, 1956, p. 55; Popper, 1963, vol. 2, pp. 216, 230, 353–65; Louch, 1969, p. 205; Walter, 1967, p. 349; Fuse, 1967, p. 249. No one familiar with the work of these writers can fail to be impressed by their unanimity on this point, which is often expressed in near identical language.

'verbal ruse'[16] which is at best trivial, while at worst it serves to disguise the relativist wolf in sheep's clothing. (Lukács expressed the common view when he suggested that 'the distinction between relativism and relationism is about the same as Lenin's distinction, in a letter to Gorki, between a yellow and a green devil.'[17]) But Mannheim's grasp of the dangers of self-referential inconsistency is far more sophisticated than this account allows, and his espousal of relationism is the conclusion of a set of theoretical moves that begin not with an innocent or ill-considered relativism but with its opposite. In his doctoral dissertation on the 'Structural Analysis of Epistemology', originally written in 1917–18 and published in 1922, the destructive consequences of relativism are uppermost in his mind. While the claims of historicity must be acknowledged, he argues, 'all too often the mistake is made of trying to explain the meaning itself with reference to the temporal features of the works in question—with reference to empirical, real factors. If we seek to validate or invalidate meanings by means of such factors, we shall inescapably fall into relativism.' This point reappears a few pages later:

...we are altogether receptive to a doctrine that tries hard to do justice—maybe even more than justice—to the meaning of history. Yet we believe that such a doctrine is bound to become entangled in difficulties which are roughly the same as beset straight historicism owing to the relativism to which it necessarily leads. The indubitable fact that everything in history is subject to change must not be carried over into the realm of meaning and validity; by doing so, we should unwittingly controvert our own assertions.[18]

In taking a stand against relativism Mannheim was also, of course, warning against the genetic fallacy. Schelting's influential dismissal of *Ideology and Utopia* ('the nonsense first begins when one believes that factual origin and social factors as such ... in any way affect the value of ideas and conceptions thus originated, and especially the theoretic value—which is to say, the truth—of cognitive achievements')[19] turns out to be a virtual paraphrase of remarks Mannheim made in his dissertation, and also in an

---

[16] Horowitz, 1964, p. 53.
[17] Lukács, 1962, p. 549.
[18] ESSP, pp. 37, 40n. (WAW, pp. 196–7, 200n.); see also, pp. 27–8 (WAW, pp. 182–4). Other than Grünwald (1934, p. 267n.) critics of Mannheim's relationism rather uniformly ignore this reference.
[19] Schelting, 1936, p. 674; cf. also his volume of 1934, pp. 157–8.

unpublished typescript (dated September 1922) 'On the Peculiarity of Cultural-sociological Knowledge':

The truth or falsity of a proposition or of the entire theoretical sphere can be neither supported nor attacked by means of a sociological or any other genetic explanation. How something came to be, what functions it performs in other contexts is altogether irrelevant for its immanent character of validity.[20]

When Mannheim moved away from this position, in the series of essays published between 1924 and 1926 on historical and sociological interpretation, it was not because of some reckless and incomprehensible lapse into philosophical *naiveté* but rather (as he puts it in the introduction to another unpublished piece which dates from this period) because he had been forced 'after extensive reconsideration, to the conclusion that even the purely methodological problems of thought cannot be solved without sociological orientation'.[21] The problem of relativism has been something of a red herring in discussions of Mannheim's work—not because it is not in itself a serious issue, but because it discourages any appraisal of the nature and function of the sociology of knowledge as Mannheim intended it to be understood. The charge of relativism provides a licence to disregard the integral meaning of the texts taken together and in the context of their development. Instead, they are merely scoured for this or that formulation which seems to convict or acquit him of the charge. The critic who finds a preponderance of the former sort of statements concludes that he is guilty as charged and that the sociology of knowledge therefore refutes itself. The critic who determines that he has avoided relativism certifies that the accused is harmless enough, but in so doing neutralizes and emasculates the substantive claims that he has made. Both judgements manage, with equal effectiveness, to avoid all that is truly challenging in Mannheim's work. The sociology of knowledge has thus suffered the classic fate of a position which questions orthodoxy in a fundamental way: if the heretic is condemned, then his position is by that fact confirmed as diabolical; if he is allowed to go free, it is because his position has

---

[20] 'Über die Eigenart kultursoziologischer Erkenntnis' p. 80. This passage, and the one that follows, are quoted from a masterful paper by David Kettler (1967) who is responsible for making these unpublished writings available. My dept to Kettler's work is enormous; his writings on Mannheim (as also those of Kurt Wolff) stand in striking contrast to the more conventional critical literature which is discussed here.

[21] 'Eine soziologische Theorie der Kultur und ihrer Erkennbarkeit', p. 1, cited in Kettler, 1967, p. 401. Both this and the essay cited in the preceding note have been deposited in the archives of the Library at Trent University, Ontario, Canada.

been either disavowed or successfully assimilated to orthodoxy and thereby rendered pointless.

This second (and basically well-meaning) verdict is also much in evidence. In fact, Mannheim's most sympathetic audience is probably to be found among those who have the least interest in the theoretical claims of the sociology of knowledge, and who are ready to jettison his troublesome ideas about 'existentiality' *(Seinsverbundenheit)* in favour of his more concrete historical investigations and policy studies. In this way, it is supposed, the ill-effects of his German philosophic heritage may be cleared away and his contributions to Anglo-American social science brought into view, 'shorn of their epistemological impedimenta'.[22] This approach to the writings is often excused by the suggestion that Mannheim himself authorized it, at least in a tacit way, when he changed his intellectual direction after moving to England in 1933. An account of this break is certainly one of the most important problems facing Mannheim's biographer, for it raises a number of interesting and still not very clearly understood questions (concerning, for instance, Mannheim's relationship to his English and American editors and translators). But the challenge it poses to a study of the sociology of knowledge is a somewhat simpler one: did Mannheim 'outgrow' his sociology of knowledge, and can we take his failure to pursue the line of thought begun in Germany as a quiet concession of defeat? (To put the question in the terms of another, more recent debate about some early writings, did Mannheim's work undergo a *coupure épistémologique* which separates a 'pre-scientific' from a 'scientific' period, with the implication that the latter repudiates the former?) Aside from the fact that the 'mature' Mannheim's assessment need not determine our own, a reading which finds in the later work justification for disregarding the central tenets of the sociology of knowledge (and in particular, the problematic notion of 'relationism') is not truly born out by the record. The difference between relationism and relativism is articulated and defended in Mannheim's 1934 survey of German sociology.[23] In the second of a series of lectures on social planning and personality delivered in 1938 he discusses patterns of social influence upon the unconscious and conscious mind of the individual in a manner

[22] Merton, 1957, p. 508. Similar assessments may be found in Salomon, 1947, Parsons, 1967, Neisser, 1965.
[23] ESSP, p. 212; cf. pp. 220–1.

designed to apply the methods of the sociology of knowledge to the
task of understanding the planning process.[24] The same concern
appears repeatedly in the English version of *Man and Society in an
Age of Reconstruction*. But the least ambiguous indication of
Mannheim's continued belief in the radical claims of his sociology
of knowledge appears in writings not intended for publication
which date from the very last year of his life. In a letter to Kurt H.
Wolff in 1946, Mannheim wrote:

On the one hand, our most advanced empirical investigations, especially
those which come from history, psychology, and sociology, show that the
human mind with its whole categorical apparatus is a dynamic entity.
Whereas our predominant epistemology derives from an age, the hidden
desire and ideal of which was stability, the traditional epistemology still
thinks of concepts as reflecting eternal ideas. . . .

Now, whereas one part of our progressive insight convinces us that
language and logic are also a part of culture which, in its turn—most people
would agree on that—is different with different tribes and in different epochs
and therefore nothing can be stated but in relation to a frame of reference; the
other part of our intellectual orientation through its traditional epistemology
cannot put up with this insight. The latter is reluctant to accept this because it
failed to build into its theory the fact of the essential perspectivism of human
knowledge. . . .

I hope this is intelligible and it at least convinces you and your seminar that
if there are contradictions they are not due to my shortsightedness but to the
fact that I want to break through the old epistemology radically but have not
succeeded yet fully.[25]

Nor is this an isolated lapse. The subject of 'relationsim' is
discussed in detail in a series of lectures delivered during the same
year—only months before his death the following January.[26]
Mannheim's late work may be distinctive, but it is scarcely
repentant.

All of this leads to the conclusion that Mannheim's early work
has simply not received an adequate hearing. The main effect of
nearly three generations of critique, whether in the form of a stern
repetition of a litany of blunders or a more mild scolding for the
indiscretions of youth, has been an almost total neglect of the spirit
and the point (as well as the letter) of the texts themselves. A
collection of critical conventions about Mannheim's views has

---

[24] ESSP, pp. 272–6.
[25] Quoted in Wolff, 1974, pp. 557–8.
[26] Again our debt is to Kettler, 1967, p. 401, who discovered this text in the file labelled
'Principles of Education Lectures, 1946' in the collection of Mannheim materials at the
University of Keele.

come to stand in the place of those views themselves; what he actually wrote in *Ideology and Utopia* and the related papers has been both faded and distorted by the critical lens that has been held up to them. To recover his meaning it is necessary to return to these texts afresh.

One final problem regarding access to the texts must by recognized by English-speaking readers. However problematic Mannheim's reputation may be, it has been established primarily by means of translation. With minor exceptions, all of Mannheim's German publications have appeared in English versions, and these translations have had far wider circulation than have the originals. The number of copies of *Ideology and Utopia* sold in the United States alone has been some twenty times greater than the number sold in Germany;[27] the essays from the twenties that became available in English editions in the early fifties were only collected in an accessible German edition in 1964. In an important sense, it is the English rather than the original German editions of the texts upon which Mannheim's reputation rests.

In the case of *Ideology and Utopia,* the pre-eminence of the English version stems from more than a matter of the size and number of editions. As was mentioned earlier, the 1936 edition was larger than the 1929 German original; it included an essay on the sociology of knowledge that Mannheim had written for the *Handwörterbuch der Soziologie* (1931) and an opening chapter 'especially written to introduce the present volume to the Anglo-Saxon reader'.[28] In addition, one of the translators (the American sociologist Louis Wirth) added a preface that was designed for the same purpose. When a new German edition appeared after the war, it followed this arrangement, reproducing the encyclopedia article and adding a German translation of both Mannheim's English introduction and Wirth's preface. The French translation which appeared in 1956 accepted the authority of the English edition in a still more astounding way: not only the new preface and introductory chapter but also the material originally published in German was translated *from the English*.[29] Needless to say, Mannheim's English-reading critics have rarely seen any point in going back to the German publications from which the far more accessible English editions were prepared.

[27] Wolff, 1971, p. lxi n.
[28] IAU, p. viii.
[29] See the discussion in Gabel, 1974, pp. 259–64.

This circumstance may have made a difference to the terms of Mannheim's reception. For in spite of the translator's promise, in the Foreword, 'to adhere as closely as possible to the German text',[30] the English version of *Ideology and Utopia* departs in many ways from the original and the translations of all Mannheim's writings are problematic. Wolff has pointed out that the Wirth and Shils version 'replaces relatively idiosyncratic German by relatively standardized English, thus presenting us with a book of a character quite different from the original'.[31] Kettler, who has examined this matter extremely carefully, claims to have found 'over four hundred shifts in meaning which do not seem to be ordinary products of translation'.[32] These shifts, some of which will be commented upon as we go along, may indeed have had the effect of making Mannheim's text more accessible to social scientists trained in England or the United States, but in doing so they seem to have weakened the emphasis of those aspects of his work which are most challenging to these traditions and which (I believe it can be shown) are at the very heart of his argument.[33]

The situation would be more straightforward were we able simply to charge these changes to Mannheim's translators. But at least in the case of *Ideology and Utopia,* the shifts in meaning were actively overseen and approved by Mannheim himself.[34] An adequate account of this problem, in consequence, requires a much fuller investigation of the biographical context in order to determine to what extent Mannheim's revisions were dictated by his ideas about the requirements of his English and American readers, and to what extent they reflected a substantive change in his approach of the sort mentioned earlier. The problems posed by the English translations are compounded in the case of a few of the texts, in particular a collection of papers published posthumously under the title *Essays on the Sociology of Culture,* for which the original German manuscripts have not been made available at all.[35]

[30] IAU, p. viii.
[31] K. Wolff, 1971, p. lxi.
[32] Kettler, 1976, p. 2.
[33] All references in the present study will be to the most accessible English edition; reference to the German edition will also be provided for those texts originally published in that language.
[34] Although Gabel, 1974, makes appropriate and helpful observations about the translation, he does not seem to appreciate the extent of Mannheim's involvement in the enterprise. The matter is greatly clarified, with supporting evidence from Mannheim's correspondence, in Kettler, 1976.
[35] See the comments of K. Wolff, 1971, p. lxxxviii.

But however troublesome these textual problems may be, they are not so severe as to make Mannheim inaccessible to readers of the English editions. I believe it can be shown that, while the existing translations often veil Mannheim's meaning, they do not (taken as a whole) leave them in any serious doubt. Students of the subject would be well served by a corrective revision of the English versions, by the publication of previously unavailable material, and above all by the further clarification of some of the puzzling features of his intellectual biography. But what is *required* of Mannheim's readers (and what, too often, he has been denied) is simply a close and attentive consideration, in the light of the intellectual context in which they were written, of the texts which are already conveniently at hand. Such a reading is the object of this book.

III

A fresh reading of Mannheim's early work is made particularly opportune by the general disarray of contemporary discussion about social theory and method. This is not because the sociology of knowledge presents itself as a comprehensive resolution of the questions contested by the rival schools, programmes, and manifestos of twentieth-century social science (even if it entails a substantial and explicit critique of many of them) but because it offers a framework within which inquiry can proceed in such circumstances without submitting either to dogmatism (in which one such position prematurely excludes all others) or scepticism (in which all are admitted indiscriminately).

It is important to emphasize from the outset the exploratory and tentative character of Mannheim's arguments, for an exposition which over-systematizes his position is likely to distort it. His sociology of knowledge is developed in a series of investigations, each of which pursues the problem from a somewhat different direction. Even the essays which compose *Ideology and Utopia,* he notes, 'were written at different times and independently of one another and, although they centre about a unitary problem, each ... has its own intellectual objective'.[36] Mannheim never tries to eliminate the repetitions and inconsistencies that may result from such a procedure (which he describes as an 'essayistic-experimental attitude in thought') for he maintains that 'a given theoretical sketch may often have latent in it varied possibilities

---

[36] IAU, p. 52.

which must be permitted to come to expression in order that the scope of the exposition may be truly appreciated'.[37] In this he remained faithful to a favourite maxim of his old mentor Lukács: 'do not stop half-way but follow uncompromisingly the idea to its conclusion; the sparks produced by the collision of your head with the wall will show you that you have reached the limits'.[38]

I have tried in this book to present Mannheim's thought in the same spirit as he developed it: not as the unfolding of a logically exhaustive, systematic, and integrated body of doctrine but as 'the exploration of the various possibilities contained in germinal ideas'.[39] This necessitates a reconstruction of the sequence of steps which led Mannheim to the sociology of knowledge and which he offered to justify it. But it also means that these arguments must be considered afresh, in the context of contemporary debate about still unsettled issues of social inquiry. For this reason, my discussion is at once expository and constructive: it attempts to provide a full and accurate account of Mannheim's ideas, but it also undertakes to *participate* in his enterprise—to reconsider his problems and to reformulate and revise his solutions in the light of more recent literature and current concerns. A reading of Mannheim which manages to be sympathetic without becoming either patronizing or uncritical and which treats his work (as one of his editors has put it) as 'invitation, not conclusion'[40] is badly needed if his texts are to recover the force and immediacy which their author clearly intended them to have. My purpose, in any case, is not to adulate a thinker of the past but to acknowledge in his thought a fertile resource for attacking the problems of the present.

It may be helpful to anticipate, briefly, the view which will be developed in the succeeding chapters. Mannheim conceived the sociology of knowledge to be a fundamental and essential tool in the service of intersubjective understanding, an achievement which he considered a primary objective of social studies. The social world is constituted by men and women acting in accord with a set of meaningful conceptions about its nature. The relationship is such that these conceptions are neither wholly

---

[37] IAU, pp. 52–3. The opening passages of his 1946 letter to Wolff, 1974, p. 557, express the same sentiment.
[38] Quoted by Mészáros, 1972, pp. 52–3.
[39] IAU, p. 53n.
[40] Wolff, 1971, p. cxxxii.

subjective and personal, nor wholly objective and universal. On the one hand, conceptions about the nature of society are shared conceptions: they permit meaningful social behaviour precisely to the degree that they are held in common with, or at least understood by, others. It is for this reason that our conceptions of the social world are constructed (if, indeed, they are constructed at all and not merely accepted as given by the social environment in which we find ourselves) in accord with the conceptions of the others who share this world. But this same reason indicates, on the other hand, that conceptions about the nature of society are specific with respect to the time, place, and situation of the social group which shares them. The same circumstances which make them general and 'objective' with respect to the individuals who hold them, make them particular and 'subjective' with respect to others who do not share the same social world.

The sociology of knowledge, as conceived by Mannheim, is designed to deal with the dilemma which results from this condition: social knowledge must be adequate to the immanent system of meaning employed by the actors being understood; but, if it is to avoid the crippling effects of relativism, it must also be capable of transcending this meaning and establishing intersubjective criteria of validity. Analysis of the relationship between society and knowledge provides both a better understanding of the immanent meaning structures upon which society is based, and also a means by which the barriers separating alternative conceptions of the social world may be transcended. The first purpose is one to which the German historical school had given considerable attention at the turn of the century, and Mannheim's earliest work shows considerable affinity with this tradition in emphasizing 'the barriers to cognitive immediacy and the need to recognize and eliminate them'.[41] Only with his 1924 essay on 'Historicism', however, does Mannheim begin to address the problem of reconciling the claim of hermeneutic adequacy (as this had been clarified by the historicists) with the need for intersubjective accessibility (a main concern of his earlier doctoral dissertation).

One could, it seems to us, venture the thesis that it is part of the essence of a historico-cultural, but also of a psychic object, that it is penetrable only in 'mental and psychic profiles', that is, by way of certain cross-sections and dimensions of depth the nature of which is dependent on the mental-

---

[41] Wolff, 1963, p. 45; cf. FKM, pp. 6–7 (WAW, pp. 89–90).

psychic perspectivic location of the observing, interpreting subject.[42]
Passages such as these only hint at the arguments which are
worked out in the essays on the sociology of knowledge during the
following years. What is important to notice, however, is that the
impetus toward this development is Mannheim's concern to
protect the insights of historicist *Verstehen* against the threat of
relativism. The fact that the sociology of knowledge was adopted
by Mannheim as a means for bridging the gap between immanent
understanding and intersubjective knowledge cannot be forgotten
if we are to make sense of his oft-repeated insistence that the
sociology of knowledge not itself be viewed as relativism.

What is true, of course, is that Mannheim rejected any attempt
to establish intersubjective criteria of validity at the expense of
immanent understanding. He viewed as inappropriate the
uncritical importation of natural scientific methodology into the
social sciences precisely because the former devalued the sphere of
meaning and identified truth with wholly formal and timeless
standards of validity.[43] In fact, he believed, it was those who
claimed for the standards of Scientific Method an absolute and
supra-temporal guarantee of validity who were the real purveyors
of relativism. 'There is no more relativistic solution', he wrote in
the essay on historicism, 'than that of a static philosophy of Reason
which acknowledges a transcendence of values "in themselves",
and sees this transcendence guaranteed in the *form* of every
concrete judgment, but relegates the material content of the
judgment into the sphere of utter relativity.'[44]

I shall argue, then, that Mannheim's sociology of knowledge
represented an attempt to do justice to the meaningful nature of
social thought without thereby surrendering the aspiration to
establish 'objective' (in the sense of intersubjectively communi-
cable) knowledge about social phenomena. He was concerned,
above all else, with developing a method of social study that would
permit both hermeneutic adequacy and intersubjective validity.
Whatever the difficulty of combining these aims, he felt that they
were to be preferred to the evasion or surrender of one in the
pursuit of the other. It is the more ironic, then, that he has been so
regularly criticized for failing to be concerned with either. On one

[42] ESK, p. 105 (WAW, p. 272). The term 'sociologist of knowledge' *(der Soziolog des
Erkennens)* is used for the first time by Mannheim on p. 96 (WAW, p. 261).
[43] See, for instance, IAU, pp. 165–71 (IUU, pp. 143–50).
[44] ESK, p. 128 (WAW, p. 301).

hand, his method is characterized as an extrinsic, non-meaning-oriented approach to human thought, and thus convicted of a debunking, reductivist, ultimately dehumanizing attitude toward knowledge. On the other, it is described as being indifferent to intersubjective criteria of validity and thus convicted of relativism. Although often presented in the same breath, it is evident that these readings of Mannheim's project do not sit easily with one another. And on the view I wish to develop here, *neither* is in fact justified. The sociology of knowledge was employed by Mannheim as an interpretative method, not as a reductive one, and by viewing his work in this light it is possible to see not only that many of the criticisms that have been levelled against it are wide of the mark, but also that his method has much wider and richer implications for the study of social phenomena than has generally been recognized.

This discussion begins, in the next chapter, with a consideration of the central problematic of any sociology of knowledge: how to characterize the relationship between thought and being. By looking closely at Mannheim's manner of formulating the question, and considering this in the light of his arguments (presented in writings prior to his turn to the sociology of knowledge) about the nature of meaning and its communication, it is possible to see that his object is the *interpretation* of thought, not its reduction to some non-meaningful 'base'. In the following two chapters, the argument for a socio-historically grounded method of interpretation is developed with reference to its most obvious sphere of application: intellectual history. Chapter 3 offers reasons for believing that adequate interpretation of a written text requires reference to a social context of meanings which is necessarily external to the evidence given directly in the textual object itself; in chapter 4 an attempt is made to characterize such a 'social context of meaning' and to consider Mannheim's suggestions about how it may be investigated. The results of these discussions are brought together in chapter 5 as the framework for consideration of the sociology of knowledge in its mature form (notably, in the arguments of *Ideology and Utopia*). Here it becomes possible to reconsider a number of the most common objections to Mannheim's methods and conclusions, and to explore some of the types of inquiry which only an interpretative sociology of knowledge makes possible. The argument is broadened, in chapter 6, to consider the application of sociological interpretation to vehicles of meaning other than written texts: in particular, to social actions. Just as Mannheim's methods preclude any intellectual history which abstracts from the socio-historical world in which ideas are embedded, so his empirical sociology and history requires that the 'facts' under investigation be recognized as conveyors of meaning, and thereby subject to essentially the same techniques of interpretation as are required in the history of ideas. (In fact, one might suggest, the argument for the methods of an interpretative sociology of knowledge is still stronger with reference to social action and the 'everyday world' since the social grounding of the ideas and conceptions that orient most such acts is far more immediate and obvious than that which is presupposed by the more abstract and formalized mode of communication characteristic of written texts.) The concluding chapter considers the question of whether an interpretative sociology of knowledge is consistent with the maintenance of adequate standards of theoretical validation and with social or political criticism. Different as these two questions may seem to be, the venerable spectre of relativism has been associated with the sociology of knowledge both by positivists (who have feared that an epistemological relativism would undermine the authority of Science) and Marxists (who have been concerned that a moral and political relativism would undermine opposition and a critical practice).

2. What is the Sociology of Knowledge?

I HAVE suggested that the main weaknesses of the critical literature on Mannheim's sociology of knowledge result from a failure to identify the essential character and spirit of his enterprise; without an adequate view of his definition of the problem, criticism of the particulars of his method becomes the pursuit of straw men. For this reason it is of the greatest importance to determine from the beginning the character and purpose of Mannheim's investigations into the relationship between 'knowledge' and 'society'.

I

What can it mean to speak of a 'sociology of knowledge'? The idea denoted by this sequence of words is anything but self-evident, and only the listener whose ear has been inured by the ease and frequency of its use can fail to find the term surprising and puzzling. The German *Wissenssoziologie* may seem at first to be slightly less awkward because the compound term makes the problematic connecting word 'of' less prominent; it does not, however, make things much clearer—particularly in light of the fact that the work generally credited with introducing the notion, a 1924 study by Max Scheler, was titled *Versuche zu einer Soziologie des Wissens* and Mannheim himself followed this example in his earliest writing on the subject. In spite of the fact that 'sociology of knowledge' is an almost inescapable choice for the translator, it is none the less (for reasons that have been widely discussed[1]) somewhat unsatisfactory. The German word *Wissen* is both more and less restricted than the English word *knowledge*. German maintains the distinction between the content of what is, in fact, known *(Wissen)* and the mental process, or act, or faculty by which knowledge is acquired *(Erkenntnis)*. While this distinction can be observed in English by the use of *cognition,* it is not unusual to find *knowledge* used in this second sense as well. (Thus, for

---

[1] I have relied primarily on the discussion in Wolff, 1974, pp. 555–6.

instance, epistemology, *Erkenntnislehre,* is understood to mean 'theory of knowledge'.) If, on the other hand, we translate *Wissen* with *science* in order to denote the quality of positive knowledge, the opposite difficulty arises: *Wissen* is considerably broader than *science* (and perhaps even than *knowledge*) in that it admits within its range forms of 'knowledge' that would not, in English, be considered 'scientific'—mystical, theological, etc. Finally, it is important to keep in mind that the German *Soziologie* reflects an intellectual tradition for which the English *sociology* may be too confining: translation by such phrases as 'social philosophy' or 'social thought' can also be appropriate.

What readers have found most troubling about the label 'sociology of knowledge', however, cannot be blamed on translation. An extremely large proportion of the ink that has been spent in this field has been devoted to the question of how it ought to be defined. The result has been all sorts of proposals (including 'sociology of cognition', 'sociology of thought or thinking', 'gnosio-sociology', even 'theory of cultural compulsives'[2]) offered not to refine the translation but to replace the original term altogether. Mannheim himself, in contrast, seems to have considered the question of terminology rather unimportant. Virtually every page of his writings on the subject can be read as an attempt to specify and elucidate the meaning of 'the sociology of knowledge', but this was not a task which he felt could be usefully pursued by argument about how the field ought to be labelled or defined *a priori.* As a result, his choice of terms often seems indifferent and casual. In his earliest appraisal of 'The Problem of a Sociology of Knowledge' *(Soziologie des Wissens)* we find him use 'sociology of thought' *(Soziologie des Denkens)* in a context for which 'sociology of knowledge' would seem just as appropriate, while forty pages later he speaks of 'this sociology of *cognition'* (Erkenntnis*soziologie*).[3] His discussions of the sociology of culture never attempt to draw sharp boundary lines from the more general *Wissenssoziologie,* and he is content, throughout his writings, to employ 'knowledge' in the broadest possible sense.

[2] Instances of these four proposals may be found, respectively, in Grünwald, 1934, p. 2 (who speaks of the theory of the relationship both of knowledge and cognition to social being, and who cites, on p. 20, Wilhelm Jerusalem's *Soziologie des Erkennens,* 1909, in this regard); Schelting, 1934, p. 85: De Gré, 1970, p. 661; and Parsons, 1936, p. 680. It should be noted that 'sociology of knowledge' also continues to find champions: e.g. Maquet, 1951, p. 4; Stark, 1958, p. 123.
[3] FKM, pp. 61, 102 (WAW, pp. 311, 368). The emphasis is Mannheim's.

Nor is he more precise in defining the relationship which connects this 'knowledge' to society or social being. Again we find in his writings a tireless investigation of the nature, extent, and implications of this connection, but a pronounced reluctance to specify such principles of derivation as would make the one 'follow from' the other. For this he has been repeatedly and roundly criticized. 'This lacuna', writes Merton, 'leads to vagueness and obscurity at the very heart of his central thesis concerning the "existential determination of knowledge" *(Seinsverbundenheit des Wissens)*.' And Hartung, after cataloguing some of the many places in which Mannheim expresses the relationship with the vague phrase 'it is no accident that...', concludes somewhat smugly: 'It is no accident that Mannheim's discussions of his fundamental proposition concerning the existential determination of thought are so vague, because he has developed no criteria by means of which a causal relation between thought and its existential basis can be recognized.'[4] What is important about this complaint is the point which it takes for granted: that the relationship at issue is a causal one. If the object of Mannheim's sociology of knowledge could be characterized as the causal derivation of knowledge from the facts of social existence, then his treatment of what he calls *Seinsverbundenheit* would indeed be inexcusably imprecise. But any such characterization is just not compatible with the evidence of his writings. Mannheim *never* describes this 'existential determination' in the language of causality, and a considerable part of his argument is devoted to distinguishing his position from such an approach. The unusual term *Seinsverbundenheit* is chosen precisely in order to escape from the restrictive and mechanical model of causal derivation (which he felt had weakened earlier discussions of the problem of ideology) and to facilitate the development of a quite different notion of relatedness which could be adequate both to the historicity and to the autonomy of thought. In this respect, the decision of the translators to use the word 'determination' (*Seinsverbundenheit* is rendered as 'existential determination', 'situational determination', or 'social determination', depending upon context) is misleading—even with their qualification that the German 'conveys a meaning which leaves the exact nature of the determinism open'.[5] For *Verbundenheit*, as Wolff has pointed

---

[4] Merton, 1957, p. 498; Hartung, 1970, p. 698.
[5] IAU, p. 267n.

out, indicates merely that there is a 'relationship' or 'connection' to existence *(Sein)* without prejudging this relation as one of determination. (Wolff recommends 'existentiality' as a more suitable translation, though he points out that this requires the rather more awkward 'existence-related' for the adjectival form *seinsverbunden.*)[6]

However the problem of translation is resolved, the crucial point is that Mannheim consistently and explicitly eschews any suggestion that the sociology of knowledge be concerned with the (in his opinion entirely futile) search for 'a causal relation between thought and its existential basis'. Those who ascribe such an intent to Mannheim cannot help but find his formulations either puzzling or evasive. Merton, for instance, seems to consider the 'it is never an accident...' phrases a satisfactory basis for supposing that 'Mannheim assumes a direct *causation* of forms of thought by social forces' (although he finds the texts inconsistent on this point). When he draws up a list of the various passages in which Mannheim describes the relationship of thought and social being, however, the idea of causality can be directly noticed in only one of them: '[This particular conception of ideology] refers to a sphere of errors... which... follow inevitably and unwittingly from certain *causal determinants.*'[7] But ironically, this passage (as its original context makes plain) tells us nothing whatever about *Seinsverbundenheit* except in the negative sense that it describes what the sociology of knowledge is *not*. Mannheim is reconstructing the concept of ideology in historical terms, and he speaks of 'causal determinants' (the German original here is not *Seinsverbundenheit* but *kausalen Zwangsläufigkeit*) in order to develop the contrast between what he calls (as Merton acknowledges) the 'particular conception' of ideology and the 'total conception'. A few pages previously he speaks of this contrast as follows:

The former [the particular conception] assumes that this or that interest is the cause of a given lie or deception. The latter [the total conception] presupposes simply that there is a correspondence between a given social situation and a given perspective, point of view, or apperception mass. In this case, while an analysis of constellations of interests may often be necessary *it is not to establish*

---

[6] Wolff, 1971, p. lii n.
[7] Merton, 1957, p. 499. (Italics, ellipses, and brackets are Merton's.) The Mannheim passage is quoted from IAU, p. 61 (IUU, p. 58).

causal connections [Kausaldeterminanten] but to characterize the total situation.[8]

In short, the model of causality is brought up by Mannheim in order to *criticize* a conception which, in his view, is entirely inadequate as an approach to the problem of the existentiality of thought, and the explicit purpose of his discussion is to show that an adequate conception (the sociology of knowledge) only becomes possible on the basis of a concept of ideology that has been made both 'total' and 'general', and in which (as a consequence) 'all elements of meaning are qualitatively changed and the word ideology acquires a totally new meaning'.[9]

It is true that Mannheim also describes this relation with the word *Seinsgebundenheit,* which conveys the idea of determination somewhat more strongly (since *Gebundenheit* suggests 'constraint' or 'subjection') and which is treated as equivalent to *Seinsverbundenheit* in the English version. But the contrast with any model of causal explanation is drawn just as sharply for this term as for the other. In the one passage in which Mannheim distinguishes between the two, he writes:

The impetus to research in the sociology of knowledge may be guided in such a way that it will not lead to the absolutizing of existentiality [*Seinsverbundenheit*], but that precisely in the discovery of the existential *relatedness* [*Seins*verbundenheit] of present views, a first step toward the resolution of existential *determination* [*Seins*gebundenheit] is seen.[10]

There is nothing in this passage to suggest that the condition of

[8] IAU, p. 58 (IUU, p. 55). (My italics.) It is noteworthy that when Mannheim intends to speak of causal necessity he does not choose evasive terms; the general oddity of the translation is apparent in the decision to render *Seinsverbundenheit* as 'situational determination' while *Kausaldeterminanten* becomes 'causal connections'.

[9] IAU, p. 76 (IUU, p. 69).

[10] IUU, p. 259 (IAU, p. 301). The German must be used here because the English version (as a result of having translated both *Seinsverbundenheit* and *Seinsgebundenheit* as 'situational determination') omits the distinction altogether. This passage is noted by Meja, 1975, p. 67n., who suggests that Mannheim adopted *Seinsverbundenheit* only after 1931 in order to correct overly deterministic interpretations of his earlier term. But we should also observe that *Seinsverbundenheit* may be found (if more rarely) in writings prior to that date: e.g. FKM, p. 225 (WAW, p. 569). In Mannheim's first published remarks on the sociology of knowledge (at the end of his 1924 essay on 'Historicism') he writes: 'Von hier aus ergibt sich ein Ausblick auf eine weitere *Standortsgebundenheit* des Erkennens wie auch der gesamten Kulturschöpfung und Lebensgestaltung: *eine Gebundenheit an und eine Verbundenheit mit* bestimmten sozialen Schichten und deren Bewegungstendenzen.' (WAW, p. 296.) This passage appears in English as: 'This suggests that "positional determination" of knowledge, culture, and life may also be conceived in a sense different from what we discussed above, that is, as *co-ordination and affinity* between styles of thought and life on the one hand, and certain social groups and their particular dynamics on the other.' (ESK, p. 125.) I have added the italics in both the German and the English versions.

Seinsgebundenheit should be understood as a relation of causal
determination; on the contrary, Mannheim's claim that this
condition can be overcome or lessened by the kind of reflective self-
awareness which the sociology of knowledge makes possible would
be unintelligible were the effects of 'existentiality' to be
understood in causal terms.

In spite of the absence of textual evidence in its favour, the view
that some kind of model of causation is entailed in Mannheim's
position has been widely accepted by his critics, presumably
because it is taken for granted that no other model of
"connectedness' can do the job that a sociology of knowledge
requires: 'either Mannheim is saying that "thought" is causally
determined by "social being",' the critics seem to conclude, 'or else
he is not saying much of anything.' This point of interpretation is
of the utmost importance, for if it is conceded that a sociology of
knowledge must treat 'thought' as a causal consequence of 'social
being', that its object is to *reduce* knowledge to some substratum of
material facts, then it is difficult to see how Mannheim's position
can free itself from the debilitating scepticism with which it has so
often been charged. The many readers who have interpreted his
work in such terms have tended to see the openness of Mannheim's
language about *Seinsverbundenheit* as an evasive and futile attempt
(however well-intentioned or ill-intentioned it may have been) to
disguise a complete and irreparable devaluation of knowledge.
Grünwald developed this line of thought with exemplary clarity in
his early critique of the sociology of knowledge. Any such
enterprise, he argued, makes a claim to grasp 'knowledge'
(understood as objectifications of the mind having an immanent
meaning which raises a claim of validity) by means of a reference
to 'society' (understood as a collection of material facts that is
extrinsic or transcendent to knowledge) in such a way that the
former is treated as a 'manifestation' of the latter.

Thus the sociology of knowledge interprets a judgment not according to its
immanent sense, but views it as a 'symbol', as the bearer of another meaning
which is unknown in principle to the positing subject. The specific feature of
the sociology of knowledge lies in the fact that it regards social being as the
most real sphere [in contrast to all other possible transcendent realms such as
race, geography, climate, etc.] to which all thinking is believed to be bound
and which is believed to be manifest in every judgment.[11]

But such an approach to knowledge, Grünwald continues, cannot

11 Grünwald, 1934, p. 63.

possibly be tenable: first, because of its wholly arbitrary selection of the social as the base from which the 'manifestation' of knowledge emanates; and second, because of its unwarranted presumption that knowledge can be considered to be determined by factors which are excluded, in principle, from access to its immanent meaning. It is, to put the matter simply, absurd (or at least metaphysically capricious) to reduce the meaningful to the meaningless, and the sociology of knowledge, on this view, does precisely this in reducing knowledge to society.

It should be clear that the question of whether Mannheim's notion of *Seinsverbundenheit* can be characterized in these terms is far more than a terminological quibble. For if the sociology of knowledge is understood as an attempt to reduce knowledge to material facts that are extrinsic to the sphere of meaning, then its effect can only be a thorough-going nihilism. Much of the vehemence and alarm which animates criticism of the sociology of knowledge can be seen to derive from precisely this belief: because the sociology of knowledge devalues thought itself, it must be judged guilty not merely of error but of contributing to a general cultural atmosphere of cynicism, distrust, and despair. Thus a volume which is devoted to depicting the modern mentality as 'an intellectual stance succumbing to the corroding influence of total suspicion' identifies the sociology of knowledge as 'a highly conscious and consistent theoretical formulation of these mental sets'.[12] Mannheim's method is held to undermine the possibility of respect for truth, and the consequences of such an attitude are seen to be not only intellectual but moral.

When the truth goes at one door, cynicism comes in at the other. But cynicism will not remain locked up in a library: it will sooner or later affect life, and affect it deeply. Whether men sink into the mire of complete negativism or whether, in revulsion, they throw themselves into the arms of some intoxicating pseudo-religion, will make little difference: the upshot will in either case be contempt for man, with the ultimate result of cruelty and sadism.[13]

These are strong words, but they would not be entirely unjustified were the reductionist interpretation of the sociology of knowledge

---

[12] Remmling, 1967, pp. ix, 10. See also, Merton, 1957, pp. 457–60, who, while not indulging in the same sweeping indictment of modern culture, does place the sociology of knowledge in this social and moral context.

[13] Stark, 1958, pp. 181–2. A similar tone (though directed at a much broader array of opponents) pervades much of Popper's work, especially 1963.

an accurate one. If knowledge is but an epiphenomenon of social being (as Mannheim is supposed, on this account, to be arguing) then human autonomy, choice, and will are deprived of all efficacy, and the subject of history—the human actor—is dissolved into the material forces which are held to have caused him. A view which devalues not only thought but any meaningful human action by making it the unwitting expression of some material substratum cannot help but devalue the human spirit itself, and it is for this reason (according to Merton) that all analyses of this kind 'have an acrid quality: they tend to indict, secularize, ironicize, satirize, alienate, devalue the intrinsic content of the avowed belief or point of view'.[14]

To demonstrate the inadequacy of this sort of characterization of the sociology of knowledge it is necessary to describe and justify the model of *Seinsverbundenheit* which Mannheim developed in opposition to the reductionist model, and to show that it is in fact possible to speak of the 'existentiality' or 'social connectedness' of thought in a way that makes sense and yields important results without indulging in any claim, implicit or explicit, to *derive* this thought from social conditions, treated as causal antecedents. But even the most preliminary inspection of Mannheim's writings should make one ill at ease with an interpretation of his motives in terms of denunciation and 'total suspicion'. The 'acrid quality' of which Merton complains is quite foreign to the style and tone of his remarks, and (as Rempel has put it) he 'makes his alliance at the outset not with the "professional debunkers" of Merton, whose main preoccupation is with unmasking illusion, deceit, delusion, and falsehoods, but rather with a positive, sympathetic, and appreciative understanding of the nature of human perception and the ultimate human quest for truth'.[15] Throughout his work, the sociology of knowledge is recommended not as a means for discrediting, undermining, or devaluing knowledge, but as a tool of *understanding*. 'The principle thesis of the sociology of knowledge', he remarks at the outset of *Ideology and Utopia*, 'is that there are modes of thought which cannot be adequately *understood* as long as their social origins are obscured.'[16] At one point he recommends the use of the term 'perspective' in place of 'ideology' precisely in order to avoid the conventional association of the

---

[14] Merton, 1957, p. 458.
[15] Rempel, 1965, pp. 19–20.
[16] IAU, p. 2. My italics.

latter word with 'suspicion of falsification' and 'moral or denunciatory intent', neither of which are implied in the 'total conception of ideology' that is employed by the sociology of knowledge.[17]

The point of investigating the 'social connectedness' of an idea, Mannheim argues over and over again, is to advance our understanding of its meaning, and it should be obvious that this goal is logically distinct from (even if it may have important consequences for) a test of its validity. Yet readers who are committed to the reductionist interpretation of his enterprise persist in ignoring this distinction. Hartung, for instance, seems to suppose that he can convict Mannheim of the genetic fallacy by citing a number of passages from *Ideology and Utopia* in which the necessity of investigating the social origins of ideas is defended, apparently unconcerned that every one of them speaks of the conditions for *understanding* an idea rather than the conditions for determining its truth or falsehood.[18] Now such a distinction might be considered immaterial if it were the case that 'understanding' in Mannheim's sociological sense directly implied or required the falsehood of the idea which is so understood: if, in other words, the sociology of knowledge were of necessity 'a theory of social roots of error'[19] exclusively. There can, however, be no doubt whatever that Mannheim rejected such a view: nothing is repeated with greater insistence and frequency in *Ideology and Utopia* than the claim that the social connectedness of an idea *cannot* be taken to imply its falsehood.[20] Mannheim does maintain that no satisfactory attempt to deal with the problem of truth or falsehood is possible in the absence of the kind of understanding which this method of investigation makes possible, and it is in this sense that the social connectedness of ideas is relevant to their validity (or, we might more precisely say, to the determination of their validity). But beyond this sense, the question of validity is left open. The sociology of knowledge prejudges neither the truth nor the falsity of an idea, much less does it undermine or debunk the possibility of making such a distinction. There can be no doubt that Mannheim himself, at least, considered his work to be the very opposite of nihilistic: an attempt to advance the possibilities for true

[17] IAU, p. 266 (IUU, p.   229).
[18] Hartung, 1970, p. 699.
[19] Horowitz, 1960, p. 183.
[20] IAU, pp. 80, 86, 125, 168, 172, 282, 296 (IUU, pp. 73, 77, 109, 147, 151, 242, 255).

knowledge about the social world without relying upon the dogmatically sanctioned illusion (religious, ideological, or scientistic) that we can escape from our position *in* that world. Defending himself on this point he wrote:

The dynamic relationism for which I stand has nothing whatever to do with nihilism. It has grown out of tendencies to overcome, as far as this is possible at all, the narrow-mindedness and encapsulation of standpoints. It is, in the first place, a method of seeking, which expressly does *not* despair of the solubility of the crisis of our existence and thought, and which for this reason alone cannot be nihilistic.[21]

Before dismissing passages such as this as disingenuous or naïve, it behoves us, Mannheim's readers, to consider far more carefully the possibility that his disavowals of a nihilistic reductionism are not only genuine but justified.

II

It is important not to lose sight of the fact that Mannheim's claims for the sociology of knowledge are presented as part of a more comprehensive argument about the nature of social inquiry. Few of his critics have shared or even paid much attention to this larger framework, tacitly accepting a set of assumptions about social science and its subject matter which Mannheim never shared and which materially affect any interpretation of what a 'sociology of knowledge' could mean. This difficulty is especially noticeable in the position of those who characterize Mannheim's work in reductionist terms. For the supposition that an account of 'knowledge' in terms of 'social being' entails a reduction of meaning to some kind of material substratum clearly presupposes that society can be characterized in naturalistic terms: i.e. as a collection of 'facts' that can be described empirically and without reference to any meaning content requiring immanent understanding. Such an assumption has, of course, been a hallmark of the various programmes for a positivist social science that have been presented from the Enlightenment to modern behaviourism, and it has been particularly influential as a part of the empiricist tradition which (at least until recently) has dominated Anglo-American social philosophy. But Mannheim was a consistent critic of this tradition. In the chapter which he wrote to introduce *Ideology and Utopia* to his English readers, he offers a preliminary diagnosis of the 'disorganization' of modern thought and

---

[21] FKM, p. 267 (WAW, p. 620).

emphasizes the debilitating consequences of 'the growth of a technique of thought by means of which all that was only meaningfully intelligible was excluded'. He continues:

Behaviourism has pushed to the foreground this tendency towards concentration on entirely externally perceivable reactions, and has sought to construct a world of facts in which there will exist only measurable data, only correlations between series of factors in which the degree of probability of modes of behaviour in certain situations will be predictable.

Under such influence, the content of social science undergoes 'a mechanistic dehumanization and formalization' in which there is a 'reduction of everything to a measurable or inventory-like describability'. The result of this tendency is that inquiry is made sterile, for 'there can no longer be any doubt that no real penetration into social reality is possible through this approach'.[22]

A critique of this kind underlies all of Mannheim's arguments about the sociology of knowledge. If his Anglo-American readers have underestimated the significance of this context, Mannheim may deserve a share of the blame, for while his challenge to the ontological assumptions of positivist social science runs like a thread through his writings, it is never brought sharply into the forefront of his argument. In England, the desire to find a way to an accommodating pluralism may have led him to diffuse the issue somewhat, although his remarks to Captain Belgion make it obvious that his views had not changed. In the German writings, on the other hand, Mannheim wrote to an audience for whom any emphasis of this kind would have been superfluous—even slightly ridiculous. From the last decades of the nineteenth century, German academic debate had been preoccupied with the problem of fashioning a satisfactory alternative to the positivist programme for the social sciences. Although the German critics of positivism argued from widely diverse positions (philosophical, ethical, and political), there was substantial agreement about the defects of the positivist programme: its one-sided cult of factuality, its objectivism, its assimilation of all knowledge to the model of physical science. Mannheim's problem, therefore, was not to make the case against positivism (other than incidentally) but rather to indicate how the construction of an alternative programme ought to proceed. Because his audience has turned out (as we have seen) to be so different from the one for whom he originally wrote, and because his own efforts to take account of this shift in the

[22] IAU, pp. 43–4.

preparation of the English version of *Ideology and Utopia* were probably more harmful than helpful, it is important to follow the development of his arguments from the specific intellectual circumstances that occasioned them.

At stake in the *Methodenstreit* (as this many-sided dispute came to be called) was the question of how to identify the distinctive characteristics, and in this way, the methods most suitable for investigating, the world created by the human spirit or mind *(Geist)*. The complex philosophical heritage that is embedded in the German word *Geist* already implies certain claims respecting the fields of study that are concerned with this realm (the *Geisteswissenschaften*).[23] Above all, it signals a determination to come to terms with the problem of subjectivity. The *Geisteswissenschaften* are concerned with the objectifications produced by human subjects in all their variety: with ideas, institutions, works of art, products etc. Thus they include disciplines such as history, jurisprudence, social science, philology, aesthetics and literary criticism, conceived as interrelated (however distinguishable) spheres of inquiry. But by conceiving this realm in terms of the activity of the subject, the *Geisteswissenschaften* are to be sharply distinguished from the study of natural phenomena. As the most influential philosopher of the *Geisteswissenschaften* put it:

Their range is identical with that of understanding and understanding has the objectification of life consistently as its subject matter. Thus the range of the human studies is determined by the objectification of life in the external world. The mind can only understand what it has created. Nature, the subject matter of the natural sciences, embraces the reality which has arisen independently of the activity of the mind. Everything on which man has actively impressed his stamp forms the subject matter of the human studies.[24]

The effect of such a characterization is to emphasize the problem of subjectivity both in respect to the ends and to the conditions of inquiry: it is the fact that the epistemological knowing subject is also an historical acting subject which makes the *Geisteswissenschaften* possible.

---

[23] Once again we must contend with a problem of translation, for in spite of the fact that *Geisteswissenschaften* seems to have first gained currency in German as a translation of John Stuart Mill's 'moral sciences', its use in the *Methodenstreit* clearly requires reference to a distinctively German intellectual tradition. Makkreel, 1975, pp. 35–44, discusses this point and gives good reasons for choosing 'human studies' as the most satisfactory English alternative.

[24] Dilthey, 1962, p. 125. The citation is taken from his 1910 study *Der Aufbau der geschichtlichen Welt in den Geisteswissenschaften*.

The participants in the *Methodenstreit* sought methods of inquiry that would be adequate to the problem of subjectivity in this dual sense: i.e. that would take account of the historical position of the knowing subject on the one hand, and prove adequate to the comprehension of the acting subject on the other. The objectivism of late nineteenth-century positivism, in which the historical position of the knower was 'neutralized' by an appeal to formalized procedures (the canons of Scientific Method) and in which the subjectivity of the historical actor was excluded, by a reductive empiricism, from the domain of inquiry altogether, was seen as an evasion rather than a solution of this problem. To this extent, the most influential currents of German philosophy and social thought at the turn of the century can be considered a reaction against positivism. This does not mean, however, that there was any consensus of views about how an alternative programme was to be constituted. Dilthey's efforts to found the *Geisteswissenschaften* upon a descriptive psychology were sharply criticized by Windelband and the neo-Kantians, who argued that such a move undermined the crucial formal distinction between the 'nomothetic' sciences of nature (concerned with establishing lawful uniformities) and the 'idiographic' sciences of culture (concerned with the description of unique historical phenomena). The Baden neo-Kantians' attempt to define the transcendentally constituted object of the cultural sciences in terms of 'relevance to values' was developed in quite different ways in the work of Rickert, Max Weber, and (somewhat more problematically) Simmel. The Hegel revival of the first decade of the century helped to stimulate a new emphasis (particularly evident in Dilthey's late work) on the intersubjective realm of objective mind. Other challenges to the neo-Kantian position appeared in Husserl's phenomenology and Bergson's vitalism. Finally, the years just after the First World War saw new efforts (primarily by Lukács) to break with the positivist orthodoxy which had dominated the Second International and to establish the pertinence of the Hegelian side of Marxist critical thought.

All of these strands of the *Methodenstreit* figure as points of departure in Mannheim's German writings, for his own position is developed as part of a critical dialogue with the writings of others. One can specify the precise terms of his relation to this complex and heterogeneous collection of positions only by taking up each of the arguments individually, but it is not difficult to identify a general orientation which Mannheim can be seen to inherit from the *Methodenstreit* taken as a whole. A passage from the 1925 essay on 'The Problem of a Sociology of Knowledge' expresses his identification with the anti-positivist objectives of this movement in succinct and unambiguous terms:

> The positivist descriptions of reality are phenomenologically false, because its adherents—as naturalists and psychologists—are blind to the fact that intended 'meaning' is something specific, *sui generis*, incapable of being dissolved into psychic acts. They are blind to the fact that perception and knowledge of meaningful objects as such involves interpretation and understanding; that the problems arising in this connection cannot be solved by scientific monism; and, finally, that their naturalism prevents them from seeing the relationship between reality and meaning in a correct way.[25]

In summarizing the case against positivism, Mannheim presents what is virtually an inventory of his fundamental claims respecting the nature of social inquiry, and it is to these claims (and to the arguments of the *Methodenstreit* which stand behind them) that we must look if the sociology of knowledge is to be characterized correctly.

(1) There is a basic disjunction, both substantive and methodological, between the *Geisteswissenschaften* and the *Naturwissenschaften*. The positivist ideal of a 'unified science' is a specious one, and the principles of investigation which it sponsors—naturalism, reductionism, and methodological monism—are simply inadequate to the human realm. This, the most famous tenet of the literature of the *Methodenstreit*, remained central to Mannheim's thinking throughout his life. When he was charged (by the critic of 'Germanization' mentioned at the outset) with neglecting to make such a distinction, Mannheim replied incredulously: 'any student of sociology would have told Captain Belgion that I am one of the most ardent protagonists of the idea that there is a fundamental difference in subject matter between the natural and the social sciences.... If I may be forgiven the analogy, he might as well have accused Freud of ignoring the Unconscious.'[26] The sociology of knowledge, then, is to be conceived as a tool of the *Geisteswissenschaften* and it must not be confused with or assimilated to procedures of inquiry appropriate to the study of natural phenomena.

(2) The *Geisteswissenschaften* are distinguished by the fact that their subject matter, their data, are invested with meaning. To

---

[25] FKM, p. 76 (WAW, p. 330).
[26] FR, p. 5.

insist that reliable knowledge is possible only on the basis of data 'whose validity cannot be questioned by offering another interpretation or reading' (what Charles Taylor has called 'brute data'[27]), as the positivist programme requires, is to eliminate the possibility of the human studies altogether. A positivist social science, in which meaningful events are treated as 'psychic acts' (or otherwise reduced to brute data) achieves reliability at the expense of the authenticity of its subject matter, for 'every fact and event in an historical period is only explicable in terms of meaning, and meaning in its turn always refers to another meaning'.[28] The sociology of knowledge is concerned with grasping historical facts and events authentically, which is to say, in terms of their meanings.

(3) The objective of an inquiry into the meaning of historical phenomena is (at least) to understand that meaning. This objective is to be distinguished from the interest of the natural sciences in discovering the cause of an event by subsuming the individual case under a hypothetically assumed general law. In the language of the *Methodenstreit,* understanding *(Verstehen)* is to be distinguished from explanation *(Erklären),* and the methodological distinctiveness of the *Geisteswissenschaften* is to be found in the fact that the former objective can only become relevant in this realm. The 'situationally determined knowledge' which Mannheim's methods are designed to investigate is precisely that 'knowledge which is not merely the simple objective accumulation of information about facts and their causal connections, but which is interested in the understanding of an inner interdependence in the life process'.[29] The sociology of knowledge undertakes to secure the understanding, not the explanation, of thought.

(4) Once the objectives of the *Geisteswissenschaften* have been posed in these terms, as the understanding of meaning, the problem of accounting for thought in terms of social reality can be seen to be a problem of interpretation. A positivist sociology of knowledge would, of necessity, be reductionistic, for an account of thought in terms of a formalized model of social relations, from which the constituent of meaning have been excluded, necessarily

[27] Taylor, 1971, p. 8; see also his discussion in 1973, p. 56, where he notes: 'Paradigmatic as brute data are states which are recognized by clear criteria and where the recourse to criteria can continue through indefinitely many stages.'
[28] IAU, pp. 68–9 (this passage does not appear in the German original; see IUU, pp. 63–4).
[29] IAU, p. 48.

involves the reduction of meaning to unmeaning. Such a procedure has nothing to do with the method recommended by Mannheim:

the problem of perspectivism concerns primarily the qualitative aspect of a phenomenon. Because, however, the content of social-intellectual phenomena is primarily meaningful and because meaning is perceived in acts of understanding and interpretation, we may say that the problem of perspectivism refers, first of all, to what is understandable in social phenomena. But in this we are by no means denoting a narrowly circumscribed realm. The most elementary facts in the social sphere surpass in complexity the purely formal relations, and they can only be understood in referring to qualitative contents and meanings. In short, the problem of interpretation is a fundamental one.[30]

Mannheim's sociology of knowledge must be conceived in terms of a hermeneutic interest: it is a method of interpretation.

This wider tradition of the German hermeneutic *Geisteswissenschaften* provides the necessary background for any consideration of Mannheim's project, for it is the set of problems embedded in this tradition—the problems of meaning, of understanding, of interpretation—which are to be found at the very centre of his sociology of knowledge.

III

This preliminary characterization of Mannheim's method as hermeneutic rather than reductive in intent can be further supported by noticing the kind of question which occupied his attention in the period that preceded his work in the sociology of knowledge. These early writings are somewhat fragmentary and inconclusive, but they clearly indicate the affinity of Mannheim's interests with the hermeneutic concerns that dominated the *Methodenstreit,* and they go a considerable way toward defining the terms of the problem which stimulated his interest in the sociology of knowledge a few years later. We find here an attempt to describe the mediating functions of culture, between the activity of subjective consciousness (at once the source, and also the ultimate end, of expression) and the objective embodiment of this activity in cultural products. (Mannheim's discussions in this early period chiefly concern works of art, but his arguments can be applied to any meaning-conveying product of cultural activity, be it a work, a text, an utterance, or even an act.) The questions which he raises

[30] IAU, p. 303 (IUU, pp. 260–1).

converge on the problem of how it is possible for such an objectification to serve as a vehicle of meaning, and what would be required of a claim to understand that meaning authentically.

Mannheim's first published work, the lecture on 'Soul and Culture' originally delivered in Autumn 1917, addresses this problem in a most comprehensive fashion: how are we to deal, he asks his listeners, with the growing estrangement of culture from the soul, or of the objectified 'work' from the subjective aspiration of its creator? Both Mannheim's question and his diagnosis show the strong imprint of his teacher Simmel, whose differentiation between 'objective' and 'subjective' culture provides the framework for his reflections.[31] 'By objective culture we understand all the objectifications of the spirit' including 'religion, science, art, the state, and the forms of life'. In contrast, 'subjective culture' indicates the activity of the soul in seeking its fulfilment by means of the appropriation of these objectifications.[32] The tension between these two aspects of culture introduces a series of paradoxes. The creative act gives expression to the soul and thus serves as a means to its self-realization; yet on the other hand, it remains dependent upon an 'alien material, the work'[33] which is external to and thus separate from its source. The objectified work acquires an independence from its creator in a double sense. It is subject to the 'lawful' conditions of its *material* existence as an object (such as the determinations of volume and perspective in sculpture, or rhythm and structure in poetry). And it is subject to further conditions of *historico-social* existence by virtue of its function as a means of intersubjective communication (it becomes part of a system of conventions, expectations, shared understandings that may become historically remote from those of its orgin). The same circumstances, Mannheim suggests, that make it possible for culture to serve as a bridge between men also make possible its alienation from the soul. The fact that a work, once created, is accessible to all; that techniques and conventions of form can outlive their original context; that humans can discover significance in a work which has nothing to do with that intended by its creator; these conditions of objectification make culture resemble a golem 'that acquires an independent existence and

---

[31] See Simmel, 1971, pp. 233-4; also his 1968, pp. 27-46.
[32] WAW, p. 69.
[33] WAW, p. 70.

leads its own life'.[34] The gap between culture and soul, between the work and the individual, has reached critical proportions in the modern period and, Mannheim concludes, the overcoming of this estrangement is the mission of his generation.

The faintly apocalyptic tone of the Budapest lecture is put aside in his 1920 review of Lukács's *Theory of the Novel,* but the problem of establishing an adequate frame of reference for the interpretation of cultural products remains his central concern. Mannheim emphasizes the multiplicity of determinations that can be assigned such an objectification, depending upon the approach taken by the apprehending subject, and he introduces the distinction between the 'dogmatic' and the 'logical' object of interpretation. While a given work might appear to be the singular object of a variety of interpretative perspectives, he argues, in fact its very status as an object changes with the frame of reference by means of which it is grasped. An individual 'dogmatic' object must be understood as a variety of 'logical' objects, depending upon the level of interpretation or explanation that is undertaken with respect to it. Thus it is a mistake to assume that a psychological and an aesthetic account of a work of art provide alternative perspectives on the same (logical) object:

The psychological, experiential context yields explanations only of psychological phenomena and explains the work of art only insofar as it contains or suggests them. The aesthetic object, on the other hand, is something essentially of the spirit [*Geistiges*]; in relation to it, the psychic element is mere material, to be ordered and formed. But it is just these spiritual aspects (such as composition, etc.) that can be adequately explained only in appropriate teleological frames of reference.[35]

Mannheim goes on to claim that these logical objects can be ordered hierarchically from the 'full spiritual-metaphysical phenomenon' to its abstract parts. Valid interpretation can never reduce the higher to the lower, but must proceed instead 'from up downward'. Thus '"attempts at interpretation" of a psychological and sociological kind' which 'have tried to derive something higher from something simpler and lower' are revealed as 'inadequate and, all too often, ridiculous'.[36]

These fragments provide no more than a hint (and, indeed, a somewhat confusing hint) of how an adequate theory of

[34] WAW, p. 74.
[35] FKM, p. 4 (WAW, p. 86).
[36] FKM, pp. 4–5 (WAW, pp. 86–8).

interpretation ought to be conceived. But they show quite clearly the direction in which he feels a solution may be found. Mannheim's rejection of what he considers the 'tendency of the modern spirit' to treat the objectifications of the human spirit purely as manifestations of material (non-meaningful) facts—the attempt 'to derive something higher from something simpler and lower'—is unequivocal and emphatic. The 'crisis' of modern culture is blamed on precisely such an estrangement of the cultural object from its source: the expressive human subject. But by the same token, he is aware that the act of interpretation requires reference beyond the material object of culture itself—the work, the text, the act—to those meanings which it presents only mediately. The problem is summarized in the Lukács review in this way:

> The meaning of a form can be adequately explained only by the spiritual [*geistigen*] content that avails itself of it. It is extremely difficult to grasp this spirit and its ultimate points of orientation, if only because it never explicates itself in its creations but only manifests itself *through* them. The task here is, not to present the explicit content of works of art of a past epoch, documenting it by appropriate quotations, but to conceptualize the spirit in which these works of art originated. It follows that in such a study in philosophy of history, observations can never be *directly* documented by quotations, for such a demonstration always presupposes the reader's capacity in a specific, separate act to read in the example presented what is essential in it.[37]

The fundamental methodological challenge facing the *Geisteswissenschaften* concerns the fact that their 'data', objectifications of culture, are (unlike the physical objects of the *Naturwissenschaften*) bearers of meaning. The object before us must be grasped not only immediately, as a 'something itself', but also mediately—as something which stands for and points to meaning which transcends the evidence given directly. The cultural object as it is given in pre-theoretical, concrete experience is always problematic; interpretation of its intrinsic meaning always presupposes extrinsic reference to a more comprehensive context of meaning. In his early work, Mannheim does not consider the possibility of conceiving this context in sociological terms, for he clearly supposes that any extrinsic reference of such a kind would imply moving outside of the sphere of meaning altogether (and, in consequence, falling into reductionism). Only when he takes the step, a few years later, of conceiving social existence itself as a

[37] FKM, pp. 6–7 (WAW, p. 89).

'context of meaning' does it become possible to affirm that
'sociological extrinsic interpretation does not serve... to abandon
the sphere of meaning as such'.[38] Without this step, extrinsic
reference can only be formulated in idealist terms—in terms of the
concept of *Weltanschauung* (world view). Mannheim's elaboration
of such an approach in his 1921–2 essay 'On the Interpretation of
"Weltanschauung"', can thus be considered the fullest articula-
tion of his position respecting the problem of interpretation prior
to his turn to the sociology of knowledge, and as such, it can be seen
to set the stage for that development.

Mannheim offers, in this essay, a 'phenomenological analysis of
the intentional acts directed towards cultural objects' in order to
show what distinguishes such phenomena (and the *Geisteswissenschaften* which study them) from the 'natural objects' investigated
according to what he calls 'the modern scientific attitude'. These
objectifications of culture are distinctive in the sense that they are
presented not only immediately, in the evidence of direct
experience, but also *mediately*. 'The distinguishing mark of mediate
presentation', he writes, 'is that a datum which is apprehended as
being there in its own right can, and indeed must, also be
conceived as standing for something else.' Two such modes of
mediation are singled out as particularly important: the object as
an *expression* of meaning (in which our attention is referred back to
its source) and the object as a *document* of meaning (in which we are
directed to a more comprehensive context).

We shall try to show that any cultural product can be fully understood only
on the following conditions: it must first of all be grasped as a 'something
itself', regardless of its mediator function, after which its mediating character
in the two senses defined must also be taken into account. Every cultural
product in its entirety will, on this showing, display three distinct 'strata of
meaning': (a) its objective meaning, (b) its expressive meaning, (c) its
documentary or evidential meaning [*den objektiven Sinn, den intendierten
Ausdruckssinn, den Dokumentsinn*].

The most important part of the essay consists of an elaboration
and discussion of these 'three kinds of meaning'.[39]

Objective meaning is given directly in the object which appears to
us; it 'is rooted in the structural laws of the object itself.... All one
needs for a proper understanding of this layer of meaning is an
accurate grasp of the necessary structural characteristics of the

---

[38] FKM, p. 123 (WAW, pp. 396–7).
[39] FKM, pp. 17–19 (WAW, pp. 102–4). See also the whole of section IV.

sensual field in question.'[40] The specification of this meaning requires reference to the framework by which the field is defined: thus the objective meaning of a painting is a matter of its visual content—its colour, texture, form, etc., but the objective meaning of paint on a canvas, treated as a physical object, concerns spatio-temporal determinations that must be articulated as a theoretical proposition. Mannheim's description of this level of meaning, involving a further distinction between objective meaning realized by means of *signs* and that realized by way of *form,* is confused by the use of some highly problematic examples, but as a foil to the categories of mediate presentation which are his chief interest, the concept of objective meaning is reasonably clear. Objective meaning is precisely that which is present prior to any interpretation, and which therefore requires no reference to whatever further meaning might lie 'behind' the object. It is the level of meaning appropriate to those sciences which treat objects as 'brute data', as 'fully cognizable without being transcended or rounded out'[41] in the expressive or documentary direction. Clearly any particular datum of this sort may have several theoretical and/or formal objective meanings, depending upon the framework within which it is defined as an 'object'. For instance, the singing of an anthem may be assigned an objective acoustical meaning, an objective musical meaning, even (though it is here that Mannheim's discussion becomes problematic) an objective social meaning, depending upon whether it is defined in terms of reference to physical measurements of sound, identification of melody, harmony, rhythm, etc., or a theoretical sociological proposition respecting 'ritual acts' or 'group identity'.[42] With each change of framework, however, the intentional object itself is altered so that (in these examples) we deal with a physical object, a musical object, a sociological object, etc. Once the object is specified, its objective meaning is governed by 'the structural laws of the object itself' but (and this is the important point) the framework adopted is determined exclusively by the interests, preferences, theoretical priorities (or whatever) *of the observer:* the

[40] FKM, p. 26 (WAW, p. 114).
[41] FKM, p. 19 (WAW, p. 104).
[42] Mannheim's example is an act of giving alms to a beggar, having the objective sociological meaning 'social assistance'. The confusion which this example engenders clearly derives from the fact that he has not yet worked out the implications of the relationships among these levels of meaning for the construction of an interpretative sociology.

object, in this sense, does not convey meaning but displays it.

While any cultural product can be assigned an objective meaning of this kind, Mannheim is chiefly interested in its distinctive capacity (in contrast to the objects of the *Naturwissenschaften*) to serve as a vehicle for the *transmission* of meaning, and thus with its different 'mediator-roles'. The *expressive meaning* of such a product refers to that which is conveyed about the intended meaning of its author or creator who, it is presumed, meant 'something' and not merely 'anything' in bringing it into existence as an object. For this reason, 'the interpretation of expressive meaning always involves the task of grasping it authentically— just as it was *meant* by the subject, just as it appeared to him when his consciousness was focused upon it'.[43] Even as a norm, this objective is clearly a highly problematic one (as we shall see in much greater detail in the next chapter). In practical terms, we face at once the serious difficulty of distinguishing the expression conveyed from the 'objective' features of the medium in which it is presented. Often, Mannheim points out, a given expression comes to be so closely identified with a particular objective content that the latter is taken automatically as an indication of the former. He offers an example from medieval religious painting:

> If the Middle Ages as a rule confined pictorial representation to sacred contents (derived from the Bible), and, furthermore, to certain selected episodes, the reason is, in part, that pictorial art was supposed to convey only a limited range of moods and feelings. Thus, a certain emotional inventory of selected subjects was gradually evolved; particular scenes from the Bible absorbed definite emotive connotations into their complex of objective meaning (into the events related as such), and these connotations became so standardized that the contemporaries could not help considering certain expressive meanings as objectively inherent in certain contents. That this cannot be the case in an *absolute* sense is clear from the fact that the same events and figures were called upon in the course of history to support many different expressive meanings. For instance, certain biblical scenes which in early paintings expressed only religious exaltation later on came to acquire an 'erotic' expressive meaning.

What this implies is that the object studied by the *Geisteswissenschaften* can never be taken as self-contained 'given', for the expressive dimension of its meaning necessarily takes us beyond the boundaries of the work as it exists 'objectively' to the larger context of experience from which it emanates in the conscious activity of a subject. To grasp the meaning of the intentional act

[43] FKM, p. 21 (WAW, p. 107).

which conferred meaning, it is necessary to make reference to more than the properties of the object in which it is conferred; 'hence, close familiarity with the attitudes and idiosyncrasies of an epoch or an individual artist is needed if we want to avoid the risk of seriously misinterpreting his works'.[44]

This makes it necessary to refer to a second and more comprehensive level of mediated meaning, that in which the cultural product is taken as a *documentary* indication of the author's 'global orientation as a whole [*seinen gesamtgeistigen "Habitus"*]'.[45] The medium of the work, in other words, conveys to the interpreter not merely an understanding of its author, but also an understanding of the age, the culture, the 'spirit' of which he partook. In contrast to expressive meaning, documentary meaning transcends all that is particular and personal about the expressive act; rather, it refers to 'the character, the essential nature, the "ethos" of the subject which manifests itself in artistic creation'. For this reason, the documentary meaning of a work 'can become an intentional object only for the recipient, the spectator. From the point of view of the artist's activity, it is a wholly unintentional, unconscious by-product.'[46] How then is it to be identified? Mannheim argues that every objectification, indeed even isolated aspects of a work (such as its distinctive formal characteristics) provides evidence of the documentary meaning as a whole. And yet such evidence requires the corroboration of a vast array of other instances before that meaning can be grasped with confidence. It takes only a few measures of a Bach cantata (even if we have never heard the particular work before) to be able to place it in the baroque. But our conception of the baroque (as a musical style) itself depends upon the corroborative evidence of its many other manifestations, in the other passages, and works, and composers, of the period. In the same way, the documentary method of interpretation proceeds in a variety of fields, bringing 'scattered items of documentary meaning together in overarching general concepts which are variously designated as the "art motive" (Riegl), "economic ethos" (*"Wirtschaftsgesinnung"*) (Sombart), *"Weltanschauung"* (Dilthey and others), or "spirit" (Max Weber and others), depending on the cultural fields explored'.[47]

---

[44] FKM, pp. 24–5 (WAW, pp. 111–12).
[45] FKM, p. 22 (WAW, p. 109).
[46] FKM, p. 30 (WAW, pp. 118–19). This characteristic of documentary meaning was already introduced in the Lukács review discussed earlier.
[47] FKM, p. 33 (WAW, p. 123).

At the end of the essay, Mannheim briefly considers and criticizes various attempts to conceptualize a 'global outlook' of this kind. What is required, he argues, is a set of concepts that are both sufficiently comprehensive (capable of bringing different cultural fields—such as philosophy and the plastic arts—and successive cultural stages into a common theoretical picture) and sufficiently scientific (subject to control and verification). Dilthey's characterization of various 'life patterns *(Lebenssysteme)*' by means of philosophical categories, and Riegl's identification of successive historical forms of the visual arts are discussed as important contributions which none the less become overly formal and abstract. In contrast, the 'historical approach' of Dvořák and Max Weber fails to resolve the difficulty of how to express the 'necessary connections' among the various cultural fields. Mannheim emphasizes the inadequacy of the category of causality, as imported from the methodology of the natural sciences, for this task. While causal explanation may have a place in the *Geisteswissenschaften* as a means of showing 'the conditions for the actualization or realization of meaning', it is not suitable to the documentary method as such, which is necessarily concerned with understanding and consequently requires 'emancipation from a methodology oriented entirely on the natural sciences'. 'At any rate', Mannheim concludes, reiterating the anti-reductionist position that we have emphasized throughout this chapter,

there can be no causal, genetic explanation of meanings—not even in the form of an ultimate theory superadded to the interpretation. Meaning in its proper essence can only be understood or interpreted. Understanding is the adequate grasping of an intended meaning or of the validity of a proposition (this, then, includes the objective as well as the expressive stratum of meaning); interpretation means bringing the abstractively distinguished strata of meaning in correlation to each other and especially to the documentary stratum.[48]

Mannheim provides no indication, in this essay, of just how this task of bringing the different strata of meaning into 'correlation' with one another is to be carried out and indeed, if we consider his discussion in the light of his later work, it would appear that his theory of interpretative method cannot advance further until he has taken the additional step of characterizing this 'global outlook' in explicitly historical and sociological terms: i.e. until he has

---

[48] FKM, p. 56 (WAW, pp. 151–2); the other references in this paragraph may be found on pp. 49–57 (WAW, pp. 142–53). Note that the paragraph on Lukács' *Theory of the Novel* on pp. 152–3 of WAW is omitted from the translation.

introduced a sociology of knowledge. Viewed in this way, however, the conceptual distinctions that are presented in the essay on *Weltanschauung* interpretation help to make the point of the sociology of knowledge more comprehensible, less puzzling. The kind of 'existential relatedness' to which they point is nothing mysterious or arcane; on the contrary, Mannheim's 'strata of meaning' reflect distinctions that are taken for granted by virtually any investigator in the humanities or social sciences—even if they are rarely articulated theoretically. No one is likely to deny that the world is presented to us in the form of evidence which has determinate physical characteristics, and that these objects can be resolved analytically into a collection of sensible elements—colours, pressures, temperatures, odours, shapes, times, etc.—specified by reference to these qualities and to whatever theoretical framework the observer may choose to adopt. No one is likely to deny, moreover, that our interest in these facts (in cultural and social studies) concerns primarily the meanings which they bear and the meaningful relations which can be found between them. There is, of course, no end of controversy (particularly as between the positivist and the interpretative traditions) respecting the question of how this 'fact' of meaning ought to be handled methodologically, but there is nothing unconventional or surprising about the claim that something more than physical description is required of the evidence that comprises the cultural and social world. Nor is one likely to deny that facts of this kind, as meaningful, refer not only to the subjective sources of expression but also to a larger pattern of interrelated meanings that can be 'located' in place and in time, and which make it possible to identify a particular bearer of meaning as somehow 'characteristic' of a group, or a period. The inexhaustible variety of expressions of meaning and the undeniable individuality of this or that instance of expression does not mean that a given objectification can appear anywhere, or at random with respect to its context. The fact that a line of Elizabethan poetry, a song from the Edwardian music-hall, a Russian joke, the actions of an industrial picket line can be identified as such on the basis of internal evidence, our strong sense (even if it cannot be clearly articulated) of the character of the experience to be expected within any sphere of cultural or social activity, testifies continually to the context-dependent nature of meaningful expression. The fundamental plausibility of the sociology of knowledge derives, above all, from this commonplace fact of socio-historical life: that bearers of meaning show the marks of their origins. (Indeed, if we can anticipate somewhat, it is precisely such marks which make it possible for objects to 'bear meaning' in the first place.) It was considerations such as these which led Mannheim to the sociology of knowledge, and which alone make the arguments of *Ideology and Utopia* intelligible.

3. Text and Context

MANNHEIM'S EARLIEST writings and the tradition of German thought which they reflect direct our attention to the identification of *meaning* as the fundamental problem of evidence in historical and social inquiry. How does communication come about? What are the conditions for a successful transmission of meaning? Is authentic communication, in principle, possible? Such questions became the business of any investigator of human *(geistige)* phenomena because some kind of answer to them is presupposed in whatever inquiry he undertakes. The hermeneutic question does not, of course, exhaust the interests or the responsibility of a *Geisteswissenschaft* but, as Mannheim often emphasized, it does concern a crucial preliminary step upon which all subsequent levels of inquiry (including the knowledge and/or the practice to which they lead) depend. The messenger-god Hermes, credited by the Greeks with the discovery of the most potent of all human tools—language and writing—but also recognized as the Master Thief, stands by the entrance gates of all avenues leading to the understanding of our shared, social world, and what is radical about Mannheim's sociology of knowledge is the fact that it compels us to return to this beginning and to acknowledge Hermes's presence in every step that we take.

The bearers of meaning are manifold, and a general hermeneutics must bring within its grasp not only the interpretation of written sentences, but signs and symbols, gestures and events, poems and symphonies. In the years since Mannheim's German writings, no realm of philosophical inquiry has seen more vigorous or more multifarious growth than the investigation of meaning and its communication. The substantive contributions and (perhaps even more important) the committed followings that have been brought into being by figures as diverse as Cassirer and Chomsky, Whorf and Gombrich, the ordinary language philosophy of late Wittgenstein and Austin and the structuralist linguistics of Saussure and Jakobson, the English and American defenders of the 'New Criticism' and the French *Tel Quel* group, testify to the breadth as well as the depth of the problem of meaning and to the centrality of this question for the twentieth-

century consciousness. Although Mannheim's original contributions to the problem of interpretation have, in my view,
continuing relevance in relation to all of these areas, it would
clearly be folly to attempt to present his position in the context of a
comprehensive evaluation of the trends and possibilities that have
been opened up in this gigantic literature. What is possible,
however, and indeed necessary for any re-examination of his
sociology of knowledge, is an attempt to describe in general terms
the problematic situation brought forward by his efforts to
characterize the different 'strata' of meaning and to indicate how
it is that a method of 'sociological interpretation' may be claimed
to offer a contribution to its resolution.

For this purpose it is both convenient and appropriate to
confine our attention for the moment to the interpretation of a
written text. Not only is an object of this kind the classic and (by
virtue of the centrality of language) fundamental concern of
hermeneutics, it also serves to bridge, both conceptually and
chronologically, Mannheim's early emphasis on the interpretation of aesthetic objects (in particular, the plastic arts) with his
later emphasis on social action and the construction of social
theory. (We shall consider later the question of whether the
interpretation of an act can properly be treated as an analogue to
the interpretation of a text.) Without losing sight, then, of the fact
that Mannheim intends to apply the sociology of knowledge to the
comprehensive field of whatever 'is understandable in social
phenomena' let us consider the hermeneutic situation, as far as
possible, in terms of its essential elements.

I

If we are to sustain the claim that the sort of evidence required in
the human studies is necessarily composed, in whole or in part, of
expressions of meaning, we must be able to show how such
meanings are to be determined: i.e. we must be able to specify
criteria for distinguishing between a true and a false account of
what any expression X 'means'. (Were such criteria not available,
were *any* account of the meaning of X as acceptable as any other,
then the concept of 'evidence' would clearly lose its force
altogether.) Mannheim's emphasis on the distinction between the
'meaning' of a natural object and that of a cultural object draws
attention, however, to an ambiguity in our use of that word that
becomes rather important once we attempt to meet this
requirement. The distinction can be readily seen by considering

examples of two senses in which some object X is held to 'mean' something:[1]

(a) What does that black cloud mean?

(b) What does that weather report mean?

In may be the case that an accurate answer to both of these questions would be 'it will rain', but it should be obvious that this 'meaning' is different in character as it applies to (a) or to (b). As a natural object, the black cloud can 'mean something' only in terms of Mannheim's 'objective' stratum of meaning. A cloud cannot, ordinarily, be understood to express anything at all, for no agent has undertaken to employ it as a vehicle of communication. To determine its meaning, it is necessary to specify a frame of reference which will establish what will 'count' as an accurate answer: in this case, a scientific or meteorological framework provides a set of theoretical propositions which provide that the meaning 'it will rain' can be accurately attributed to the black cloud only if the latter event is a sufficient condition for the occurrence of the former. Other frames of reference (e.g. magical, aesthetic, psychological) may establish other 'objective meanings'.

The second example presents a quite different sense of meaning. It is true, of course, that a cultural object (in this case, let us assume, a written document) also possesses 'objective' meaning or meanings. The weather report, for instance, may be said to 'mean' that 'the strike at the weather bureau is over'. But in as far as we take question (b) in the more normal sense of 'what did the author of this report mean?', 'what does it *express*?', our determination of its meaning is governed by a different type of consideration: our question is oriented not to the requirements of a frame of reference (theoretical or otherwise) nor to the objects so indicated, but rather to the agent from whom the expression emanated. Thus the accuracy of our attribution of the meaning 'it will rain' to the weather report is affected not at all by whether or not it does, in fact, rain. Weather forecasters might like to have the meaning of their reports determined in this way, but alas, it is perfectly possible that the (accurate) meaning of an expression is itself an inaccurate proposition. Thus, whereas our determination of the

---

[1] There are, of course, any number of other senses of 'meaning' in ordinary usage, for instance: 'Did he mean it when he said he was going to retire?' in the sense 'was he sincere and honest in saying he was going to retire?'; 'does his work mean anything to him?' in the sense 'is his work important to him?'; etc. While these and other senses may be important to a general theory of meaning, they are not of consequence to the problem considered here.

meaning (sense [a]) of the black cloud is materially affected (in the scientific framework assumed above) by whether or not rain falls, the meaning (sense [b]) of the weather report is affected not at all by this outcome: the weatherman may have been mistaken.

Stated thus, this distinction is scarcely a remarkable one, and something like it is acknowledged in many different philosophical approaches to the problem of meaning. Husserl's distinction between 'indication' and 'expression' clearly influenced Mannheim's thinking, and recent discussion of Grice's theory of meaning, which rests on a differentiation between 'natural' and 'nonnatural' meaning, observes the same boundaries.[2] What is important about the distinction is the implications that may be drawn from it about how to determine expressive meaning. As we have seen, Mannheim's position in the essay on *Weltanschauungen* is that meaning in sense (b), as the expression of another subject, can only be determined by reference to 'the intentional object in the artist's mind', a requirement which of necessity entails reference to the 'historical background' associated with the object in question—in other words, to evidence which is not 'self-contained and hence ascertainable' in the object taken by itself.[3] The text which is presented to us in the immediacy of its 'objective meaning' is always 'incomplete'; 'if we are to have any access to the other subject, it can only be through these dimensions of meaning [i.e. the expressive and the documentary]. It is impossible to see how a subject could be constituted out of objective meaning alone.'[4] It is precisely for this reason that an interpretative method is required by a science that would undertake to comprehend a world composed of cultural (expressive) objects.

This conclusion is not, however, immediately or obviously evident. 'It is perfectly true', it might be argued against Mannheim's scheme, 'that there is a distinction to be made between the meaning of clouds and the meaning of texts. But that distinction concerns exclusively the "frame of reference" (to use Mannheim's terminology) that is appropriately brought to bear upon the objective evidence presented in each type of object. Expression is to be distinguished from other instances of objective meaning only in so far as a particular frame of reference, the rules governing the grammatical and semantic use of language, is

² Husserl, 1970, 1:269 ff.; Grice, 1957.
³ FKM, p. 29 (WAW, p. 117).
⁴ FKM, p. 34n. (WAW, p. 124n.).

shared by the writer and the reader of the text. The weatherman employs certain rules to express his meaning, we employ the same rules to grasp it. Once he has employed this frame of reference to construct his report, however, its meaning is to be found "objectively" in that text—and exclusively in that text. Our purpose in contemplating the object before us is to understand the text, not its author. In so far as information about the intentions of the author are present, objectively, in the text itself we may have access to them. But there is no reason to suppose that it is necessary, in order to understand expressed meaning, to go "behind" the text to any historical facts that "transcend" or "round out" (as Mannheim put it) the evidence presented in the expressive object by itself. Indeed, to insist upon such a procedure is to renounce objectivity in the human studies altogether and to resign the objects of culture to the obscure and mystifying methods of intuition, empathy, and wanton subjectivism.'

There is an undeniable plausibility about this view, and it has exercised considerable influence over interpretative practice in a wide variety of human studies during the past fifty years. It was espoused with a militant vigour in the manifestos of the 'New Criticism' which insisted upon the autonomy of the text and left the impression that any external reference whatever (other, perhaps, than to a good grammar text and the *Oxford English Dictionary*) reflected a grievous failure to appreciate either the function of criticism or the essential integrity of the literary object. It has been tacitly assumed by countless intellectual historians and commentators on the 'great books' of the Western tradition, who eschew 'excess' historical baggage in favour of a close examination of the 'texts in themselves'. And I believe that it underlies, in a more deep-seated fashion, the many different programmes that have been developed, in the name of a behavioural science of society, for purifying data of all interpretative reference and defining them exclusively in formal and quantifiable terms. (The 'language' of numbers is never in need of interpretation for meaning 'expressed' quantitatively is always precise, unambiguous, and trans-historical.)

But in spite of the surface plausibility and the substantial and continuing influence of this argument for the autonomy of the text, there are very powerful reasons for deciding that it is mistaken. Mannheim, it is true, did not himself develop the case against a doctrine of textual autonomy (though the materials for such a case are clearly present in his work) but then, neither was the prejudice in favour of such a case as pronounced or influential during the period in which he wrote. In order to understand his argument for a sociology of knowledge, therefore, it is necesssary to see why the ideal of the autonomous text is a specious one and why, in consequence, the arguments based upon it fail to obviate the need for expressive and documentary reference (as Mannheim claimed) in the interpretation of a cultural object.[5]

We begin to discover difficulties in the notion of the autonomy of the text when we reflect upon just what sort of an object is so presented to us. The whole advantage of the recommendation that we confine interpretation to objective meaning presented directly in the object is precisely that it is immediate, palpable, before us: 'the poem', Leavis remonstrated against Bateson, 'is a determinate thing; it is *there*'.[6] But as a matter of fact, it is a confusion to suppose that a poem (or any written text) is so obviously 'there'—in the sense, for instance, that a piece of paper with ink markings is certaily *there*. What is the text? What are its boundaries? Can the interpretation of an individual line of the poem make reference to another line of the same poem? Can it refer to other poems in the same volume? To other volumes by the same poet? What about other versions of the same text: is it legitimate to refer to earlier editions, to corrected proofs, to manuscripts or notebooks?[7] The fact that we can find any number of instances of such forms of interpretative reference in the writings of the proponents of textual autonomy indicates either that the 'texts' to which their interpretations are confined cannot be easily specified or else that their practice departs from their doctrine. But the problem of deciding what is 'there' is still more serious. How, we must ask, are we to ascertain that the 'text' before us really is the text? The question appears ridiculous in relation to the most common situation, in which we have no reason to question the 'text' as it appears before us. But the elaborate and complex process, be it art or science, by which a problematic text is 'fixed' shows that the question is by no means frivolous. Surely it would not be deemed necessary by a proponent of textual autonomy to account, in his interpretation, for whatever printer's errors might appear in the textual object before him. What then do we make of a text in

---

[5] This case is also presented, in a slightly different way, in Simonds, 1975.

[6] Leavis, 1953, p. 174.

[7] Both the arguments and the example presented in this paragraph are taken from an extremely valuable essay by Cioffi, 1963, pp. 96–7 and 101 ff.

which such an error is not immediately evident? Certain editions of Yeats's *Among School Children* present the sixth stanza thus:

Plato thought nature but a spume that plays
Upon a ghostly paradigm of things;
Soldier Aristotle played the taws
Upon the bottom of a king of kings.

The reference to 'soldier Aristotle' in this text was then interpreted by one critic to allude to a legend that Aristotle had accompanied Alexander on his military expedition to India. As it turned out, a compositor's error had led to the tranposition of two letters, such that Yeats's 'Solider Aristotle' came to be printed 'Soldier Aristotle'—an error which was not immediately apparent since it did not obviously violate any rules of language. What does this imply about the status of the text as a self-sufficient and autonomous expression of meaning? One might be inclined at first to answer that the example confirms the thesis of textual autonomy: the objective text 'Soldier Aristotle' means one thing, the different text 'Solider Aristotle' means another, but in neither case must the interpretation refer to anything lying outside or 'behind' the text as it stands. But the question cannot be settled in this way.

In the first place, it can now be seen that reference beyond the text as 'a determinate thing' is necessary to establish that it is in fact a cultural object (and not merely an arrangement of marks on paper). Were the act of interpretation confined strictly to the evidence presented in the text as an autonomous object, we would have no basis whatever for acknowledging any difference of *kind* between these two 'texts' (or between, for instance, a cloud in the shape of the letter 'I' and the written expression 'I'). This would have the damaging consequence that it would no longer be possible to make any distinction (even the provisional one suggested earlier in terms of the choice of the rules of language as a frame of reference) between meaning in sense (a) and meaning in sense (b). In the second place, the fact that the misunderstanding of Yeats's text was brought about, in this case, by a physical alteration of the object (the transposition of the letters 'i' and 'd') only draws our attention to the problem that would have arisen had the words in question been homonyms with identical spellings. Would the poem (Yeats's poem) in that case change meaning? Must a text be interpreted, then, to 'mean' everything that the dictionary definitions of its constituent words make possible?

This question leads to the heart of the problem: a difficulty in
the thesis of textual autonomy which would not be evaded even
were there never any problem in the constitution of the text as a
'determinate thing'. The reason that the defenders of this thesis
find the notion of a determinate text so important is that they
suppose that this alone makes it possible to speak of determinate
meaning: 'if interpretation is not grounded in the objective
evidence of the text itself,' they ask, 'then how are we going to
adjudicate among conflicting accounts of what it means? The
'meanings' of a text will become as disparate as the external
sources in terms of which it is interpreted.' It would be a mistake, I
believe, to dismiss this concern for the determinacy of meaning as
nothing but an ill-founded objectivist bias—a mistake which is
often found in relativist versions of hermeneutic method. On the
contrary, if expressive meaning is to prove suitable as evidence in
the *Geisteswissenschaften,* determinacy is an inescapable requirement, for evidence that is indeterminate (that is nothing in
particular) is no evidence at all. The problem, then, with the
interpretative doctrine of the autonomy of the text is not that it
insists upon the identification of determinate meaning but rather
the opposite: that *it is in principle incapable of* attaining this goal.
Ironically, the position which treats the text as an autonomous
object can be shown to undermine rather than to assure the
possibility of assigning determinate meaning to an expression; by
drawing on the conclusions of a vigorous recent literature on this
problem, it is possible to show that extra-textual reference is in fact
a *prerequisite* for the determination of expressive meaning, and that
therefore consideration of the determinacy of meaning must be
understood to require rather than to prohibit our 'going behind'
the text in the manner recommended by Mannheim.[8] A complex
set of arguments may be briefly summarized by means of three
general observations.

First, the rules of language as they are provided in dictionaries
and grammars do not suffice to establish any determinate

---

[8] Two writers must be especially credited with the bulk of the arguments to be
presented here (though they must not, for that reason, be assumed to approve of the use
to which they are put): E. D. Hirsch, Jr., whose critique of the assumptions of the New
Criticism is developed in the form of a general theory of interpretation in 1967 and
1976; and Quentin Skinner, who has published an extraordinary collection of papers
on the nature of intellectual history and social theory (in particular, see 1969, 1970,
1971, 1972b, 1972c, 1974b) that have unfortunately not yet been collected in book
form.

meaning but only to indicate meaning possibilities. Every sentence is composed of words which have a variety of possible determinations, and these determinations alter with the passage of time. Every grammatical arrangement of words affords the reader opportunity to distribute emphasis in more than one way. This does not mean, of course, that the rules of language authorize *any* reading; it is only that they never permit one to determine which, among a variety of options, is correct. In the normal business of life this 'limitation' poses no serious obstacles to understanding because numerous extra-textual references are taken for granted from the beginning: the man who remarks 'my watch is not working properly' is not likely to be understood to mean that his sentinel is loafing on the job. If ambiguity does arise, it is quickly resolved by dialogue. When communication occurs by means of a text or other 'mediator' that traverses widely different life situations however, the possibilities for misconstrual grow. The difficulties tend to become especially severe with respect to the language of social and political thought, which requires the use of terms that are highly abstract, connotatively rich, and laden with theoretical and axiological assumptions. It is this characteristic of language which makes Mannheim insist upon the inadequacy of the textual object as a sufficient indicator of expressive meaning:

If earlier philosophers, say Plato, Augustine, or Nicholas of Cusa, appear to have maintained something akin to present-day theses, then, if one looks more closely, they will always be seen to have meant something different. For in their system, and, more fundamentally, in the vital context of their life, every sentence and every thought pattern necessarily had a different function and hence a different meaning.[9]

Skinner has been particularly resourceful in amassing examples of the muddle which befalls debate in the history of ideas when texts are taken as timeless contributions to a standard or uniform collection of 'problems'.[10] It is quite true that the vocabulary employed, say, in the European tradition of political thought since the sixteenth century has shown considerable surface stability, but it does not take very elaborate historical research to show that words such as 'obligation', 'contract', 'property', 'consent' function in quite different ways in the writings of different theorists. 'Only the relative rigidity in the sound of words', Mannheim notes, 'can hide the fact that behind the same words there is a

---

[9] ESK, p. 100 (WAW, p. 226). In the original, 'Cusa' is misprinted 'Cuse'.
[10] See especially 1969, but also his historical essays such as 1972a and 1974a.

constant change in the actual meanings. A closer inspection shows us again and again that the historical denotations of the various words are always different.'[11] Obviously no proponent of the doctrine of textual autonomy is going to deny the existence of ambiguity in language; the point, however, is that his only means of resolving such ambiguity (by reference to the context established *within* the text itself) is inadequate to the task of affixing meaning—partly because of the earlier-mentioned uncertainty about how the boundaries of this 'internal' context are to be established, but also because of the many examples we can point to (such as those discussed by Hirsch and Skinner) in which such internal evidence, however broadly conceived, still fails to establish any determinate reading.

A second reason for holding that the autonomous text is insufficient to secure determinacy of meaning concerns the nature of the 'speech act' which is performed whenever a text or an utterance is expressed. In order to understand a text, it is necessary to grasp not only what it is that its words and sentences refer to, but also the nature of the act that is being performed in that expression. 'In this respect,' Mannheim writes, 'it is not the content, the "What" of objective meaning that is of preponderant importance, but the fact and mode of its existence—the "That" and the "How".'[12] In expressing himself, a person is also doing something, and knowing what it is that he does makes a difference to our understanding of what his expression *means*.[13] An utterance such as 'I beg your pardon', to take a modest example, can be understood as an entreaty ('please commute my sentence'), an apology ('forgive me'), a rebuke ('I object to your stepping ahead of me in line'), or a request for attention ('would you listen to me?'). The author of such an expression must be presumed to *mean* to express only one of these senses (or perhaps some further possibility), and we cannot claim to understand him unless we can, with good reason, decide which one. But there is nothing whatever in the words or in their grammatical arrangement that provides us with any clue: the relevant evidence must be external to the text itself.

[11] ESK, p. 113 (WAW, p. 281).

[12] FKM, p. 42 (WAW, p. 134).

[13] It will be obvious that this discussion draws heavily on the large literature stimulated by Austin, 1962, and especially on his notion of 'illocutionary force'. To conform to Mannheim's usage, however, I speak of both 'meaning' and 'force' in a somewhat broader sense than does Austin.

It might be objected that examples such as these are artificial because they are so brief, while in a text of any substance ample indication of the force of the author's remarks could be given internally. Now this may be quite true in most cases, but it is certainly not always true (as, again, many of Skinner's examples testify) and it is not difficult to see why. A text is written with a certain audience in mind. (True enough, this audience may be more or less consciously in mind, more or less precisely defined by the author. None the less, it is not possible to write intelligently for every conceivable audience.) In most cases, questions about what the writer is 'doing' are determined by what that audience can expect him to do—and this is not something which one is likely, with any stylistic effectiveness, to explicitly announce in his work. For instance, it is of the greatest importance to the determination of meaning to know whether a text is written as an act of affirmation and endorsement of the 'conventional wisdom' of the day, or whether it is to be counted a challenge to it. To judge whether its content (its specific arguments) support one reading or the other, however, it is necessary to know whether such arguments were commonplace or unheard of at the time—and this information is something that the author is not likely to find it necessary to assert. Similarly, whether a text should be taken as descriptive or evaluative, serious or humorous, inflammatory or pacific, depends very often on information which is not provided in the text because to do so would be either superfluous or counter-productive in relation to its original audience. In the rather intriguing case of irony, moreover, one can argue that an internal declaration of force is excluded *in principle* from the text: to say 'I am being ironic' is to cease to be so. (Hirsch makes the point nicely in his discussion of Defoe's *The Shortest Way with the Dissenters?*[14]) It is no wonder that failure to appreciate ironic intent is responsible for the most ridiculous of all interpretative blunders.

Reference to audience expectations suggests, finally, a third sense in which determinacy of meaning proves inconsistent with interpretation confined to the autonomous text. The more complex the expressive object, the more essential it becomes that we construe its *point* correctly: we must be able to assign appropriate weights to the various passages and sections which make up the whole; we must be able to distinguish between what the text implies and what it does not imply; we must be able to

[14] Hirsch, 1976, pp. 24–5.

specify the nature of the relationship that brings the various (not always consistent) parts of an argument together; we must be able to decide what is essential and what is incidental and ornamental among the many different timbers that the author has fashioned into a single structure. Judgements of this kind are possible only if the project as a whole is taken in view—something which is difficult if not impossible to do from a position *within* the text itself. Against the figure of the objective content of an expression there always lies a ground in terms of which the problem has been conceived and defined. If we are excluded from considering that ground, it becomes impossible to discern the shape of the figure. This, I believe, is the problem raised in the celebrated passage of R. G. Collingwood's *Autobiography* in which he describes his path to the 'logic of question and answer'.

I began by observing that you cannot find out what a man means by simply studying his spoken or written statements, even though he has spoken or written with perfect command of language and perfectly truthful intention. In order to find out his meaning you must also know what the question was (a question in his own mind, and presumed by him to be in yours) to which the thing he has said or written was meant as an answer.[15]

There may be some dispute about the *logical* status of this position, but Collingwood's hermeneutic insight is of the greatest importance. Intellectual history cannot be conceived as merely a vast and randomly arranged collection of minds, from which ideas shoot forth at irregular intervals and in arbitrary forms. Tradition is, after all, an empirically observable feature of the history of expressive acts; behind what is said there is a background of what is left unsaid and taken for granted, and it is this background which both informs and makes possible the act of communication in the first place. The extreme parochialism of the many misguided attempts to make the classics 'relevant' to the solution of contemporary problems only has the effect of confirming the sort of 'tough-minded' behaviourism which would relegate such texts to the dustbins or to the museums.[16]

The problems that are raised by Collingwood's position cannot be satisfactorily answered in the compass of a survey of considerations for supposing the doctrine of textual autonomy to be incapable of securing determinacy of meaning. (The issue will reappear, of course, in the later discussion of Mannheim's methods

---

[15] Collingwood, 1970, p. 31.
[16] Some examples may be found in Skinner, 1969, pp. 11 ff.

of historical understanding.) My immediate purpose is to draw attention to the consequences of this view for the question of interpretative method. For it should be clear that the internal evidence of the text is almost never a *sufficient* indicator of the question or set of questions to which that text stands as an 'answer'. Authors write, as Collingwood observes, 'for their contemporaries, and in particular for those who are "likely to be interested", which means those who are already asking the question to which an answer is being offered; and consequently a writer very seldom explains what the question is that he is trying to answer'.[17] In order to discriminate between what is central and what is peripheral in a complex text, in order to be able to identify with any confidence the point of the position adopted, in order to determine the range of implication authorized by the argument, we must be in a position to inform our judgement and to adjudicate among the various conflicting possibilities on the basis of a grasp of the nature of the question that lies behind the text. To exclude such reference for reasons of methodological purity is to protect the appearance of determinate meaning at the expense of its substance.

If there is any merit to these suggestions, then the objective meaning of the autonomous textual object must be judged insufficient to determine the sense, the force, or the point of an expression (as these are described above), and therefore we must conclude that the interpretative injunction to respect the autonomy of the text cannot be justified by the goal of securing determinate meaning, and that in fact it must be rejected precisely for the reason that it precludes the achievement of this goal. It is important to be clear about just what this 'goal of determinacy' in the interpretation of an expression entails, for it is obvious that a full and correct interpretation of the meaning of certain expressive objects need not yield a 'determinate' meaning in the sense of being singular or even precise. It is perfectly possible to express an ambiguous meaning, or a vague one, or an open-ended one. It would obviously make no sense to insist that the meaning of a double entendre be interpreted as either one possibility or the other, for if it is in fact a double entendre then its meaning consists in the joint presence of both. But in this acknowledgement we have not the denial but the confirmation of the determinacy of its meaning: a reading of such a text which treated one of the

---

[17] Collingwood, 1970, p. 39.

possibilities as its singular and exhaustive meaning would be, in fact, a misreading of what was meant. To require that meaning be determinate is to require only that it be possible to distinguish between what an expression means (however vague, ambiguous, or open-ended that may be) and what it does not mean. If we make the simplifying assumption, for instance, that there are only two meaning possibilities authorized by the rules of language for the earlier example 'my watch is not working properly', then the interpreter of such a text *must* choose one of the following possibilities:

(1) it means 'my portable timepiece malfunctions' and only this;

(2) it·means 'my sentinel is loafing on the job' and only this;

(3) it means both 'my timpiece malfunctions' and 'my sentinel is loafing on the job';

(4) it means nothing (i.e. it is not an expression at all).

Any of these possibilities is determinate in that it excludes the others; to deny that the meaning of an expression can be indeterminate is only to deny that it can mean both 'just this' and 'just that', or both something and nothing.[18]

Nor is the insistence that the object of interpretation be determinate meaning a denial of *fallibility* in interpretation. It is always possible that the determinate meaning which we attribute to an expression is a mistaken attribution. But to admit this is, once again, to affirm the principle of determinacy, for if the meaning of a text were indeterminate it would be impossible to be mistaken or indeed to distinguish, even in principle, between understanding and misunderstanding its meaning. It may be true that, in the strictest sense, no complete, verifiable act of communication is possible. But the weight of practical evidence for supposing that communication does take place is overwhelming, and an interpretative method can only proceed on the assumption that it is possible to secure a sufficiently probable reading of the meaning of a text to warrant the belief that we have, in fact, understood it. In any case, between a position of total scepticism and the position which affirms the determinacy of meaning no middle ground is possible.

It is important not to lose sight of the fact that this question of the determinacy of meaning is a fundamental one not only for logical reasons but because it pertains so crucially to the initial

---

[18] For a more elaborate discussion of this matter, see Hirsch, 1967, pp. 44 ff.

hermeneutic problem confronting the *Geisteswissenschaften:* how do we go about securing knowledge in a field which must take expressions of meaning as its data? The distinctive attribute of such meaning (in terms of the contrast with 'natural' meaning posed at the outset of this chapter) is that it is somehow grounded in the intentional act of another subject: a text is presumed to mean something, and not just anything, because our interest in it is not with the variety of meaning possibilities that linguistic rules may authorize but with what it *communicates.* Once the idea of communication is taken seriously, the interpretation of meaning assumes an unavoidable reference to *another.* Determinacy of meaning becomes important because we want to know (no matter what the proponents of textual autonomy claim we *should* want to know) what it is that the other *means* and not what it is that his text *could* mean according to the range of possibilities allowed by the rules of language. To insist upon this is not to deny that the latter object is an essential means of achieving the former, but only to keep sight of the fact that the text is only a means (and, for the reasons we have seen, not in itself a sufficient means) for reaching our goal. Considered in this way, the ideal of determinacy is but a different way of conceiving what might be called the ideal of faithfulness: the object of interpretation is to grasp not *a* meaning but *the* meaning which has been expressed. Our reference to the 'meaning of a text' is but shorthand for the 'meaning of an author which is communicated by the vehicle of the text'. In so far as we are interested in expression, we want to know what *he* means, not what *it* means.

However dubious this distinction may appear to (certain) academic theorists of interpretation, it is immediately and easily accepted in the interpretative practice that accompanies the communication of everyday life. No one pauses to entertain the alternative possible 'readings' of a message from a friend which says 'I'll pick you up at the corner for lunch'—unless for some reason the extra-textual indicators of the intended meaning are confusing. So strong, in fact, is our customary reliance upon extra-textual evidence for what the other means that we often do not hesitate to understand him to express a certain meaning even when that interpretation is actively *countermanded* by the rules of language. The conversational situation is familiar, for instance, in which the speaker in a slip of inattention says something which is so obviously not what he meant that the hearer automatically corrects the mistake (without even bothering to confirm the correction) and replies to what he understands the other to have *meant* rather than to what he actually *said*. This tendency to attend to what is meant rather than to what is said can also be seen from the standpoint of the speaker. If we are asked (because, let us say, someone else has just walked into the room) to repeat what we just said, we are unlikely to do so with precisely the same words or in precisely the same (objective) manner; we are likely, indeed, to have forgotten just what it was that we said, but we know very well and are capable of reproducing what it was that we meant.

Now it must be conceded that a more complex and difficult interpretative situation is posed by the cultural objects of the *Geisteswissenschaften* (not least because the opportunity offered in dialogue for securing immediate confirmation or disconfirmation of a 'reading' is not usually available). But it does not follow from this that the ideal of a faithful reading should be abandoned. Those who insist that the expressive medium be considered an autonomous source of meaning seem to suppose that the everyday communicative goal of understanding what someone means must be replaced, in science, by the quite different goal of understanding the text as an object in itself. And such an assumption (which is very widespread even if it is not always explicitly affirmed) has a predictable and easily observable consequence: alternative 'interpretations' of individual texts proliferate—seemingly without limit. The argument for textual autonomy would seem to be disconfirmed simply by the empirical existence of so many different 'readings' of major texts: if the internal evidence of the text were capable of establishing the determinate meaning expressed therein, then it should not be possible for intelligent and accurate readers to come forth with the array of disparate accounts of the work of writers like Hobbes, Rousseau, or Marx, which can be found on any library shelf. But not only does this kind of proliferation occur, it seems to be accepted as natural and unproblematic. The idea that a classic text will inspire a steady stream of further texts which offer 'A Reading of...' has ceased to be considered an embarrassment to scholarship; on the contrary, highest marks are accorded those 'interpretations' which depart most sharply from what had previously been *thought* to be the meaning of the text and yet manage to remain consistent with the rules of language. Against such 'readings', external evidence about what the author can plausibly be assumed to have *meant* in his text is considered inadmissible or irrelevant.

Now at least by the standards of everyday communication, this is a very odd situation indeed. Except for those sceptics who would deny the possibility of communication altogether (and, like most forms of radical scepticism, such would be a trivial argument), the scholar as well as the conversationalist is interested in the expressive object not as an end in itself but as a means by which to reach the other: he is interested, in the end, in 'what Hobbes meant' and not in 'what variety of readings can be shown to be consistent with the text of *Leviathan*'. But a hermeneutic method that sanctions indefinite variety in interpretation, that does not make it possible for inquiry ever to converge upon a single most plausible view of 'what Hobbes meant', can never be of real service to such an interest. In so far as the doctrine of textual autonomy authorizes multiple readings of specific expressive acts and fails to provide any basis for deciding which, among these possibilities, is most likely to correspond to the meaning intended by the author, it cannot serve as a guide to understanding the communications of others.

Where then are we to turn? Mannheim's theory of interpretation, in directing attention from objective meaning to the expressive and documentary levels of mediate presentation, makes essentially two claims. (1) The expressive meaning of an object is governed by the intentions of its author; interpretation can respect the ideals of determinacy and faithfulness only by reference to this standard. (2) Recovery of the intended meaning of the author is possible only if the evidence presented directly in the object is supplemented by reference to an external (ultimately social) context of meaning which the author of an expression must always presuppose and without which no successful act of communication would be possible. Let us consider the problem of intention and the problem of context in turn.

II

The problem of fixing the relationship between authorial intention and expressed meaning has been much confused, especially in discussion about literary interpretation, by failure to distinguish among the different *kinds* of 'intention' that may be involved in any act of expression: for instance hope, desire, purpose, ulterior motive, deliberation, etc. It is necessary to be quite specific, therefore, about the sense of 'intended' that is required to make expressive meaning (Mannheim's *indendiert Ausdruckssinn*) determinable. Mannheim's use of the term clearly derives mainly from Husserl's analysis of meaning in the *Logical*

Investigations (although he emphasizes that Husserl's 'procedure
has been modified for our purposes'[19]). Following Brentano,
Husserl employs the concept of intentionality to elucidate the
structure of consciousness, and in particular, to specify the
'directedness' of consciousness toward its object. Whatever form a
particular act of consciousness may assume (be it perceiving,
imagining, stating, loving, hating, desiring, etc.) it can be
characterized only with reference to the object it *intends* (what is
perceived, imagined, stated, loved, hated, or desired).[20] Thus the
intentional object exists only by virtue of the intentional act of an
experiencing subject; as Husserl puts it in his later work, the
intentional object is 'constituted' in the intentional act. The
intentional object is therefore to be distinguished from the
particular, psychological act in which it is experienced, as well as
from any independently existing object that is 'out there'. When I
turn a box over in my hands I have the experience of seeing a
singular, unified object, not a collection of different, unconnected
sense impressions. But this intentional object remains the object as
experienced by me: 'it makes no essential difference to an object
presented and given to consciousness whether it exists, or is
fictitious, or is perhaps completely absurd'.[21] Thus an intentional
object can as easily be a unicorn, the god Jupiter, or the tower of
Babel as a box, Mount Everest, or Queen Victoria.

The meaning that is conveyed in any expression, then, is
determined by the intentional act of the subject just as any
intentional object is determined. It must be distinguished both
from the personal, unique, psychological act of the expressing
subject and also from those real occurrences or phenomena to
whose existence it may refer. Meaning can be communicated
because such contents of thought are objective (though unreal),
self-identical, sharable intentional objects: I can express my
meaning on more than one occasion (i.e. in different psychological
acts) and usually in more than one way, but the intentional object
remains self-identical and as such, may be reproduced by the
intentional acts of others. Thus, Husserl writes, 'the essence of
meaning is seen by us, not in the meaning-conferring experience,
but in its "content", the single, self-identical intentional unity set
over against the dispersed multiplicity of actual and possible

---

[19] FKM, p. 18 (WAW, p. 103).
[20] Husserl, 1970, 2:554.
[21] Ibid., 2:559.

experiences of speakers and thinkers'.[22] The phenomenological concept of intentionality makes it possible to affirm the dependence of meaning upon the conferring act of an expressing subject, without thereby surrendering it to purely private, inner, psychological experience such as would make communication and the successful reproduction of specific meaning contents incomprehensible.

Although Husserl's analysis of intentionality has been one of the most influential chapters in twentieth-century continental philosophy, it has (in common with most of the rest of the phenomenological tradition) been little noticed on the other side of the English Channel. None the less, the concept of intention and intentionality has come to occupy an important place in post-Wittgenstein analytic philosophy, and in spite of the fact that the problem is approached from a wholly different background (and Husserl's name is scarcely ever so much as mentioned), the descriptive account which emerges is remarkably complementary.[23] What is established in this discussion, above all, is the necessity of employing the concept of intention in any satisfactory description of an 'action'. The quality of 'directedness' which distinguishes action from any other kind of behaviour or physical movement, is intelligible only with reference to the notion of agency, to a 'locus of responsibility' which is somehow 'inside' the actor and yet inseparably linked to the 'outside' event which is his action. Charles Taylor suggests, on account of this, that an adequate characterization of such an event requires what he calls an 'intentional description' of it.

What is essential to this notion of an 'inside'... is the notion of consciousness in the sense of intentionality. To speak of an 'intentional description' of something is to speak not just of any description which this thing bears, but of the description which it bears for a certain person, the description under which it is subsumed by him. Now the notion of an action as directed behaviour involves that of an intentional description. For an essential element involved in the classification of an action as an action of a certain type, i.e., as directed to a certain goal, is the goal to which it is directed by the agent, i.e., the description it has *qua* action for the agent.[24]

Reference to intentions provides a form of description that is indispensible to any accurate account of what people do. This

[22] Ibid., 1:327.
[23] See Anscombe, 1963; Hampshire, 1960 (especially chapter 2); Taylor, 1964 (especially chapter 3); Meiland, 1970. (Of this group, only Taylor, p. 69n., makes explicit reference to the phenomenological analysis of intentionality.)
[24] Taylor, 1964, p. 58.

descriptive form is necessary even for the identification of acts that we commonly regard as 'unintentional', for to say (let us assume correctly) that 'I didn't intend to do that' (e.g. to offend you) is intelligible only if intending to do so were a *possible* description of my act.[25] The intention that is described in an 'intentional description' can therefore be said to 'belong to' the act so characterized; it is not an antecedent, contingent event that is causally (or otherwise) related to the action but something that is executed in the action itself. It is for this reason that an inability to offer an intentional description of an action means that one has failed to identify just what sort of an action it was, or even that it was an action at all.

Speaking, writing, communicating by means of any expressive medium, must be seen as a special kind of action which requires a particular (potentially quite complex) form of intentional description. The behaviour of someone who is applying ink to paper may have the intentional description 'he is writing'. But if this description is understood to identify the act as an act of expression, then it can be resolved into a description of a further intention, his 'intention to be understood by some audience as meaning that which he is expressing'. In other words, it is in the nature of the act which the writer intends (is conscious of performing) that he intends (has the purpose) to achieve a certain result, sc. comprehension by another of what he has expressed. Intention in this last sense has been taken, by Grice and others, as the basis of a general theory of non-natural (i.e. expressive) meaning, in which the formal analysis of communication-intention is used to explain the concept of linguistic meaning itself.[26]

Each of the uses of 'intention' here mentioned, i.e. that of phenomenology, of theory of action, and of theory of meaning, is discussed in a large, technically elaborate, and distinctly controversial literature, but it would be an unnecessary diversion at this point to pursue the question of intentions very far in any of these directions. It is important, however, to recognize the connection between these senses and their contribution to the interpretative problem of fixing the determinate meaning of an expressive object. The meaning of an expression may be said to be governed by authorial intentions in the threefold sense that: (a)

---

[25] Cf. Anscombe, 1963, p. 84.
[26] See Grice, 1957, 1969; Strawson, 1970; Schiffer, 1972.

the expressive act must be intended (the author must understand himself to be expressing something); (b) the goal of communication must be intended (the author must, at least with respect to *some* real or potential audience, intend to be understood as having expressed something); and (c) a determinate content of meaning must be intended (that 'something' must be graspable as a 'self-identical unity of meaning' which can, at least in principle, be the object of any number of different concrete acts of consciousness). Although these senses of 'intention' are analytically distinguishable, they implicate one another in such a way that it is permissible to speak collectively of authorial intentions determining the expressive meaning of any object. If the notion of authorial intention is understood in these terms, the most common objections to an interpretative method which makes reference to intentions may be seen to miss the mark. Three such objections deserve some comment.

(1) *Intentions are unknowable.* In its broadest terms, this objection reflects the materialist disinclination to attribute any evidential status to mental entities, processes, or events. The text (as we have seen it emphasized by the proponents of textual autonomy) is palpably *there;* intentions, in contrast, are hidden within the personal psyche and remain unavoidably private. An argument of this kind has long been the hallmark of neo-positivist objections to *Verstehen* as a method of investigation: an empathetic or imaginative attempt to share the experience of another, or to make sense of his actions by comparing them to the introspective evidence we have about our own, may serve some heuristic purposes in suggesting possible explanatory hypotheses, but it can never in itself provide knowledge because no method of verification is applicable to what are essentially and irremediably subjective experiences.[27]

But intentions of the sort we have been describing cannot be considered to be private events, and the method by which they are recovered (and, *mutatis mutandis,* the method of *Verstehen* itself) relies neither on empathy nor on introspection. Undertaking to understand another does not involve attempting to experience or even to identify the particular set of feelings, the 'state of mind' that was present in his individual psychological act of expression, but simply to discover what he meant. (Were these two objectives indistinguishable then it would be impossible, as Husserl's

---

[27] A celebrated statement of this case against *Verstehen* may be found in Abel, 1953.

analysis brings out very clearly, to express the same meaning in two different psychological acts of expression.) The intentions that must be identified in order to determine what is meant are necessarily public in character: the intention to communicate requires (logically requires) reference to norms, rules, conventions, expectations, etc. that are already shared by the relevant community of potential listerners, and were this presupposition incapable of being fulfilled, communication would be, in principle, impossible. Now it is true (as mentioned earlier) that such a possibility can never be strictly disproved, but the position which denies the possibility of communication must ultimately be judged (along with most other forms of radical scepticism) a trivial argument because it leads to nothing but resignation; it is capable of telling us nothing at all.

(2) *Intentions are irrelevant.* The second common objection consists in the claim that intentions, however interesting and significant they may be in their own right, are just not the business of an interpretation of meaning. Reference to intentions may rationalize, glorify, vitiate, disparage, or dignify the meaning of a text, but it cannot alter that meaning. Our responsibility, in interpretation, is to determine not what someone intended to express but what he did in fact express. To suppose otherwise is to commit the 'intentional fallacy'.[28]

I hope that it has already been shown that the question of 'what someone did in fact express' is left thoroughly problematic in the absence of reference to authorial intentions. But beyond this, the various versions of the argument from the 'intentional fallacy' can be shown to rest upon a confusion about the relevant sense of 'intention'. We have already noticed the variety of senses of 'intention' that are authorized by common usage (design, purpose, motive, hope, etc.) and more than one of these senses is very likely to be involved in any act of writing or speaking. It is clear that the author of a text may intend any number of different things when he sits down to write: he may intend to be electrifying; he may intend to prove, once and for all, the existence of God; he may intend to escape from his family; he may intend to make money, or get tenure, or receive a Nobel Prize. It is also clear that he may fail to accomplish any of these intentions in (or by means of) the text

---

[28] The *locus classicus* for this charge is Wimsatt and Beardsley, 1954. For a more comprehensive discussion of the inadequacy of this thesis, including a profusion of examples and further references, see the work of Skinner and Hirsch.

that he produces and, more to the point, that whether or not he does accomplish these things is quite irrelevant to the *meaning* of the text that he produces. But however many such examples may be suggested, they fail to weaken the case for the relevance-to-meaning of authorial intentions in the sense stipulated above. Every version of the argument from the 'intentional fallacy' of which I am aware establishes only that certain kinds of intentions are irrelevant to meaning, and that (so fas as I know) has never been denied by anyone.

(3) *Intentions may contradict meaning.* The third objection draws attention to certain special cases in which it can be shown that authorial intention, even in the restricted sense stipulated, does in fact contradict the meaning of the text. If such cases (which are indicated by the possibility of a situation in which one would claim 'he did not say what he meant' or even 'I did not say what I meant') exist, then surely we must conclude that the relation between intention and meaning is a contingent one, and therefore that meaning can be characterized, at least in principle, without reference to authorial intention.

The first thing to notice about this objection is that it cannot be made on the assumptions of a doctrine of textual autonomy. For unless reference to authorial intention (or at least to *some* kind to extrinsic factor) is admitted, then there is no basis for ever supposing that the meaning of the text departs from what 'it says'; the whole point of this position is, after all, to insist that meaning is to be found in 'what is there' and in nothing else. None the less, the possibility of justifiably claiming that 'he did not say what he meant' is familiar to everyone, and it is important to be clear about the situations in which such a claim could be intelligible and appropriate. It seems to me that there are two such situations: error and deception.

We may say that there is an error in the execution of an author's intentions when the text or utterance in which he endeavours to express them violates the relevant rules and conventions that the expressive act presupposes. This may be an error of grammar or of definition (i.e. the rules that are acknowledged as governing the 'autonomous text') or an error with respect to conventions that are external to textual considerations (as, for instance, in some form of verbal *faux pas*). In the case of such an error, interpretation may issue in one of three possible readings of what was meant. (1) The interpreter may fail to 'catch' the error, and conclude (mistakenly) that what was said was meant, i.e. he may misidentify authorial

intentions and therefore misunderstand the meaning expressed.
(2) The interpreter may manage to correctly identify authorial
intention (for reasons extrinsic to the autonomous text) and
'correct' the error; i.e. he may substitute the correct meaning of the
expression for the meaning that would otherwise appear to be
required by the relevant rules and conventions. We noticed earlier
that this outcome is a common feature of interpretation in
conversation (e.g. I judge by the movement of your right arm that
in the directions you just gave me you *meant* to say 'turn right' even
though you *said* 'turn left'). It is also a common and appropriate
response to expressions couched in sub-standard but still, in a
limited sense, 'conventional' uses of language (e.g. since you told
me 'I don't want no potatoes' I will comply with your request and
give you no potatoes). (3) The interpreter may notice the error but
fail to identify the intentions that would allow him to correctly
identify the meaning. In this case, he may conclude either that an
intention to communicate failed (I'm sure he means something,
but I haven't any idea what it is') or else that the object before him
is not an expressive object at all ('this note means [objective sense]
that my cat jumped on the typewriter keyboard'). Thus the
situation of error in the execution of an intended expression can be
seen to confirm rather than undermine the thesis that authorial
intentions govern the meaning of a text.

We must also acknowledge the possibility that the author of a
text may himself, in reporting upon his intended meaning, be in
error. It is for this reason that while the author of a text must
normally be considered a privileged authority on what he
intended to express he cannot *invariably* be considered as such. It is
possible that he has forgotten his intended meaning. It may also be
possible (though here we must tread very cautiously) that he is,
and was at the time of expressing himself, unconscious of his
intended meaning. (For instance, it is possible that a speaker who
in a certain situation utters the statement 'I want you to live your
own life' could be correctly understood by his listener as having
expressed the meaning 'You don't pay enough attention to me',
even if the intention governing this expression were consciously
disavowed by the speaker.) In such a case it would seem to be a
requirement, even from a psycho-analytic perspective, that the
unconscious intention could, in principle, be avowed; this
possibility would be, in fact, the goal of therapy. The important
point, however, is that it requires a rather extraordinary kind of
external evidence about an author's real intentions to suffice to

override his own account of his intended meaning. There is always a strong presumption in favour of the latter type of evidence, and indeed it is obvious that there must be such a presumption if intersubjective communication, in the normal sense of that word, is to occur.

The case of deception is different and simpler. If a man reports to his wife 'I am going to spend the evening at the office' when in fact he intends to go out for drinks with a friend, the gap between his meaning and his intention is apparent rather than real. For even though he intends, by his communication, to deceive, still he does not intend to *mean* 'I am deceiving you'. On the contrary, it is a condition for the success of his deception that no such meaning be expressed; hence his authorial intentions fully govern the meaning of his expression, and the 'intention to deceive' is but a red herring. (Should his wife see through the deception she will not conclude that his expression really meant 'I am going out for drinks' unless this way of speaking is a private convention between them. But in the latter case, of course, the utterance is no longer to be counted as an attempted deception.)[29]

III

As some of the above-mentioned examples may suggest, the debate over hermeneutic method continually brings us back to the fundamental tension between intention and convention in the act of communication. On the one hand, the resources of linguistic (and other) media of communication can be seen to be the *servants* of authorial intentions: they can be employed to communicate original, individual, unprecedented contents of thought, and they make it possible for us to understand such thoughts as they are expressed by others. But on the other hand, the very effectiveness of these resources depends upon their *authority over* intentions: the rules, the norms, the conventions that communication presupposes cannot be made subject to personal whim or the imagination of the individual 'expressive soul'. The challenge that has been posed by Wittgenstein (as well, of course, as by Humpty Dumpty) therefore strikes at the heart of the question of how communication is possible at all: 'Make the following experiment: *say* "It's cold here" and *mean* "It's warm here". Can you do it?—And what are you doing as you do it?'[30] The answer must certainly be

[29] Cf. Hirsch's comments on lying, 1967, pp. 54–7.
[30] Wittgenstein, 1958, p. 140e (para 510).

something like 'it all depends'—but to see on what it depends is, I hope, to summarize some of the results of the discussion this far.

One part of the answer is certainly 'no, you cannot'. The intention to communicate entails a commitment to respect the rules and conventions that govern the linguistic medium chosen. Assuming that the speaker knows the rules of grammar and the public definition of 'cold' (and how, if he does not, could he make this 'experiment' at all?) then he cannot decide to make it mean something else. The impossibility of doing this, as Hampshire has stated very clearly, is a logical one.

He could not (logically) have meant it to be understood in a way in which he knew that no one would in fact understand it; this would be the same as to intend that he should be misunderstood. He could not (logically could not) *make* the word mean in his own mind, or to him, something that he knows that it does not mean, by rule or custom. If this feat was possible, it would be no more than thinking of something else while uttering the word. If I use a word, or conventional symbol, seriously meaning something by it, it must be true that I expect it to be understood in a certain way, and that I believe that the recognized rules governing its use allow it to be understood in the way that I intend.[31]

The necessity of respecting the 'objective' rules and norms of language thus reinforces the authority of authorial intentions in the sense stipulated by the preceding argument. We cannot at once intend to communicate and refuse to respect the conventions which make it possible for us to do so. Thus there can be no objection to the claim that consideration of the norms proscribed by a grammar and the O.E.D. is to be counted a necessary condition for the expression of meaning, at least in the overwhelming majority of cases.

We have seen, on the other hand, that this is not a sufficient condition. The autonomous text provides insufficient evidence for the determination of expressive meaning, because recovery of the author's intentions requires consideration of the external meaning context that he presupposed: conventions governing use, shared understandings, customary expectations, mutual definition of the stituation, etc. To determine what it is possible to express and to be understood as having expressed by virtue of these resources cannot be settled by examining a reference book; there is no dictionary or grammer of conventions that can remotely be considered as exhaustive. Hence, a further answer to Wittgenstein's challenge

---

[31] Hampshire, 1960, pp. 136–7. (The first 'to' in the last sentence has been erroneously printed as 'so' in the text.)

must be at least 'maybe'. It is possible to imagine a circumstance, for instance, in which it might be correct to interpret the utterance 'It's cold here' as meaning 'It's warm here'. (Irony is the most obvious possibility, but there are others as well in which a conventional situation might be established such as would make this reversal of normal sense a reasonable and appropriate expressive tactic). The extra-textual context which makes such expression possible is a socio-historical context: it is founded in shared experience, in a common life world, in a common fund of 'pre-understandings' ('prejudices' as Gadamer bravely calls them[32]) that can be taken for granted by both speaker and listener. Only by utilizing the background that is already shared is it possible to express and to comprehend meaning content that has not previously been shared.

But the latter possibility shows that the authority of rules and conventions over expression must not be overstated. It is obviously not the case that in order to understand what you express I must already know what you mean. Expression is not simply the reactivation of already shared meanings, as in the club of joke-lovers who, being familiar with every existing joke and wishing to spare themselves the tiresome effort of retelling what is already familiar, amuse one another by the simple expedient of calling out the number by which each joke has been catalogued. On the contrary, the real power of the text is to be found in its ability to overturn old conventions, to express what has hitherto been inexpressible. Thus it is a strength and not a weakness of the rules governing any living language that they are open-ended and cannot, taken in themselves, mandate a single, univocal, unchallengeable meaning. Specialized technical languages that are designed for the latter purpose can never serve as an adequate vehicle of expression, for their capacities are always instrumental: i.e. their application always presupposes that the question of what it is possible to 'express' has already been settled.[33] In a living language, this question is never settled, and this means that even if I cannot say 'It's cold here' and mean 'It's warm here' I cannot rule out the possibility that meaning contents which cannot be intended by the use of such a phrase now could become such objects in the future. The authority of the rules and conventions which govern expression is legitimate and substantial, but it is not

---

[32] Gadamer, 1975, pp. 238 ff.

[33] Cf. Gadamer's remarks on 'technical language', ibid., pp. 373–7, 404–5.

omnipotent. Unless such a strict conventionalism is rejected, it is impossible to account for (or indeed to make sense of) the historical character of these very rules and conventions.[34] What is, in the last analysis, most wondrous about the communication of expressive meaning is this dialectic of invention and convention. The socially constituted rules, conventions, shared understandings, that must be assumed to be stable and obligatory from the perspective of the individual expressive act are themselves historical: in the course of the ongoing social process of communication they continually change, develop, alter, and expand the resources of communication.[35]

This is why inquiry into meanings must always be sociohistorical inquiry. And this is why Mannheim's hermeneutic method is a sociology of knowledge. In order to be in a position to grasp what an expressive object means it is necessary to have access to the context of meaning which it presupposes. When a common context of meaning is already shared by speaker and listener, it can be taken for granted. When, however, we listen to the voice of someone who speaks from a very different socio-historical location, this context must become the object of deliberate and extremely careful investigation. The distinction between these situations is, of course, a matter of degree, and from communication between two intimate and life-long companions to communication between a contemporary American reader and the author of an ancient Chinese manuscript there is a very wide spectrum of possibilities. None the less, it was one of Mannheim's most frequently reiterated convictions that the problem of cross-contextual communication has become increasingly severe in the modern period. 'Ours is a world', he writes in *Ideology and Utopia,* 'in which social groupings, which had hitherto lived more or less isolated from one another, each making itself and its own world of thought absolute, are now, in one form or another, merging into one another.' This has led to what he believes to be an increasingly common condition: 'talking past one another'. This is the situation which makes a sociology of knowledge necessary; indeed, it is *only* this situation, for 'as long as discussion proceeds from the

[34] For some very suggestive observations about the way in which the conventions governing expression change, see Strawson, 1970, pp. 7–8; Hirsch, 1967, pp. 102–11; Skinner, 1974b, pp. 289–301.
[35] This historical process may also lead to the atrophy and decay of these resources: cf. Steiner, 1975, pp. 21 ff. and *passim.*

same basis of thought, and within the same universe of discourse, it [the sociology of knowledge] is unnecessary'.[36]

It is not difficult to see the reasons for the tendency to 'talk past one another' that Mannheim considered such an important and distressing characteristic of his age. Both the increased frequency of communication with 'outsiders' (i.e. with members of different class, regional, linguistic, generational groupings) and the increased rapidity of social change make the maintenance of a common 'universe of discourse' difficult. The structural consequences of what Mannheim called 'the democratization of culture'[37] reinforce this tendency. In as far as such trends issue in the overcoming of parochialisms of various kinds, the beneficial consequences can be considerable. But Mannheim was greatly concerned about the effects of a cosmopolitanism of appearance only, in which rival groups sought not to understand but to undermine and dominate one another. It is extremely ironic that the sociology of knowledge, which is founded on the general thesis that meaningful phenomena can be understood only by reference to a social context that is extrinsic to the object presented directly, has been criticized so widely for opening the door to indeterminacy, relativism, scepticism, and the devaluation of thought and meaning. In fact, as we have seen, the method is recommended precisely in order to avoid such dangers, or at least to open the way to the kind of research that is necessary if such dangers are to be minimized.

What is to be said, then, about the 'social context' which the sociology of knowledge is designed to investigate? The question is difficult to answer *a priori*, because a major point of the research project which Mannheim recommends is precisely to determine the nature and the parameters of the condition of 'context dependency' which is relevant to the adequate interpretation of expressive meaning. It is obvious from the outset, however, that not any kind of 'background' is relevant to the determination of authorial intention. Critics of the intentionalist approach to interpretation and of the sociology of knowledge sometimes ridicule such inquiry by pointing to obviously insignificant

---

[36] IAU, pp. 279–81 (IUU, pp. 239–41). It is incomprehensible how any reader of this section, which is titled 'The Special Approach Characteristic of the Sociology of Knowledge', can attribute to Mannheim the motives of a debunker.

[37] FKM, ch. 8.

'extrinsic' considerations, such as Marx's carbuncles,[38] but clearly an argument for the necessity of extrinsic interpretation is not the same thing as the (plainly silly) argument that *any* extrinsic reference is appropriate to this task. What the sociology of knowledge must investigate is the kind of evidence that affects the plausibility or the probability of any reading of the text's intended meaning. Applied to the history of ideas, this implies analysis of the kind of use to which relevant concepts are put in the writings of other members of the socio-historical location in which the author is situated, consideration of the relationship of the text to the arguments presented by contemporaries, examination (where possible) of such interactions as have been recorded between the author and others in which the self-interpretative moves characteristic of dialogue may be discovered, etc. In the course of such inquiry, adequate interpretation is most often secured through a process of approximation: i.e. through the gradual exclusion of implausible or impossible hypothetical 'readings' and the development of a reinforcement of accounts that parallels, as far as possible, the hermeneutic procedures that are employed automatically in discourse.

But to consider the question of meaning context from the perspective of an immediate interest in identifying the authorial intentions that inform this or that text is to take an overly narrow view of the problem. The structures of meaning relations that stand behind communication are historical structures: their existence and character can be 'documented' in terms that transcend the particular senses in which they are employed in any individual expressive act. And the context which is so identified is not some absolute and universal 'context of possible thought' but a historically delimited and determinate entity. This historical dimension is of the utmost importance to Mannheim's method. Without it, the interpretative problem of the relation of intention to convention (in the sense that we have been discussing it here) is not adequately mediated: on one hand we have a purely individualistic term, on the other hand, a purely abstract and general term. The contribution which Mannheim envisioned for the sociology of knowledge involved not merely investigation of the relationship of interdependence between such terms but the attempt to determine and characterize the specific historical 'situation' in which the relationship was effected. In the

---

[38] See Hacker, 1954.

introduction to the English version of his essay on 'Conservative Thought', Mannheim describes the two kinds of ahistorical assumption that must be avoided:

One is that Thought is one, the same for all men, except for errors or deviations which are of only secondary importance. At the other extreme, there is the assumption (which in fact contradicts the first one) that the individual thinks independently and in isolation from his fellows. Thus the unique qualities of each individual's thought are overemphasized, and the significance of his social *milieu* for the nature of his thought is ignored. . . .

But this intermediary level between the most abstract and the most concrete is just what is lacking in the history of thought.[39]

To cease to treat thought as autonomous is not to deny or denigrate the individuality of the other subject but to respect it by recognizing that his resources of communication, indeed the very materials with which he fashions his thought, depend for their effectiveness upon reference to a specific socio-historical context of meaning. Unless we are capable of re-establishing that reference, access to the other is closed off and 'communication' becomes a mere pretence. In a world of 'talking past one another', the expressive object functions not as a vehicle but as a reflector in which we hear, however strangely, just an echo of our own voice.

[39] FKM, p. 134.

4. Investigating Socio-historical Location

HOW CAN we come to grips with the historicity of thought and expression? Any attempt to do so must confront from the outset the troublesome dilemma of self-reference: 'True historical thinking', as Gadamer has put it, 'must take account of its own historicality.'[1] But from what Archimedean point is this possible?

The question is taken up in Mannheim's 1924 essay on 'Historicism' and it leads him, in this and the associated papers of mid-decade, directly to the sociology of knowledge. The principal contribution of historicism, he argues, has been to resist the claim of the 'philosophy of the Enlightenment' to transcend history by claiming a privileged position for 'the formal categories of Reason'.

What we have to show, as against Enlightenment, is that the most general definitions and categories of Reason vary and undergo a process of alteration of meaning—along with every other concept—in the course of intellectual history. It is rather questionable in general whether 'form' can be sharply separated from 'content'. We always ask to what extent the particular content, which, after all, is unqualifiedly historical, determines the particular formal structure. If, however, one tries to evade the problems involved in historicity by assuming a timeless 'form as such', 'concept as such', 'value as such', and similar 'as such' structures, then it becomes impossible to say anything concrete in methodology at all.[2]

But if the dilemma of self-reference cannot be evaded by claiming to stand 'above' history, neither can we afford to resign ourselves to the relativist conclusion that one is somehow entirely imprisoned within his own historical context of meaning. The most common weakness of the historicist position has been its inability to provide a convincing account of how cross-contextual communication occurs or a clear indication of the methodological criteria for securing authentic interpretation. The purpose of the sociology of knowledge is to undertake the kind of socio-historical investiga-

---

[1] Gadamer, 1975, p. 267.
[2] ESK, pp. 90–1 (WAW, p. 254).

tion that is needed in order to avoid the damaging consequences of either an ahistorical formalism or a subjectivistic historicism. Such inquiry, Mannheim believes, makes it possible to show both how cross-contextual communication is possible and in what (other than arbitrarily personal and private acts of 'empathy') it consists. Much of the groundwork for such a clarification has already been presented. But whereas the problem of interpretation has thus far been considered primarily with reference to the cultural object (and its expressive meaning), we must now turn more directly to the problems posed by its necessary reference to a socio-historical context (and thus, to documentary meaning).

I

Let us look more closely at this notion of context and the manner in which it may be identified. It is important, first of all, to keep sight of the fact that to speak of the socio-historical context of any expressive meaning is always to make reference to a further collection of meanings. If on occasion such a context is characterized by reference to events or physical objects, then it is taken for granted that the meaning of these events or objects from the perspective of the occupants of that location has already been clearly and authentically grasped. Much of the confusion, nonsense, and misrepresentation that is to be found in writings which claim to 'disprove' any relation between social position and ideas is based on the mistaken assumption that 'social position' (or 'material base' as it is often labelled in Marxist debate) can be characterized by empirical description, as a collection of physical objects alone. But only the shallowest kind of empiricism would attempt to define social or historical position, or class membership, or place in the system of production, in such a fashion, and it was precisely against such a version of objectivist empiricism that Mannheim (and, though Mannheim does not seem to have fully appreciated this, Marx as well) directed the most devastating critique. Social position is constituted in relations of meaning (which include mutually understood conceptions of status, expectations respecting behaviour, manner of characterizing the situation, definitions of relevant norms, obligations, etc.) and unless such meanings can be identified, the notion of 'social position' reveals nothing whatever about thought (nor, for that matter, about much else). To investigate the 'social rootedness' of

ideas is to investigate their rootedness in *social* existence, and these
roots are never 'brute data identifiable'.

Being conceptual, the context of meaning which makes it
possible to communicate must also have an identifiable structure.
This does not mean, of course, that it must take the form of a
theoretical system nor that it must reflect any rational design:

also open to rational analysis are those fields which are not limited to the
manipulation of the reflective and conceptual but still constitute vital systems
permeated by a rational structure in spite of their non-rational, non-reflective
origin. The economy, the legal system, the mores of an epoch do not arise in
their entirety on the basis of a reflectively thought out plan of one individual.
Nevertheless, they do have an actual meaningful, systematically understandable structure—in virtue of the rational, meaningful orientation of human
conduct in general.

Fields of a 'psychic-cultural' nature may resist even this kind of
retrospective 'logification', being 'understandable less as *systems*
than as "parts" of a unified psychological *Gestalt* of the various
epochs'. A structured interrelationship of elements is required in
any case, for the unstructued 'primordial stuff of experience' can
neither serve expression nor be comprehended as meaning at all.[3]
The boundaries of such a structure can be determined only by
reference to the process of communication itself; i.e. the limits of
the socio-historical context of meanings is established by the
expressive use to which it can be put in successful acts of
communication. For this reason, it is often easier to identify the
relevant context in situations in which communication has broken
down and the participants endeavour to achieve the kind of metacommunication which is directed at the re-establishment of a
common universe of discourse. When dialogue is unimpeded, the
presupposed context of meaning seems to become transparent:
nothing is more difficult to grasp than the structure which is taken
for granted.

If the socio-historical context that is presupposed by any act of
expression is to be grasped as a conceptual, structured entity, it is
evident that we must consider such a context to be itself a form of
meaning. But, as Mannheim's early tripartite classification of
meaning recognizes, it is a distinctive form. Objective meaning is
conferred entirely by the knowing subject (or the scientific
community of knowing subjects): the object to be known (even if

---

[3] ESK, pp. 110–11 (WAW, pp. 278–9). See also the section titled 'Rationalism v.
Irrationalism' in the essay on *Weltanschauung*, FKM, pp. 12–17 (WAW, pp. 97–103).

that object happens to be another subject) is treated as mute, passive, given. Expressive meaning is conferred by the intentional act of the expressing subject: the object to be known (which is always the product of such a subject) must be *read,* its meaning recognized, discovered. But the form of meaning that appears as the context of communication, documentary meaning, conforms to neither of these models. On the one hand, it is surely determined by (or, it might be more accurate to say, in) the acts of the subject-to-be-known rather than by the knowing subject; in this sense it is, like expression, a meaning which must be read, which must be interpreted. But, on the other hand, documentary meaning (unlike expressive meaning) cannot be governed by the intentional act of the other subject, for no single individual is in a position to establish such a context: one cannot (logically cannot) decide to 'express' those conventions by means of which one intends to have this expression understood! The socio-historical context of meaning is thus established as a 'by-product' (as Mannheim puts it[4]) of the intentional acts of expression of the many different participants in a common universe of discourse. It is not itself the intentional object of any of these acts, and indeed, in the typical case, it never becomes such an object for the individuals who employ (and in employing, reflect) it.

The context of meaning relations which makes communication possible is thus a construct which (like any metalanguage) can only be considered 'from the outside'—by a reflexive or retrospective act of consciousness. On the other hand, its determination is fully governed by its use 'inside' the acts of communication. This means that no *a priori,* categorical determination of the structure of documentary meaning is possible (a conclusion which Mannheim considers confirmed by the failure of the Enlightenment programme to transcend history). The variety of documentary contexts is evident not only in historical shifts of meaning, but in the many different strata of reference that are to be found within a single universe of discourse. As some of the earlier examples indicate, an individual act of expression many depend upon many different types of meaning context: it may employ a particular set of stylistic conventions, it may invoke prevailing visions of the normative order of society or of the institutional past, it may draw upon any number of conventional points of reference—categories, ideas, attitudes, symbols, priori-

[4] FKM, p. 30 (WAW, pp. 118–19).

ties, anxieties. Throughout the essays of his German period we find
Mannheim taking up this problem of the determination of socio-
historical context again and again, tacking from one approach to
another, redesigning his analytic tools, refocusing his arguments.
Thus the discussion of the comprehensive 'spirit of the age' and its
documentation (in the essay on *Weltanschauung*), his analysis of
'forms of historical movement' (in 'Historicism'), his investigation
of 'styles of thought'—both conceptually (in 'The Problem of a
Sociology of Knowledge') and empirically (in 'Conservative
Thought'), and his ultimate emphasis upon the conditions of
political discourse as presented in his analysis of the 'public
interpretation of reality' (in 'Competition as a Cultural Phenomenon') and of course in the central theoretical arguments of *Ideology
and Utopia,* the whole of this discussion addresses the problematic
situation posed by the contextual presuppositions of expression. In
the process of refashioning his approach, Mannheim moves
continually toward greater concreteness, greater specificity of
reference, and the main emphasis of his analysis shifts from the
determination of thought as manifested in the outstanding
achievements of culture (i.e. history of ideas) to thought as it
informs the activity of everyday life (i.e. social theory). Thus we
find his early interest in the problem of context conceived at the
most abstract and idea-oriented level *(Weltanschauung),* whereas in
the sociology of knowledge his analysis focuses upon socially
differentiated contexts determined by concrete interests and
political orientation. The key step in this shift of emphasis comes
at the end of the essay on 'Historicism', in which he argues for an
explicitly sociological sense of 'positional determination'.

The philosophy of history which mostly treats historical periods as units,
overlooking their inner differentiation and stratification, must be supplemented by a socially differentiated view of the historic-social process as a
whole, explicitly taking into account the distribution of social roles and its
significance for the dynamics of the whole. No one social stratum, no one class
is the bearer of the total movement; nor is it legitimate to assess this global
process merely in terms of the contributions of one class. It may indeed be that
one class carries, so to speak, the 'leitmotiv' of evolution, but the harmony of
the whole can be grasped only by taking into account the whole contrapuntal
pattern of all the voices.

   We see emerging, at this point, an entirely new dimension of historico-
philosophical interpretation: the social stratification of the cultural process,
and the identification of cultural trends with social classes; but we cannot
pursue this subject here any further.[5]

[5] ESK, p. 125 (WAW, pp. 296-7).

The subject is taken up here, as we see, only to be abruptly dropped, but it becomes the centre-piece of all Mannheim's subsequent writings on the sociology of knowledge. Thus his theory of ideology must be considered the ultimate issue of the theory of documentary interpretation developed in his first substantial publication.

If the socio-historical context of thought cannot be identified from a privileged position 'above' history and, at the same time, cannot be discovered as the intentional object of an expressive act, how then is it to be grasped? It is clear, if the arguments of the preceding chapter are well-founded, that documentary reference is an integral part of successful interpretation, for the determination of expressive meaning depends upon access to the context of meaning that it has presupposed. But how is such access to be secured if we can neither step outside of the historical process nor look to the meaning expressed by the cultural objects that are within that process? Mannheim's answer, as we saw in his essay on interpretation of *Weltanschauung,* is to explore the extra-expressive dimension of communication, in which evidence of an object's socio-historical origin is *displayed* even if it is not *presented.* This means that any cultural product, a text, an aesthetic work, an action, must be interpreted in a double sense: as an expression and as a document. Considered in relation to the second objective, the object takes on a new character. In expressing an intended meaning, the text also indicates the nature of the means by which that meaning is expressed, just as a sentence which conveys a message by means of grammatical rules can also be 'read' as an indication of what those very rules are. To provide such evidence, of course, the cultural object cannot be considered in isolation; meaning contexts must always be identified inductively, and confirmed by a continuous process of trial and error. This process is not, however, a random and accidental search for patterns within chaos. As we have seen, it is a logical requirement of successful communication that a shared context exist (even if this structure cannot be consciously identified or articulated by those who employ it). Hence the greater our collection of instances of expression articulated in a common socio-historical environment, the more confidently can we identify the documentary reference that they share. The general nature of this experience of entering into a 'foreign' universe of discourse is familiar to the learner of a foreign language: we study the model sentence of our textbook not because its expressed meaning has any particular interest for us but because its documentary reference (to linguistic rules and conventions which govern such expressions) does—and precisely in order that we may arrive at a position in which any number of other sentences employing the same linguistic means will be accessible.

Those who are familiar with the notion of a 'hermeneutic circle' will recognize at once the nature of the relationship between expressive and documentary interpretation. Mannheim himself called attention to this 'paradoxical result': 'we understand the whole from the part, and the part from the whole. We derive the "spirit of the epoch" from its individual documentary manifestations—and we interpret the individual documentary manifestations on the basis of what we know about the spirit of the epoch.'[6] The hermeneutic circle is inextricably a part of any interpretative method. The fact that there is not, and by the logic of communication cannot be, any code-book by which all meanings can be identified or any metalanguage from which all language in use can be derived, means that we must always begin in the middle: we must take the earth under our feet as *terra firma* in order to have a position from which to survey *terra-incognita,* but we must turn our gaze back to what has been taken as fixed as soon as we have a further position from which to do so. Such a procedure, it is true, seems to offend against the most fundamental logic of method according to the Cartesian assumption that one begins with what is indubitable and proceeds with sure steps to conquer the unknown, and it is the grip of such assumptions that accounts for much of the hostility, among positivist philosphers of science, to the use of an interpretative method in the first place. But the only alternative to such an approach is the (dogmatic) denial of historicity: the observer in the social and historical sciences is, unavoidably and irremediably, a part of the structure which he observes. However awkward the task may seem, he must manage to extricate himself from his position of ignorance by pulling on his own bootstraps, and he does not advance his condition a bit by assuming a rock to stand on when there is none. Once this condition is recognized, moreover, the fruitfulness of interpretative inquiry is quite striking: the communicative powers of human beings seem to be very little constrained by the 'vicious circle' that might appear to belong to the logic of the situation. It is evident, with a moment's consideration, that the 'hermeneutic circle' is

---

[6] FKM, p. 49 (WAW, p. 142).

actually a familiar and not particularly destructive feature of the process of inquiry in many different areas of life and science. What is puzzling or obscure about a chapter or section of a book may become clear once the entire argument becomes familiar, but the entire argument is made familiar by the cumulative effect of the chapters and sections which make it up. I attribute a friend's act of kindness to his thoughtful and generous personality, but how do I know anything about his personality if not from acts such as this one? The art historian uses his knowledge of the style of a period to date a newly-discovered piece of work, but the same work becomes the source of new knowledge about the style of the period. Recent philosophers of science show, persuasively, that empirical observation and description is 'theory laden', but it is from these observations and descriptions that theory is constructed. A judge comes to his decision by construing the requirements set by judicial precedent, but this authority comprises decisions no different than his own. In none of these cases (and, of course, dozens of others suggest themselves) is the element of circularity in the process of arriving at a judgement necessarily debilitating, and this leads one writer to suggest that the hermeneutic circle, far from being vicious, is a 'circulus fructuosus'.[7]

Any item of shared experience, be it a sign, an act, an institution, or some other feature of the human environment, can only be considered 'meaningful' in the first place because of its position in a pattern of interrelated structures of other meanings. The global whole of human experience *is* a closed circle, but since we are all, understanders and understood, within that circle it cannot be considered a damaging constraint. The problems faced in interpretation are to be found instead within 'local' complexes of experience, and these can be elucidated only by reference to one another. As long as the fabric of experience is seamless, the boundaries of the hermeneutic circle are no prison.

The significant problem for interpretation, therefore, is a rather different one: is the fabric indeed seamless? May it not be the case that, even if we reject the argument of radical scepticism against the possibility of *any* communication, we must still accept the argument that communication which crosses the boundaries of different socio-historical contexts is impossible? If the hermeneutic circle is no obstacle to successful interpretation from any point within it, can we suppose that there is any means of entry other

[7] Radnitzsky, 1973, p. 215 (from whom some of these examples have been borrowed).

than the accident of birth and 'citizenship' within an age or a social location? To answer such questions, and the more limited form of historical scepticism toward which they point, it is necessary to consider more carefully the implications of the fact that the method Mannheim recommends is not merely *historical* but simultaneously and necessarily *self-reflective*.

II

We have seen that while the cultural object may provide documentary evidence of its presupposed socio-historical context of meaning, this context can be an intentional object 'only for the recipient, the spectator';[8] from the perspective of the intentional act of the expressing subject, such documentary reference is employed without being an object of conscious awareness. (Those who think it absurd to suppose that we can apply contextual conventions without knowing what they are should reflect on the commonplace capacity of native speakers of a language to apply rules—even to novel cases—without knowing them.[9]) We have also seen, however, that no comprehensive solution to the problem of interpretation can be achieved from the position of spectator alone: at some level, the spectator must also be in the position of participant, for to be purely 'outsider' would mean to cease to be a member of the human community at all. Such a 'tactic', it might be noted, would not only be unfeasible but also impractical since a wholly alien consciousness—whatever that might mean—would have no basis, no point of entry, from which hermeneutic reconstruction could begin. The observer who undertakes to interpret a text or some other cultural object is not and cannot be an empty vessel; his reading of the documentary evidence given in the object before him is itself a document of his own socio-historical context. 'To understand the "spirit" of an age,' Mannheim writes, 'we have to fall back on the "spirit" of our own—it is only substance which comprehends substance.' For this reason, because the argument for the historicity of thought applies as fully to the interpretative as to the expressive act, 'documentary interpretation has the peculiarity that it must be performed anew in each period, and that any single interpretation is profoundly influenced by the location within the historical stream from which

---

[8] FKM, p. 30 (WAW, p. 118).
[9] See the remarks and the example in Searle, 1969, pp. 41–2.

the interpreter attempts to reconstruct the spirit of a past epoch'.[10]

Plainly this conclusion is an inescapable consequence of the arguments presented earlier. The interpreter cannot rid himself of the marks of his own socio-historical location—his background of experience, his preconceptions and presuppositions, his very language—without disappearing altogether. But what does this imply for the ideal of interpretative determinacy, for the attempt to understand the other authentically—as he intended to be understood? According to one version of hermeneutic theory, the implication is devastating. In his monumental inquiry into *Truth and Method,* Gadamer argues as follows:

Every age has to understand a transmitted text in its own way, for the text is part of the whole of the tradition in which the age takes an objective interest and in which it seeks to understand itself. The real meaning of a text, as it speaks to the interpreter, does not depend on the contingencies of the author and whom he originally wrote for. It certainly is not identical with them, for it is always partly determined also by the historical situation of the interpreter and hence by the totality of the objective course of history.[11]

If the doctrine of the autonomy of the text can be characterized (loosely) as a positivist case against the relevance of authorial intentions, Gadamer shows that there is a historicist case as well: the interpretative goal of identifying the intended meaning of an expression is rejected not because it affirms the historicity of expression but because it is held to neglect it. Since the merits of the sociology of knowledge depend critically on its claim that it is possible, at least in principle, to achieve cross-contextual understanding, and since, as we have seen, this claim implies the possibility of distinguishing between a correct and an incorrect (or at least, in view of the fallibility of any reading, between an adequate and an inadequate) interpretation of the intended meaning of that expression, we must consider very carefully the suggestion that there is 'something absurd about the whole idea of a uniquely correct interpretation'.[12]

Mannheim draws attention throughout his writings to two aspects of interpretative procedure that are required if cross-contextual understanding is to be possible. First, the interpreter must supplement his investigation of the relation between objects of expression and their socio-historical context of meaning with

[10] FKM, p. 36 (WAW, p. 126).
[11] Gadamer, 1975, p. 263.
[12] Ibid., p. 107.

investigation into the nature of the historical relation between different contexts themselves. The possibility of successful interpretation from one socio-historical location to another is founded in the fact that these contexts are historically related to one another: by tracing the process by which one context evolves from another, and by identifying the points at which different contexts overlap and implicate one another, it is possible to broaden the circumference of the hermeneutic circle. The most fundamental minimum of common ground is established in the fact that all possible contexts of meaning are human contexts. Since shared human problems and shared human needs are addressed in any social context, some level of understanding can begin on the basis of reference to those common problems and needs. In the case of interpretation of objects of great cultural remoteness, as in some anthropological or historical research, this may be the only hermeneutic resource available. As we have seen, however, such a beginning does not take us very far and it is a serious mistake to jump from our common 'human condition' to the assumption of a universal and timeless context of meaning. The problem can be dealt with in a more satisfactory way if we are able to reconstruct the historical steps by which one socio-historical context (having stable and determinate structure for one group of persons at one period of time) evolves into something essentially different.

The historical structure of consciousness itself is guarantee that some understanding of the intended meaning may be possible even in respect of works remote in time, the reason for this being that the range of emotions and experiences available to a given epoch is by no means unlimited and arbitrary. These forms of experience arise in, and are shaped for, a society which either retains previously existing forms or else transforms them in a manner which the historian can observe.[13]

This is why the analysis of the sociology of knowledge must always take place in two dimensions: on one hand, the interpreter attempts to secure an authentic grasp of intended expressive meanings by looking 'behind' each work to its documentary context; on the other hand, he attempts to secure an authentic grasp of a foreign socio-historical context by investigating, at a more comprehensive level, the evolution of such structures of meaning in order to bring what is distant and foreign into an intelligible historical relation with what is intimate and familiar.

[13] FKM, p. 30 (WAW, p. 118).

Change can be observed (and thus distinct contexts related to one another) because it occurs continuously. The historian of ideas, just as the historian of art, can identify the transformation of 'mental sets' because innovation is never total: 'variations can be controlled and checked only against a set of invariants'.[14] Were it not possible to do this, were the novel not assimilable to the conventional in the short run, no change in conceptual context would be possible, for the innovator would be incomprehensible in his own time no less than in another. Thus the historical structure of meaning which makes it possible for the conceptual means of communication to change over time also makes it possible (assuming the task of historical reconstruction is carried out) to re-establish communicative contact with systems of thought which have become remote.[15]

This kind of analysis is exemplified in Mannheim's important essay on nineteenth-century German conservative thought.

We want to look at the thinkers of a given period as representatives of different styles of thought. We want to describe their different ways of looking at things as if they were reflecting the changing outlook of their groups; and by this method we hope to show both the inner unity of a style of thought and the slight variations and modifications which the conceptual apparatus of the whole group must undergo as the group itself shifts its position in society.[16]

Such an investigation clearly differs from the interpretation of the expressive meaning of a specific, individual work, in which a documentary context is imputed to the author in order to establish 'the background against which the specific intent of the work, the unique contribution of the individual artist [or author], will stand out in sharp detail'.[17] Those who criticize such constructs as illegitimate substitutes for the interpretation of individual intended meanings are, from Mannheim's point of view, simply confusing the task of interpretation as reconstruction of intended expression with the task of interpretation as reconstruction of the

---

[14] Gombrich, 1969, p. 323. The concept of 'mental set' is not, of course, original to this work but it is employed by Gombrich to particularly illuminating effect.

[15] This process is easiest to grasp in respect to distances of time in which a *tradition* can be reconstructed. It is also possible, however, to establish an intelligible relationship between documentary contexts separated in other ways (e.g. geography, class, culture) by proceeding from one intermediary context, in which some overlap occurs, to another.

[16] FKM, pp. 134–5. (This passage is part of Mannheim's revisions for the English version of the essay.)

[17] FKM, p. 30 (WAW, p. 118).

documentary context of expression.[18] Not only does the latter kind
of investigation make an essential contribution to the success of
the first, it is a legitimate form of historical inquiry in its own right,
no less 'objective' for having structures of meaning rather than
collections of physical 'fact' as its subject matter. One passage in
the essay on 'Conservative Thought' may be taken as a summary
of Mannheim's view of the historical structure of contexts of
meaning, what he here calls

a dynamic, historical structural configuration; a concept implying a type of
objectivity which begins in time, develops and declines through time, which is
closely bound up with the existence and fate of concrete human groups, and is
in fact their product. It is nevertheless a truly 'objective' mental structure,
because it is always 'there' 'before' the individual at any given moment, and
because, as compared with any simple range of experience, it always
maintains its own definite form—its *structure*.... The particular form and
structure of these related experiences and elements can be indicated only
approximately and only for certain periods, since the structure is *dynamic* and
constantly changing. Moreover, it is not merely dynamic, but also historically
conditioned. Each step in the process of change is intimately connected with
the one before, since each new step makes a change in the internal order and
relationships of the structure *as it existed at the stage immediately before,* and is not
therefore entirely 'out of the blue' and unconnected with the past.[19]

The model of cross-contextual understanding that Mannheim
defends, and attempts to substantiate in his historical research, is
not dissimilar to the idea of a 'fusing of horizons' which Gadamer
conceives as the task of 'the effective-historical consciousness'.[20]
The conceptual distance that separates the interpreter's contextual presuppositions from those of the object he undertakes to
comprehend may be bridged by a careful and conscientious
investigation of the historical relationship between these two
structures of meaning. What this investigation must avoid above
all is 'the overhasty assimilation of the past [or other] to our own
expectations of meaning'.[21]

Such a danger accounts for Mannheim's emphasis on the other

---

[18] This distinction is pertinent, I think, to criticisms (such as Skinner's) of the kind of
inquiry undertaken by Macpherson, 1964, whose concept of 'possessive individualism'
can be treated as a reading not of any specific intended meaning of Hobbes,
Harrington, or Locke, but of the historical origins of a particularly significant (in terms
of the resourses it provided following thinkers) documentary context.

[19] FKM, p. 155 (WAW, p. 415).

[20] Gadamer, 1975, esp. pp. 267–74.

[21] Ibid., p. 272.

aspect of hermeneutic method which he attributes to the sociology of knowledge: it must always permit, and indeed encourage, critical self-reference; it must be a method of self-reflection. The concept of reflection which he inherits from the Hegelian tradition affirms the possibility of a double orientation of consciousness; in being aware of the object before it, consciousness is also presented to itself. The act in which the subject 'reflects on' something may also be grasped as a self-directed act in which the subject is 'reflected' in its relation to the object. The documentary reference of one's own intentional act of expression cannot, as we have seen, stand as the intentional object of that act, but it is possible for us to undertake to 'see ourselves as others see us' by allowing the historical investigation of documentary contexts to reflect back on to our own position, and to attempt to secure a measure of 'self-recognition', as Mannheim puts it, 'as if in our own objectifications we were brought face to face with a total stranger'.[22] By giving explicit attention to the changing structure of what others have taken for granted in their thought, it may be possible to get some kind of perspective on at least aspects of what we ourselves take for granted. The hermeneutic significance of the ability to bring one's own position into question is considerable, for the obstacle to securing an authentic grasp of an expression foreign to our own location is a function not merely of the fact that its context of meaning is remote but also of the correlative circumstance that our own conceptual presuppositions are familiar. This is not, it scarcely needs to be emphasized, an easy task, but to acknowledge that it is a necessary one is the single most important step toward achieving it. Once we adopt the position that our own conceptual environment has no position of privilege with respect to the historicity of thought, then we can be on guard against the error of attributing our own assumptions, norms, questions, and concerns to the author whom we wish to understand. A self-reflective awareness of the world that is familiar is a prerequisite to the ability to gain access to a world that is strange. Thus we find, once again, that Mannheim's counsel conforms closely to the position urged by Gadamer:

a person trying to understand a text is prepared for it to tell him something. That is why a hermeneutically trained mind must be, from the start, sensitive to the text's quality of newness. But this kind of sensitivity involves neither 'neutrality' in the matter of the object nor the extinction of one's self, but the conscious assimilation of one's own fore-meanings and prejudices. The important thing is to be aware of one's own bias, so that the text may present itself in all its newness and thus be able to assert its own truth against one's own fore-meanings.[23]

What conclusions, then, may be drawn respecting the claim to understand another as he intended to be understood, the notion that the goal of the interpretation of expression must be the identification of a determinate meaning, and thus the insistence upon recognizing standards by which adequate, faithful interpretation can be distinguished from misinterpretation? A number of observations must be made about the case for indeterminacy offered by Gadamer.

First, we must re-emphasize the fact that to reconstruct the intended meaning of an expression is not to reconstruct or somehow relive either the experience of creating it or the experience of its original audience in understanding it. If understanding is taken to require this sort of reconstitution of experience, it is clearly and patently impossible for a twentieth-century reader to understand a sixteenth-century work. But then again, in this sense it is impossible for *any* two readers to read the same work, to identify an identical meaning (for *every* reader brings a different background and experiences a different psychological 'impact' in what is read) and indeed it could be said with equal accuracy that it is impossible even for a single reader to read the same meaning on different occasions since, whatever other differences there may be in his two states of mind, his second reading is informed (as his first was not) by the prior reading. The question, with all such examples, is whether they support the conclusion that the intended *meaning* of a work is indeterminate, and for the reasons we surveyed earlier, it appears to make no sense to suppose that they do. We come back to the view, which seems to be essential in order to make any sense at all of the process of communication, that it is possible to identify, out of a multitude of substantially different individual psychological experiences of a text, a common core: a self-identical meaning. Were this possibility not a real one, it is difficult to comprehend in what understanding would consist. Gadamer himself describes herme-neutic understanding as 'a sharing of a common meaning' and speaks repeatedly of the importance of allowing the past 'to make its own meaning heard'. But if it were true that 'the real meaning

[23] Gadamer, 1975, p. 238.

of a text...is always partly determined also by the historical situation of the interpreter' then it would be impossible to know what it is that ought to be shared, or heard.[24]

It is quite true, of course, that to affirm the possibility of understanding the intended meaning of a work in principle is not to assure its possibility in this or that specific case. Interpretation is always fallible, and in situations in which the historical evidence that might permit a reconstruction of the relevant context of meaning is lacking, we may well have to conclude that no determination is possible at all. The limits to understanding, on this view, are perfectly intelligible: they are established by the state of the available historical evidence. Gadamer's (qualified) scepticism about 'correct' interpretation, on the other hand, leaves a certain confusion about where and why the possibility of recovering authorial intentions disappears. Presumably a 'uniquely correct interpretation' of the meaning expressed by another is possible in direct dialogue with him: we can discriminate accurately between what he means and what he does not mean. At what point, however, does the intervention of historical distance make the meanings of an expression multiple? When does interpretation become indeterminate? When does a shared horizon have to be replaced by a 'fusion of horizons'? Obviously qualitative differences in the degree of remoteness of an object-to-be-interpreted can and must be recognized, but it is extremely difficult to specify a point at which interpretation of a determinate expression must give way to interpretation of an historically changing complex of meaning elements.

Gadamer is certainly right to insist, as did Mannheim in the passage cited earlier, that interpretation of any particular object must continually be performed anew; indeed, what he says about the meaning of a text would be perfectly unobjectionable applied to its *interpretation*, which certainly 'is always partly determined also by the historical situation of the interpreter and hence by the totality of the objective course of history'. But to say that the interpretation of a text must change is not to say that the meaning of that text must change; on the contrary, it is precisely because its meaning does *not* change that it is necessary, for a reader in a new socio-historical location, to employ a new interpretation in order to recover that meaning. Thus Gadamer's remark that 'a text is understood only if it is understood in a different way every time' is

[24] Ibid., pp. 260, 272, 263.

entirely consistent with the thesis of the determinacy of expressive meaning if it is seen to refer (as he puts it) to 'the tension that exists between the identity of the common object and the changing situation in which it must be understood'.[25] What is important is the recognition of a common object—a self-identical meaning that remains itself for all who would open themselves to its expression.

Thus it would appear that Gadamer's arguments against the interpretative relevance of authorial intention[26] do not really affect the case that was presented in the last chapter and which can be said to justify the sociology of knowledge. What is perhaps most important in discussions of this kind is to clearly distinguish among the different sorts of claims that might be made for the intentional determination of meaning. To say that the author of a text has privileged authority in the determination of its expressive meaning does *not* mean (as we have seen) that he has privilege, or even an awareness, respecting the documentary context which his expression presupposes. It also does not mean that he has any kind of privilege respecting the determination of the *validity* of the content that he expresses. All that the hermeneutic norm of determinate intended meaning entails is the supposition that the author of a work meant to express something, and that it is our responsibility to identify what that something was, to the best of our ability.

One final point is suggested by this reference to the question of validity. Generally speaking, the establishment of a shared socio-historical context of meaning cannot be understood to imply *agreement* about any proposition of substance that is expressed in terms of that context. Reciprocal understanding is certainly a prerequisite to the establishment of consensus or agreement, but it is just as surely a prerequisite to any genuine disagreement. It is for this reason that Mannheim always insisted that the sociology of knowledge be understood as a *preliminary* level of analysis, designed to establish a common universe of discourse in which discussion (whether in agreement or in disagreement) might proceed unimpeded. Successful interpretation of meaning always stops short of the final determination of validity although (as we shall see further in chapter seven) it must be counted a consequential precondition of the ability to reach such judgements.

These comments do not, of course, exhaust the problems

[25] Ibid., pp. 275–6.
[26] Ibid., pp. 169–70, 299–301.

associated with providing a satisfactory general account of the concept of a socio-historical location of thought. But it may be more enlightening, and certainly more in keeping with the style of Mannheim's own analysis, to put aside the question at this most abstract level and consider the problem of meaning contexts in the more immediate, practical, and familiar situation that Mannheim himself took up in his theory of ideology.

III

The concept of ideology refers to a particular type of socio-historical context: the conceptual presuppositions of political thought and expression. As we have mentioned, Mannheim's main interest shifts, during the period of his German writings, from the interpretation of aesthetic and theoretical objects (the history of art and the history of ideas) to the interpretation of thought and expression as it orients the activities of everyday life. The latter focus is particularly characteristic, of course, of *Ideology and Utopia,* and when Mannheim wrote the introductory chapter for its English edition he began by describing its objectives as follows: 'This book is concerned with the problem of how men actually think. The aim of these studies is to investigate not how thinking appears in textbooks on logic, but how it really functions in public life and in politics as an instrument of collective action.'[27] The kind of interpretative method which is developed in the sociology of knowledge is particularly suited to the political sphere for a number of reasons.

First, political activity depends in a peculiarly critical way upon the character of the meaning constructs that are presupposed by the actor. The language of politics presents 'objects' which are not directly in evidence but which none the less direct, justify, and render intelligible much of what the member of any modern society does and thinks. In orienting ourselves to phenomena such as 'class', 'law', 'the free market', 'the democratic state', we employ the elaborate structures of meaning which stand behind them. All forms of expression, as we have argued, are mediated by shared intersubjective meanings, but these mediations have especially decisive significance when they inform decisions about how to act *on* a situation (i.e. to influence or change it) rather than simply within it. Politics is the realm of the most comprehensive and therefore abstract forms of practical activity, and for this

---

[27] IAU, p. 1.

reason interpretative analysis of its content is unsually telling.

Second, politics is characteristically directed towards ends which implicate others—outsiders to the socio-historical location of the actor. The problems associated with cross-contextual understanding are particularly severe in this realm because the discourse of politics is essentially public: it is discourse among strangers and not just among the friends, associates, and familiar co-participants who share the environment in which an individual's life experience takes place. Because politics comprises, at least in large part, decisions respecting the allocation of limited collective resources, it tends to be located in an arena in which different groups, interests, nations, traditions, cultures meet. This makes the interpretative problem of intersubjective understanding a matter of pressing practical concern, a concern which Mannheim came to feel was the predominant challenge before modern social science. It is not merely the text or artifact of a distant age which we must understand but the strangers in our own midst, individuals of other countries, of other races, of other classes, of other occupations, of other generations.

Politics, finally, can be distinguished from other areas of investigation in the *Geisteswissenschaften* by its orientation toward the future. 'Political conduct', Mannheim writes, 'is concerned with the state and society in so far as they are still in the process of becoming.'[28] The problem of the relation between thought and social position is especially acute in connection with political phenomena because the conceptual resources available to any group must (if they are to be effective) be oriented to its *interests* in the essentially political task of shaping its collective future. Mannheim continually emphasizes the fact that the quest for political knowledge is necessarily a form of moral inquiry: we ask not only 'who, or what are we?' but also 'what are we to do, what can we become?'. The notion of the scientist as a privileged observer, standing outside of the historical process, must be particularly resisted in the political sphere, where such an attitude serves not to eliminate the distortions of parochial interest but to disguise them.

When … we enter the realm of politics, in which everything is in process of becoming and where the collective element in us, as knowing subjects, helps to shape the process of becoming, where thought is not contemplation from the point of view of a spectator, but rather the active participation and

²⁸ IAU, p. 112 (IUU, p. 97).

reshaping of the process itself, a new type of knowledge seems to emerge, namely, that in which decision and standpoint are inseparably bound up together. In these realms, there is no such thing as a purely theoretical outlook on the part of the observer.[29]

It is in such a situation that the self-reflective interpretative procedures of the sociology of knowledge have their most important contribution to make. By making the perspectival character of knowledge (even his own) a matter for scrutiny rather than denial, the sociologist of knowledge has resources for securing political knowledge that are denied to the observer who proclaims his value neutrality.

The concept of ideology is not defined with any univocal precision in Mannheim's writings. His use of the term is consistent only in the sense that it is applied (as I indicated above) to those forms of socio-historical context of meaning that are relevant to political thought and behaviour. But in common with his procedure elsewhere, Mannheim is less interested in elaborating the category in terms of a set of definitional specifications than in identifying and characterizing different ways in which the comprehensive concept (context of meaning) can be specified in the course of investigation. Thus his concept of ideology acquires content mainly in the course of a series of historical investigations, to be found in the essays on generations, competition, economic ambition, democratization, and the concept of the state. Confusion about Mannheim's use of the term in *Ideology and Utopia* is a result of the fact that his purposes shift, among the different essays, between the historical and the methodological. In the essay on 'The Utopian Mentality' he attempts to describe the fundamental opposition, within the conceptual context of political discourse at any historical period, between a justificatory and a critical interest in 'things as they are', and he distinguishes between the terms 'ideology' and 'utopia' in order to emphasize the significance of this difference. From the perspective of this argument, then, the future-orientation of utopias means that 'they are not ideologies in the measure and in so far as they succeed through counteractivity in transforming the existing historical reality into one more in accord with their own conceptions'.[30] Since this outcome can only be finally determined in retrospect, Mannheim's distinction has

---

[29] IUU, p. 170 (IUU, p. 149).
[30] IAU, pp. 195–6 (IUU, p. 172).

often been judged a methodological solecism.[31] Mannheim claims, on the other hand, that a position which *fails* to make such a distinction, which indiscriminately regards *any* vision in opposition to the *status quo* as lacking reality, itself indicates an ideological position committed to maintaining the present as it is. 'By calling everything utopian that goes beyond the present existing order, one sets at rest the anxiety that might arise from the relative utopias that are realizable in another order.'[32] But to pursue this argument (which is, I think, of considerable significance) would require a substantial and unnecessary digression: what is important to notice is that Mannheim's restricted concept of 'ideology' is designed to illuminate a particular feature of the conceptual presuppositions of political discourse. When this feature is not in the forefront of discussion, a wider concept of ideology (which would include the 'utopia' of this restricted argument) is employed.

Mannheim's main theoretical objective, which is evident especially in the title essay of *Ideology and Utopia,* is to subject the concept of ideology to the full implications of a method of historical self-reflection. The argument is developed by tracing the history of the concept of ideology in relation to the rise of what he had earlier called the 'unmasking turn of mind' *(enthüllende Bewusstsein).*[33] Although distrust and suspicion of the expressions of others 'is more or less evident at every stage of history,' he suggests, it is only when it 'becomes explicit and is methodologically recognized that we may properly speak of an ideological taint in the utterances of others'.[34] An attitude which seeks not to refute but to 'disintegrate' opposing ideas becomes systematically apparent in the thought of the Enlightenment but, Mannheim claims, it 'found its first conscious, reflective formulation in Marxism'.[35] Thus Mannheim presents his position, which can be taken as an application of the theory of interpretation examined

---

[31] For instance Wagner, 1952, p.   320.

[32] IAU, p. 197 (IUU, p. 173).

[33] FKM, p. 65 (WAW, p. 315).

[34] IAU, p. 61 (IUU, p. 57).

[35] FKM, p. 65 (WAW, p. 315). In spite of the considerable influence of Lukács's *History and Class Consciousness,* which was a favoured text in his Heidelberg tutorials at mid-decade, Mannheim's view of Marxism never really reached beyond the version of mechanical orthodoxy preached by the theorists of the Second International. If we turn to Marx's writings themselves, from *The Holy Family* to *Capital,* we discover a conception of ideology that is closer to the position adopted in *Ideology and Utopia* than either Mannheim or his many Marxist critics would seem to believe.

above, as an explicit response to Marxism. Two key steps in the development of a self-reflective theory of ideology are singled out: the shift from a *particular* to a *total* conception (which Mannheim credits to Marxism), and the shift from a *special* to a *general* formulation (which Mannheim supposes to represent a transcending of Marxism).

Unmasking is based on the particular conception of ideology when it uncovers more or less conscious acts of distortion in the service of interests. Distortion in this sense refers to a psychological act: it is specific, individualized, and related solely to the *content* of the expression unmasked. In contrast, the total conception of ideology refers 'to the ideology of an age or of a concrete historico-social group, e.g. of a class, when we are concerned with the characteristics and composition of the total structure of the mind of this epoch or group'.

When we attribute to one historical epoch one intellectual world and to ourselves another one, or if a certain historically determined social stratum thinks in categories other than our own, we refer not to the isolated cases of thought-content, but to fundamentally divergent thought-systems and to widely differing modes of experience and interpretation. We touch upon the theoretical or noological level whenever we consider not merely the content but also the form, and even the conceptual framework of a mode of thought as a function of the life-situation of a thinker.[36]

The contrast between 'content' and 'conceptual framework' makes it clear that the interpretative distinction between the expressive and the documentary meaning of an object is very much to the point here. To 'unmask' a position in the sense of the particular conception of ideology does not imply that its conceptual context is brought into question; it is assumed, in fact, that unmasker and unmasked share a common conceptual environment. In such a situation, discussion in good faith is all that is necessary in principle (however difficult it may be to achieve in practice) to re-establish dialogue, for 'the suspicion that one's opponent is the victim of an ideology [according to this particular conception] does not go so far as to exclude him from discussion on the basis of a common theoretical frame of reference'.[37] An entirely different situation prevails when unmasking proceeds according to the total conception of ideology, for here it is not the content of the ·expression which is at issue. The unmasker of total ideology repudiates not *what* is said, but the

[36] IAU, p. 56 (IUU, pp. 54, 55).
[37] IAU, p. 57 (IUU, p. 55).

conceptual means *by which* it is said. He attacks precisely the context of meaning which his unmasked opponent has taken for granted. Thus the universe of discourse is broken and direct communication becomes impossible. By such means, the unmasker supposes, his adversary's position has been annihilated for it has been 'dissolved' into its socio-historically determined presuppositions.

As suggested by this last way of putting the matter, the use of the total conception of ideology implies the repudiation of whatever thought is subjected to such an 'analysis'; indeed, the very term 'unmask' establishes this negative objective. The idea of the historicity of thought thus becomes nothing but a weapon for undermining one's adversary. Such a position, Mannheim argues, is completely unsatisfactory. First, it requires an unwarranted (and unwarrantable) presumption on the part of the 'unmasker' to be in a position to absolutize his own context of meaning, and thus to place himself outside of history. Second, it achieves nothing in a practical sense because the technique of unmasking can always be (and, it can be observed historically, always is) generalized: the 'unmasked' can always turn the same weapon back upon the 'unmasker'. Third, by breaking the universe of discourse, such a position eliminates the very *possibility* of understanding; and where social relationships can no longer be founded in communication, there is left only the alternative of isolation or forceful imposition. Hence the total conception of ideology, conceived in this *special* formulation, can be shown to lead to both a theoretical and a practical dead end.

As long as one does not call his own position into question but regards it as absolute, while interpreting his opponent's ideas as a mere function of the social positions they occupy, the decisive step forward has not yet been taken.... In contrasts to this special formulation, the general form of the total conception of ideology is being used by the analyst when he has the courage to subject not just the adversary's point of view but all points of view, including his own, to the ideological analysis.[38]

With the transition from the special to the general formulation of ideology (which Mannheim also expresses as the transition from the theory of ideology to the sociology of knowledge), the 'unmasking turn of mind' turns back upon itself, and in doing so (in truly Hegelian fashion) both obliterates and transcends itself. By unmasking one's self, unmasking comes to an end. By directing

[38] IAU, p. 77 (IUU, p. 70).

one's analysis toward a self-reflective grasp of his own conceptual context of meaning, communication is reinstated as a goal of knowledge on a new and more comprehensive level. The total and general formulation of the theory of ideology, the sociology of knowledge, affirms the possibility of communication across the boundaries of differing socially constituted conceptual environments because it neither takes for granted a common frame of reference (in which case communication becomes illusory) nor does it seek to impose a common frame of reference (in which case communication is repudiated) but rather attempts to mediate the distance between subjects by investigating in good faith the conceptual means employed on both sides. Only after this interpretative task has been performed is it possible to address substantive differences, and this is then no longer a matter of unmasking or debunking. This represents, of course, a radical shift in the customary (pejorative) definition of 'ideology', and Mannheim himself seems unable to decide whether it is appropriate to retain the word. In the 1931 encyclopedia article on 'The Sociology of Knowledge' which was appended to the English version of *Ideology and Utopia,* he writes:

Since the suspicion of falsification is not included in the total conception of ideology [understood in its general formulation], the use of the term 'ideology' in the sociology of knowledge has no moral or denunciatory intent.... In the realm of the sociology of knowledge, we shall then, as far as possible, avoid the use of the term 'ideology,' because of its moral connotation, and shall instead speak of the 'perspective' of a thinker. By this term we mean the subject's whole mode of conceiving things as determined by his historical and social setting.[39]

This terminological question is never entirely resolved in Mannheim's writings on ideology; both evaluative and non-evaluative uses of the word may be found. His indecision, however, can be understood to reflect the dual intentions of his argument: on the one hand, to affirm what he felt to be the distinctively modern insight into the historicity of thought (thus emphasizing continuity with the conception of ideology employed in the Marxist tradition), and on the other hand, to insist upon the self-reflective application of this insight (which, he believed, fundamentally and essentially transformed the Marxian conception).

The value of ideological analysis in the service of comprehension rather than unmasking can be established only on the basis of

[39] IAU, p. 266 (IUU, p. 229).

the accomplishments of an interpretative sociology of the kind Mannheim recommended. Many of his essays of this period endeavoured to map out, in a preliminary way, the domain of the sociology of knowledge. Thus an investigation such as his 'Conservative Thought' can be considered not only as a substantive contribution but as an example of the style of analysis that Mannheim wanted to encourage. In this essay, Mannheim exploits the documentary evidence of a variety of nineteenth-century German texts to extract 'a number of characteristic features of the conservative form of experience and thought': its 'qualitative nature', its 'emphasis on concreteness', its acceptance of 'enduring actuality', its spatial conception of history, its preference for 'organic social units', etc. These features are related (conceptually and historically) to a common 'basic intention' of the conservative movement: the defence of the past against the challenge of the bourgeois-revolutionary epoch. Thus the 'theoretical core of conservative thought' amounts to a 'counter-system' to the content and methodology of bourgeois natural law thought.[40] Mannheim's complex discussion of the various strands of conservative thought in the period has the purpose of bringing this common conceptual structure into clear relief. Attitudes toward nation, state, law, land, 'life' are shown to reflect a persistent affirmation of being over thought, particularity over universality, organism over mechanism, etc. The relationship between the romantic celebration of the irrational and historicist emphasis upon synthetic 'mediation' is explored and contrasted with the counter-system of liberal abstraction, conceptualization, contemplation, atomization. More generally, in this and the other empirical essays, Mannheim develops a picture of the conceptual context of thought by investigating (a) how different ideas in a given social location reflect a common context of meaning, and (b) how ideas adopted in a new social location change their meaning by virtue of the new context. An example of the first is his effort to identify the conceptual coherence tying such spheres as romantic culture, feudalistic social values, historical philosophy. An example of the second is his description of the changing fortunes of concepts such as 'property' and 'liberty', or his comparison of the significance of pantheism in its Renaissance and romantic incarnations.[41]

---

[40] FKM, pp. 160–77 (cf. WAW, pp. 423–46; the last part of this section is original to the English version).
[41] FKM, pp. 162–7, 189–90, 217–19 (WAW, pp. 427–35, 461–4, 501–3).

But perhaps the most important point to emerge from these essays is a recognition that analysis which 'goes behind' the expressive object need not, after all, entail such a radical or bizarre interpretative procedure. Reference to the conceptual presuppositions of contending positions is a familiar and probably unavoidable feature of political discourse. And it is reasonably clear that the continuing grip of ideological categories (such as liberal, conservative, radical) is based upon their reference not to purely conceptual alternatives present in the timeless 'nature of being' but on their reference to historically specific positions and the interests associated with them. The main claims of the sociology of knowledge, in other words, are entirely consistent with conventional political discourse. What is novel about such a method is only its insistence that the implicit be made explicit, that meaning contexts usually taken for granted be treated as problematic.

This, on the other hand, is no inconsiderable challenge. A social science based upon a method of historical reflection threatens every kind of egocentric world view, be it the unreflective confidence of the ordinary agent or the epistemological self-righteousness of the social scientist. But by proposing a process of inquiry in which the conditions of discourse are examined, held up to one another, illuminated and tested, such a challenge eschews the fruitless path of historical scepticism and affirms the competence of public, intersubjectively accessible, methods for securing knowledge. The interpretative ideal of a community of subjects, capable of undistorted, luminous, free, and (in virtue of this freedom) rational discussion becomes the model not only for the *Geisteswissenschaften* but for the political order itself.

5. The Sociology of Knowledge as an Interpretative Method

WE ARE now in a position to return to the question with which we began: how should Mannheim's sociology of knowledge be characterized? To this point Mannheim's interpretative method has been described in terms of the series of arguments that begin with his earliest writings on culture and its objectifications. These steps have been discussed primarily on the basis of suggestions that are gradually elaborated and refined in the collection of essays that precede publication of *Ideology and Utopia*. It is in the latter work, however, that his 'mature' formulation of the method of the sociology of knowledge is to be found, and it is obvious that any reading of the point of this method must be tested against the contents of this work. In this chapter I propose to consider the problem of a sociology of knowledge as it can be seen to emerge from Mannheim's work as a whole, and in particular, as it is expressed in his most celebrated book. This is turn will provide the basis for a reconsideration of some of the more significant, or at least more frequently reiterated, criticisms of that method.

I

The arguments collected in *Ideology and Utopia* defend a coherent view of the nature and responsibilities of a social science, and can be taken as Mannheim's resolution of the central issues posed in the German *Methodenstreit*. In common with that tradition, he rejects any approach that would attempt to pattern social inquiry on the model of the natural sciences. Behavioural methods must be rejected, he argues, because they are incapable of acknowledging either meaning or history in the constitution of the world that we endeavour to comprehend: i.e. they restrict access to the material surface of phenomena, to only such evidence as can be perceived directly and without mediation, which can be measured, quantified, and thence assimilated to entirely formal and timeless categories of 'explanation'; and they offer no resources whatever for dealing with the problems that result from the fact that the observer, the scientist himself, is a participant in the historical process he seeks to comprehend. In the place of such methods, procedures of inquiry are required in which words and acts are recognized not as autonomous facts, but as vehicles of meaning. It is the nature of its subject matter, Mannheim makes very clear, which necessitates that social science be conceived as a hermeneutic and self-reflective discipline.

It has become clear that the principal propositions of the social sciences are neither mechanistically external nor formal, nor do they represent purely quantitative correlations but rather situational diagnoses in which we use, by and large, the same concrete concepts and thought-models which were created for activistic purposes in real life. It is clear, furthermore, that every social science diagnosis is closely connected with the evaluations and unconscious orientations of the observer and that the critical self-clarification of the social sciences is intimately bound up with the critical self-clarification of our orientation in the everyday world.[1]

Although Mannheim does not continue to employ the tripartite interpretative distinction between 'objective', 'expressive', and 'documentary' meaning, the substance of that distinction is emphasized repeatedly. To treat an object or an act as a vehicle of meaning is to 'look behind' it in the two directions we have discussed. It is first, to attempt to identify the intentional meaning conferred by its author. Since 'a human situation is characterizable only when one has also taken into account those conceptions which the participants have of it', the sociology of knowledge can accept 'no theoretical contention as absolutely valid in itself, but reconstructs the original standpoint, viewed from which the world appeared thus and such, and tries to understand the whole of the views derived from the various perspectives through the whole of the process'.[2] And it is, secondly, the concurrent attempt to identify the wider context of intersubjective meanings that is implicated in any expressive act, since 'every fact and every event in an historical period is only explicable in terms of meaning, and meaning in its turn always refers to another meaning. Thus the conception of the unity and interdependence of meaning in a period always underlies the interpretation of that period.'[3] The sociology of knowledge is, then, the methodological consequence

---

[1] IAU, p. 45.

[2] IAU, pp. 44, 170–1 (IUU, p. 149).

[3] IAU, pp. 68–9 (Mannheim added this passage to the English version, presumably in the belief that it might assist an audience alien to the Hegelian tradition; cf. IUU, pp. 63–4).

of the determination to treat social events as meaningful in the intersubjective (rather than in the merely objective) sense. Thus it is against the background of the preceding discussion of interpretation that the formulations of *Ideology and Utopia* must be read. The following passage, for instance, summarizes much of that discussion:

in order to be transmuted into knowledge, every perception is and must be ordered and organized into categories. The extent, however, to which we can organize and express our experience in such conceptual forms is, in turn, dependent upon the frames of reference which happen to be available at a given historical moment. The concepts which we have and the universe of discourse in which we move, together with the directions in which they tend to elaborate themselves, are dependent largely upon the historical-social situation of the intellectually active and responsible members of the group. We have, then, as the theme of this non-evaluative study of ideology [i.e. the sociology of knowledge], the relationship of all partial knowledge and its component elements to the larger body of meaning, and ultimately to the structure of historical reality.[4]

It is now possible to indicate the principal characteristics which distinguish Mannheim's conception of social science method from what he felt to be the defects of its alternatives: historicism on the one hand, and positivism on the other.[5] There is general agreement, first of all, that the ability of men to communicate with one another depends upon their being in a position to refer to a common means of communication; barring telepathy, an individual requires some medium by which to convey his thoughts to others, and for the medium to be effective it must be shared with others (i.e. grasped in essentially the same way by them) prior to making the attempt at communication. In fact, it is this ability to share meanings that makes both society and knowledge possible. This much of the interpretative argument would seem to be quite generally acceptable.

The difficulties raised in the methodological discussions of the social sciences, however, result from the fact that the problem of intersubjective communication is both a first order and a second order problem. We can say, first, that society itself depends upon the possibility of intersubjective communication among its members. If effective social action is to be possible, an actor must

---

[4] IAU, p. 86 (IUU, p. 77).
[5] These are rough and imprecise, but none the less convenient labels. I use them much in the spirit of Miller, 1972, with the obvious qualification that I wish to stress (as Miller does not) the elements of Mannheim's position that constitute a critique of historicism.

be able to assume with reasonable confidence that his act will be (a) seen to be a socially meaningful act by other members, and (b) understood by them to convey essentially the same meaning as he intends it to convey. As soon, however, as this act becomes the datum of social science investigation, a different intersubjective community becomes relevant. For social knowledge to be possible, the observer must be able to assume with reasonable confidence that his datum will be (a) seen to be theoretically meaningful by other observers, and (b) evaluated and/or validated by them according to essentially the same criteria as he employs. This distinction between the first order and the second order problem of intersubjectivity has generated many kinds of conceptual problems, and it is at the root of the methodological alternative addressed in Mannheim's writings. How do we go about gaining knowledge of meaningful social acts?

The historicist answer gives priority to the intersubjective community of participants in the social process. The meaning of a social act can be ascertained only by reference to the shared historical experience of which it is a part, for it is that shared life experience which constituted the medium by which the act conveyed meaning in the first place. An observer who cannot in some way 'enter' this context of shared experience can never hope to grasp the meaning content of the act, and without such a grasp his account of it is as shallow as accounts of Egyptian hieroglyphics before the discovery of the Rosetta stone. Historicism wavers on the methodological consequences of this position. For some, it implies that intersubjective communication is irremediably confined to its original socio-historical location, and knowledge of outsiders is therefore precluded in any but the most superficial sense. For others, knowledge of a foreign social environment may still be secured if it is preceded by a direct, personal, empathetic leap of understanding, in which the knower 'puts himself in the place' of the known.

Positivist discontent with this answer is based primarily upon its disregard for the intersubjective community of observers. If a social act depends upon the possibility of intersubjective agreement among members of the social community, it is argued, surely knowledge depends upon the possibility of intersubjective agreement among the community of observers. But this community, unlike the social community, is in principle universal. A method which makes access to knowledge dependent upon the historical position of the knower (which is, after all, only an event of chance from the perspective of an interest in truth), or upon certain subjective and unshared acts of *Verstehen* on his part, undermines the public character of knowledge. It acknowledges no common standards of evidence or coherence that can be appealed to in the event of contradictions among alternative claimants to 'understanding', and for this reason it would seem to permit no possibility of evaluation or critique. But this, in turn, overthrows the possibility of knowledge itself, for unless it is *possible* to show that some claim is false, it can never be held to be true. To avoid such a crippling defect, social science method must be based solely upon such elements of social action as *can* be identified and understood in a universal context of meaning: viz. the theoretic context of science. Whatever social 'knowledge' cannot be grasped in this 'objective' (because universal) context of meaning is not knowledge at all and should be rigorously excluded from the field. It is, in fact, the commitment to expel such subjective, impressionistic, unverifiable pretenders to 'knowledge' that distinguishes social *science* from the humanistic speculative methods that preceded it.

Mannheim's position fits into neither of these camps. He agrees with the historicist that a method which abstracts the content of a social act from its original (historical) context of meaning has the effect of altering and distorting that content. As he points out, this commitment to take 'expressive meaning' seriously does not imply any indifference to the 'objective facts'.

No one denies the possibility of empirical research nor does any one maintain that facts do not exist. (Nothing seems more incorrect to us than an illusionist theory of knowledge.) We, too, appeal to 'facts' for our proof, but the question of the nature of facts is in itself a considerable problem. They exist for the mind always in an intellectual and social context. That they can be understood and formulated implies already the existence of a conceptual apparatus.[6]

It is precisely because of his respect for the 'facts' of social experience that Mannheim finds it necessary to understand them in terms of the context of meaning constituted by the intersubjective community of participants. Moreover, as our earlier discussion of the thesis of textual autonomy sought to demonstrate, the methodological claim to replace the participants' historically-located context of meaning with an absolute and universal context appears in practice to amount merely to replacing one historical

[6] IAU, p. 102 (IUU, pp. 89–90).

context (the subject's) with another (the observer's). 'The absoluteness of thought is not attained by warranting, through a general principle, that one has it or by proceeding to label some particular, limited viewpoint (usually one's own) as supra-partisan and authoritative.'[7]

On the other hand, Mannheim acknowledges the cogency of the positivist's insistence that 'knowledge' cannot be subjective: it must be publicly accessible to the intersubjective community of observers. I cannot defend my interpretation of a distant writer simply by claiming that I am able, through a private act of understanding, 'to think as he thought'. Rather, I must undertake (a) to give an explicit account of the context of meaning in terms of which I claim that he thought (and by means of which I am able to have access to *what* he thought) and (b) to provide intersubjectively accessible evidence to support this hypothetical construct (evidence which, as our discussion of documentary interpretation indicated, is simultaneously historical and conceptual). Only in this fashion is a method of understanding also a method of intersubjectively accessible knowledge. Thus Mannheim insists that the sociology of knowledge, in contrast to historicism, must

work out criteria of exactness for establishing empirical truths and for assuring their control. It must emerge from the stage where it engages in casual intuitions and gross generalities (such as the crude dichotomy involved in the assertion that here we find bourgeois thinking, there we find proletarian thinking, etc.) though even this may involve sacrificing its slogan-like clearcutness. In this it can and must learn from the methods and results of the exact procedure of the philological disciplines, and from the methods used in the history of art with particular reference to stylistic succession.[8]

Furthermore, Mannheim rejects the historicist's suggestion that the question of the validity of a proposition can be resolved by reference to *its* context of meanings alone. Neither, however, does he accept the positivist claim that such reference is irrelevant to the question of validity. Adequate understanding of an expression is a necessary prelude to judgement about its truth, for the problem of validity can be addressed only after the problem of meaning has been settled. Sociological analysis of the meaning context may reveal that apparent conflicts about truth are in fact differences of meaning. But it may also bring to light contradictions which, in order to be resolved, require the critique of the

---

[7] IAU, pp. 42–3.
[8] IAU, pp. 306–7 (IUU, p. 263).

presupposed context itself by reference to a more comprehensive and adequate framework. In this case, the sociology of knowledge reaches a point where it also becomes a critique by redefining the scope and the limits of the perspective implicit in given assertions. The analyses characteristic of the sociology of knowledge are, in this sense, by no means irrelevant for the determination of the truth of a statement; but these analyses, on the other hand, do not by themselves fully reveal the truth because the mere delimitation of the perspectives is by no means a substitute for the immediate and direct discussion between the divergent points of view or for the direct examination of the facts.[9]

Mannheim does not, then, reject the positivist's definition of the goal of science, viz. knowledge that is intersubjectively accessible irrespective of the knower's social or historical location, by virtue of a comprehensive, universal, and (as near as investigation can make it) absolute context of meaning. What he resists is the claim that this context can be established by methodological fiat. Instead, he insists, it must be discovered in the laborious process of inquiry itself, a process in which the investigator must be attentive to the views of others and critical of his own to a far more radical and thoroughgoing extent than is commonly implied in the injunction to 'keep an open mind'.

By making the concept of a socially-constituted context of intersubjective meanings the centre of its analysis, the sociology of knowledge distinguishes itself from the methods of both historicism and positivism. For in spite of their divergent positions in almost all other respects, the historicist and the positivist are equally guilty (though each in his own way) of begging the question of how cross-contextual communication is possible. (The radical historicist, who denies that it *is* possible, does not beg this question of course.) The historicist asserts that it is possible for an observer to enter another historical context but since this is a private and intuitive act, there are no intersubjective criteria for determining that a given observer has in fact done what he claims. The goal of understanding is affirmed, but the goal of shared knowledge is relinquished. The positivist, on the other hand, asserts that it is possible for a suitably trained observer to step out of *any* historical context, with the consequence that the specific meaning content of the historical period he studies is no longer of interest to him. The goal of shared knowledge is affirmed, but the goal of understanding is relinquished. Both approaches take it for granted that social knowledge is possible only within a single context of meaning: for the historicist, it is the local context given in history; for the positivist, it is the universal context given by Scientific Method. The problem of reconciling contexts is resolved dogmatically in each case. For the historicist, social knowledge is made possible by the assumption that the investigator has managed to enter the historical world of his subject, making the context of his own world irrelevant. For the positivist, social knowledge is made possible by the assumption that the investigator has managed to construct a supra-historical, universal meaning context (Scientific Method), making the original distinction between the two worlds (in terms of systems of meaning) irrelevant. But according to Mannheim's position, assumptions of either kind are illegitimate except as they are established by inquiry. An investigation of the content of a meaningful social act is possible only after its conceptual context has been grasped, for it is no help that the facts 'speak for themselves' as long as we do not understand the language in which they speak. Were it the case that all observers and all subjects of observations in history shared a common context of meaning, the science of society could proceed directly and simply to the 'facts'. But since this is not the case, it is necessary to proceed 'in a more roundabout fashion' (as Mannheim puts it) by directing attention first to the alternative contexts themselves. It is insufficient simply to pronounce the priority either of the context of meaning employed by a community of subjects (as do the historicists) or of that employed by a community of observers (as do the positivists). Rather, we must make the attempt to identify and compare the alternative contexts so that the content of one can be re-expressed (as authentically as the ultimate limits of communication permit) in terms of another. 'An effort must be made to find a formula for translating the results of one into those of the other and to discover a common denominator for those varying perspectivistic insights.'[10] The sociology of knowledge directs attention to the context, rather than the content of thought because intersubjective communication of the latter is possible only by means of the former. What other methods of social science take for granted, the sociology of knowledge makes a deliberate, conscious, critically important stage of investigation. It is still, of course, only a preliminary stage; but since whatever subsequent knowledge we may attain depends on the care and accuracy with which this investigation is carried out, it is of absolutely fundamental importance.

II

To identify and overcome the obstacles to intersubjective communication is, perhaps, the single most pervasive and deeply-held purpose of Mannheim's writings on social science. It is a purpose which he espoused as a member of the scientific community and as a member of the social community at the same time. Much of the fervour and also, I think, the poignancy of his constant reformulations of the method of the sociology of knowledge derives from his conviction that we must pursue the ideal of intersubjectivity not only as a norm of science but as a norm of social life. Indeed, for Mannheim this is a single pursuit. A scientific methodology which attains a high degree of intersubjective communication between observer and observer (by means of a formal, privileged, technical language) at the expense of obstructing intersubjective communication between observer and subject endangers the larger responsibility of social science to contribute to intersubjective communication among *persons*. Mannheim continually cautions the social scientist against adopting the self-image of an observer standing outside history, removed from the fabric of social experience which he claims to explain. For

in so far as the world does become a problem it does not do so as an object detached from the subject but rather as it impinges upon the fabric of the subject's experiences. Reality is discovered in the way in which it appears to the subject in the course of his self-extension (in the course of extending his capacity for experience and his horizon).[11]

It is for this reason that the pursuit of social knowledge—knowledge of other men, other groups, other historical problems and the efforts to solve them—is 'bound at every step to the process of individual self-clarification'. As observers, we acknowledge our place in the historical process not by absolutizing it but by subjecting it to critical scrutiny. As long as our methods make of others merely a reflection of our own concerns, attitudes, and categories, we are unable to understand either them or ourselves. This is why Mannheim, throughout *Ideology and Utopia*, describes the sociology of knowledge in reflexive terms: it is a method of 'self-criticism', of 'critical self-awareness', of 'self-clarification', of 'self-

---

[11] IAU, p. 49.

extension', etc.[12] The point, which Mannheim seems to regard as both an epistemological and a moral truth, is that if the social scientist is to take the ideal of intersubjective communication seriously, his method must treat his own position—as well as the positions he studies—as problematic.

We have already commented upon the implications of this self-reflective method in relation to Mannheim's search for an alternative to an historicist relativism. But it is important also to notice (and this is particularly clear in the arguments of *Ideology and Utopia*) implications of such an attitude for the political status of the scientist within society. A method which takes its own position for granted, which is content to reduce all other positions to its own terms, precludes the notion of knowledge as shared experience. Implicit in such a model of knowing is a relation of power, or at least of superiority, of knower over known. Mannheim is thoroughly hostile to such a vision of science (a fact which may surprise those who are familiar with the conventional accounts of his theory of the intelligentsia—to which we shall return shortly), and the hermeneutic model is defended in major part because it checks any presumption of this type. This does not, however, make Mannheim hostile to knowledge, anti-intellectual, indifferent to standards, etc. He is as committed as any positivist to the search for a 'total view', for knowledge that is not bound to the transient and partial and distorted positions that are found to change from one individual or group to another. But he insists that we cannot claim to have attained such a view simply by reducing all other perspectives to our own, absolutized position—even if that position be the position of Science. As social scientists and as citizens we are engaged in a 'continuous process of the expansion of knowledge, [which] has as its goal not achievement of a super-temporally valid conclusion but the broadest possible extension of our horizon of vision'.[13] The method of the sociology of knowledge is an invitation to extend our knowledge of society by learning how to listen to others. It is an invitation to reflect upon the nature of our own beliefs and historical position by attempting to grasp (in so fas as this is possible as an intellectual act) other positions. It is an affirmation of our ability to transcend (through intersubjective communication) the limits of understanding born of personal experience, and to know and learn from the experiences of others.

---

[12] IAU, pp. 2, 47–9, and *passim*.
[13] IAU, p. 106 (IUU, p. 93).

Thus the hermeneutic aspirations of the sociology of knowledge must be treated as part of a larger 'moral-philosophic' concern that animated Mannheim's work from his first lecture on the crisis of culture to his last reflections on education and the prospects for democracy.[14] In his essay on 'The Concept of Ideology', George Lichtheim describes such a concern from the larger perspective of a two-hundred-year tradition in historical philosophy:

it responded to a practical purpose which in our own age has become more urgent as the globe shrinks, and historically divergent and disparate cultures press against one another. Because these pressures are experienced as ideological conflicts among people holding different and incompatible aims in view, it remains the task of the critical intellect to evolve modes of thought which will enable men to recognize the common purpose underlying their divergencies.[15]

Certainly this is an accurate description of what Mannheim wished to accomplish. There is a long passage (to which we have already alluded) in the encyclopedia essay at the end of *Ideology and Utopia* which clearly attempts to establish such a programme for the sociology of knowledge. The modern world is distinguished, he writes, by the sudden and forced breakdown of the traditional structure of human separation and heterogeneity.

Not only Orient and Occident, not only the various nations of the west, but also the various social strata of these nations, which previously had been more or less self-contained, and, finally, the different occupational groups within these strata and the intellectual groups in this most highly differentiated world—all these are now thrown out of the self-sufficient, complacent state of taking themselves for granted, and are forced to maintain themselves and their ideas in the face of the onslaught of these heterogeneous groups.

The result, Mannheim continues, is the proliferation of acts of pseudo-communication, in which the utterances of speaker and listener go 'past one another' and in which all participants 'overlook the fact that their antagonist differs from them in his whole outlook, and not merely in his opinion about the point under discussion'. Such is the situation in which the sociology of knowledge becomes of crucial political significance; it offers a means by which the conditions of communication may be re-established. Mannheim acknowledges the criticism, which had greeted the original German edition of *Ideology and Utopia,* to the effect that the sociology of knowledge, in 'going behind' the

---

[14] See the excellent discussion of Mannheim's place in a moral philosophic tradition in Kettler, 1967.
[15] Lichtheim, 1967, p. 44.

immediate expression, *undermined* authentic discussion and failed to take the other subject seriously. But this, he insists, is to misread entirely the purpose of such analysis, which is employed in precisely those circumstances in which authentic discussion cannot occur and is, moreover, designed to establish those conditions that make communication possible.

The sociology of knowledge seeks to overcome the 'talking past one another' of the various antagonists by taking as its explicit theme of investigation the uncovering of the sources of the partial disagreements which would never come to the attention of the disputants because of their preoccupation with the subject-matter that is the immediate issue of the debate. It is superfluous to remark that the sociologist of knowledge is justified in tracing the arguments to the very basis of thought and the position of disputants only if and in so far as an actual disparity exists between the perspectives of the discussion resulting in a fundamental misunderstanding. As long as discussion proceeds from the same basis of thought, and within the same universe of discourse, it is unnecessary. Needlessly applied, it may become a means for side-stepping the discussion.[16]

Those who maintain that the sociology of knowledge is guilty of undermining and devaluing thought will not be persuaded, of course, by a passage which establishes only that Mannheim did not *wish* to do so. The road to the genetic fallacy, after all, may be paved with good intentions. It is therefore necessary to re-examine the central problem introduced in the second chapter: what is *Seinsverbundenheit?* What sense does it make to interpret the *meaning* of any expression by reference to *social existence?* As we saw then, the answer of Grünwald and his successors has been that it makes no sense. In his critique, Grünwald makes a sharp distinction between understanding an expression in terms of its immanent meaning *(Geistverstehen)* and understanding it as a manifestation of some absolute which is external to this meaning *(Manifestationsverstehen)*. The sociology of knowledge is alleged to be concerned exclusively with the latter, with the additional qualification that for it, the absolute sphere is (arbitrarily) identified with social being. To believe, however, that extrinsic factual circumstances can in any way determine the meaning or truth status of instrinsic meaning is to commit the genetic fallacy. Since the sociology of knowledge interprets expressions extrinsically (i.e. by reference to factors

[16] IAU, pp. 279–81 (IUU, pp. 239–41).

which are not part of the immanent—intended—meaning of the subject of the expression), it is guilty of the genetic fallacy.[17]

It is evident (as Mannheim would be the first to admit) that this criticism carries decisive weight against any attempt (such as has sometimes been attributed to Marxism) to 'reduce' ideas to material existence, *Idealfaktoren* to *Realfaktoren*. But as we have seen, such an enterprise has little to do with the sociology of knowledge which is, in fact, very much concerned with the immanent meaning of ideas. Extrinsic analysis of thought is used by Mannheim as a means of access to immanent meaning, not as a means of replacing ideas with material facts. 'What must be stressed', he writes, 'is that not all genetic "derivations" are un-meaning: there are not only genetic *explanations*, which are, but also genetic *interpretations*.'[18] The significance of treating the sociology of knowledge as an interpretative method is seen in the critical distinction between two very different types of extrinsic analysis: causal explanation of the preconditions of thought on the one hand, and meaningful interpretation of the presuppositions of thought on the other. It is the former type of analysis which, if offered as an account of the meaning of an expression, commits the genetic fallacy. For

it is impossible to confirm or refute the validity of, for instance, a proposition on the ground of its causal, un-meaning preconditions. But it is erroneous to locate sociological (or other extrinsic) interpretations in this sphere of un-meaning causal explanations and to apply to them the axiom that genesis can determine nothing about meaning and validity.[19]

Mannheim never swerves from the view which he saw expressed in the early essay on *Weltanschauung,* that 'there can be no causal, genetic explanation of meanings—not even in the form of an ultimate theory super-added to the interpretation'.[20] The point, however, is that the methods of the sociology of knowledge 'cannot be considered causal explanations in terms of un-meaning phenomena'.

Every sociological 'explanation', then, whenever it functionalizes intellectual phenomena—e.g. those found in a given historical group—with respect to a 'social existence' that lies behind them, postulates this social existence as a context of meaning more comprehensive than, though different from, those

[17] Grünwald, 1934, pp. 62–4, 67–79.
[18] FKM, p. 122 (WAW, p. 396).
[19] FKM, p. 122 (WAW, p. 395).
[20] FKM, p. 56 (WAW, p. 151).

phenomena, whose ultimate significance is to be understood in relation to this context....

Sociological extrinsic interpretation does not serve in this case to abandon the sphere of meaning as such. But only by abandoning *immanent* interpretation is it possible to see those meaningful existential presuppositions which, although the theory itself that is to be interpreted was not capable of seeing them, nevertheless were the presuppositions (albeit not immanent) of its validity.[21]

These remarks, from a short essay on interpretation that Mannheim published in 1926, are confirmed in the analysis of *Ideology and Utopia,* and they show that the importance which Mannheim's critics attach to the genetic fallacy is justifiable but misapplied. A social theory which reduces meaningful acts or expression to physical events is indeed epistemologically self-destructive and even dehumanizing. But to determine whether such a reduction has occurred the relevant distinction is not between extrinsic and intrinsic reference but between extrinsic causal explanation of thought (which is guilty of the genetic fallacy as charged) and extrinsic meaningful interpretation of thought (which is not). At no point in Mannheim's argument does he posit a causal link between un-meaningful phenomena and the meaningful content of expression. It is absolutely essential to the sociology of knowledge, as he develops it, that the 'existence' of *Seinsverbundenheit* be understood to have a conceptual structure: his method (as the passage just quoted puts it) relates thought to 'social existence as a context of meaning', not to some conception of 'social existence as brute data'.

What Mannheim means by 'social existence as a context of meaning' or, as he puts it in *Ideology and Utopia,* simply 'social existence' *(soziales Sein)* should, by this point, be reasonably clear. But so much of the discussion of *any* version of the sociology of knowledge is preoccupied with this notion of a 'base' (or 'substructure' or 'real factors') that we should pause for a moment to emphasize the point which is at issue. One of the fundamental notions propounded in the positivist version of the Marxian tradition is that the ideas of a social class are determined by the 'material conditions' which characterize its place in the system of production. In vulgar accounts of historical materialism, this thesis is expressed as the dependence of thought upon certain kinds of material entities—e.g. resources, machines, physical character-

---

[21] FKM, pp. 122, 123-4 (WAW, pp. 396n., 396-7).

istics of productive activity, etc. Such a thesis (which is extremely difficult even to expound, much less defend) has little relation, however, to Marx's own account of 'material conditions' of production, and indeed, would seem to commit the very error of confusing social relations for physical things which he so effectively criticized—in his theory of commodity fetishism and in his critique of political economy in general. Marx made it very clear that the material substructure of a society is constituted in social relations. The forces of production are no mere collection of things: they are objects and persons standing in a determinate social relationship to one another, and they can be characterized only by reference to those relations. Capital itself, to take the most fundamental example, is not a class of objects (such as machines) but objects utilized in a certain way and determined in terms of a particular form of social relations; indeed, it is not improper to say that capital *is* a social relation. This is not the place to deal with Marx's theory of ideology, but it is important not to confuse Mannheim's notion of 'social existence' with a vulgar materialist account of 'base' that is quite foreign, even to Marx's view of the 'material conditions' that underlie thought.

Mannheim conceives 'social existence' in the most general terms, on the basis of his historical observations about the nature of expression and its communication. The conceptual means by which thought is formulated and expressed is, as we have seen, neither handed down from heaven as a timeless and absolute vehicle of communication available to all men, nor created afresh by each individual independently from others. Since it is instead constituted by the social process of sharing meaningful experience, by life, it can be identified and grasped only with reference to that (social) experience. It is for this reason that 'a position in the social structure carries with it the probability that he who occupies it will think in a certain way. It signifies existence oriented with reference to certain meanings *(Sinnausgerichtetes Sein)*.'[22] This is the most general characterization of 'social existence'; it is left to historical research to determine the constitution of the social groups and their forms of activity, which may (for instance) follow Marxian analysis in terms of class structure and the forces and relations of production. The important point, however, is that irrespective of the nature of that determination (i.e. whether one pursues a Marxian sociology of knowledge of a non-Marxian one), the entity

[22] IAU, p. 293 (IUU, p. 252).

which is posited as 'standing behind' thought is itself constituted in social relations, which is to say, it is invested with meanings. This is why the charge of the genetic fallacy (meaning derived from un-meaning) misses the mark:

'Social existence' is thus an area of being or a sphere of existence, of which orthodox ontology which recognizes only the absolute dualism between being devoid of meaning on the one hand and meaning on the other hand takes no account. A genesis of this sort could be characterized by calling it a 'meaningful genesis' *(Sinngenesis)* as contrasted with a 'factual-genesis' *(Faktizitätsgenesis)*.[23]

The dualism of which Mannheim complains characterizes almost all discussions of attempts to relate thought to social experience. The critics of Mannheim (and of Marx as well) refuse to take seriously the notion of a context of meaning (or an ideology) as a mediating entity—a structure of meanings constituted in shared social experience on the one hand, but providing the means by which an individual's thought is formulated and expressed on the other. Talcott Parsons, for instance, has quite properly defended the position

which considers cultural and social systems, not as completely 'concrete' systems, nor merely as 'interdependent', but as *interpenetrating*. The failure to clarify the problem of interpenetration is one of the major sources of the difficulties in which discussions about the sociology of knowledge have become enmeshed. The key to the relation is the proposition already reiterated—the patterning of the structure of social systems *consists* in institutionalized culture. If this be granted, the question of 'which is more important' becomes nonsensical on a certain level.

But he goes on to suggest (and here, I think, he goes astray) that this conception of interpenetration was *not* understood by Marx (who is held to have engaged instead in the vulgar practice of reducing ideas to 'material facts') and that Mannheim followed suit.

Mannheim was so preoccupied with what he regarded as his great discovery of certain patterns of interdependence, that he tended to adopt and work with the Marxian level of analysis of the structure and functioning of social systems (the *Realfaktoren*). He did not even seriously utilize the much higher level of theoretical differentiation in this field that Max Weber's work made available.[24]

This view is, I have suggested, a double misrepresentation. But

[23] IAU, p. 294 (IUU, p. 252); it is noteworthy that Mannheim refers, in this passage, to his earlier essay on interpretation cited above.
[24] Parsons, 1961, pp. 990, 991.

Mannheim's view of Marx was itself guilty of the same kind of over-simplification, with the result that we find, in his essay on 'German Sociology', almost a reproduction of Parson's argument!

If we take into account the whole of Max Weber's work, and not only his previously mentioned book [*The Protestant Ethic*], then we come to that conclusion . . . that *the manner in which the question was formulated by the materialists and the idealists was wholly wrong*. We cannot separate spheres of economic and social change on the one hand from the sphere of a change in mental development on the other.[25]

It is possible to conclude, I think, that the argument from the genetic fallacy, popular as it has been among Mannheim's critics, has scant application to the sociology of knowledge as he understood and recommended it.

III

Many of the other traditional criticisms of the sociology of knowledge rest on the same misconstruction. The unsatisfactory state of discussion about the problem of imputation, for instance, reflects this disinclination to recognize the 'reality' of a mediating structure of intersubjective meanings. It is clear why, on the conventional dualistic view mentioned above, the business of 'imputing meaning' looks absurd. If the sociology of knowledge reduces the meaningful content to social facts, all we need to do is show that very different meanings are expressed by persons in the same or similar 'material positions'—and vice versa—and its claims are shown to be spurious. One scarcely needs to undertake an empirical investigation to know that expressions which are related to common social locations are not on that account identical in content. Thus Mannheim's claim is considered to be based upon patent nonsense. W. G. Runciman, for example, considers it an objection to Mannheim (whom he joins with Lukács on this score) when he notes

that it is illegitimate to talk of classes as having opinions or ideas; it is individual members of classes who have opinions and ideas, and intellectuals or proletarians can be too easily observed to disagree with each other about precisely those topics on which Lukács and Mannheim assign to them an ideal-typical unanimity.[26]

---

[25] ESSP, p. 219. This argument for 'interpenetration' is presented even more forcefully in his 1929 lecture on 'Economic Ambition' (ESK, p. 235 [WAW, pp. 631–2]) and in his original essay on 'The Problem of a Sociology of Knowledge' (FKM, pp. 86–9 [WAW, pp. 343–7]).

[26] Runciman, 1971, p. 164.

But nowhere does Mannheim speak of such a thing as 'classes having opinions or ideas', and nowhere does he deny that disagreement may be found within any social group. What is clearly confused, in such a line of criticism, is the distinction between imputing to a group (or to a social location) a common *content* to its members' expressions, such as common beliefs, opinions, etc., and imputing to them a common context of shared meanings. In terms of Mannheim's earlier language, the error is to confuse expressive meaning (which is individual and unique, and thus cannot be imputed to a group) with documentary meaning (which is necessarily shared and therefore must be imputed to a group). The notion of intersubjective meanings is not the same as that of consensus; common terms of reference imply no identity of content. Where these distinctions not valid ones, the phenomenon of communication itself would, as we have seen, become quite incomprehensible.

It is incorrect, moreover, to suppose that by imputing even a general conceptual context to a group we can assume that it is employed *in toto* in any instance of expression or by any individual member.

The individual members of the working-class, for instance, do not experience *all* the elements of an outlook which could be called the proletarian *Weltanschauung*. Every individual participates only in certain fragments of this thought-system, the totality of which is not in the least a mere sum of these fragmentary individual experiences.[27]

Any specific imputation, therefore, represents an attempt to characterize the particular context of meanings which a given social location makes available to the individual thinker. To impute such an ideal-typical construct to a group (whether defined in historical, social, occupational, or any other terms) is to make the claim that its members employ this conceptual framework of presuppositions in their thought and expression. This claim is always hypothetical in that we can never be certain that our investigations have been sufficiently extensive to guarantee that the imputed context of meaning is an accurate and sufficient description of the conceptual framework which a given thinker does indeed employ. On the other hand, the claim is categorical in the sense that *some* such imputed context (if not our own, then a more adequate one) must be attributable to the

---

[27] IAU, p. 58 (absent from the German). See also the important passage in the essay on *Weltanschauung*, FKM, pp. 33–6 (WAW, pp. 123–6).

thinker, since otherwise he would be unable to communicate with others at all and his expression would cease to be meaningful.

As these remarks indicate, the problem of imputation can only be understood in relation to the general method of interpretation which has been presented earlier. An inspection of the arguments of *Ideology and Utopia* on this subject shows that the conception of documentary interpretation remains in the background of Mannheim's views. Imputation, he writes, may proceed at two levels. The first 'reconstructs integral styles of thought and perspectives, tracing single expressions and records of thought which appear to be related back to a central *Weltanschauung*'. It attempts to make explicit the documentary referent which is implicit in any single expression. The hermeneutic circle is then closed by employing the ideal-types constructed in such investigation as a hypothesis for the interpretation of concrete expressions, by asking for example, 'to what extent liberals and conservatives did think in these terms, and in what measure, in individual cases, these ideal-types were actually realized in their thinking'. Finally, Mannheim suggests, on the assumption that such styles of thought are constituted by and hence reflected in the common experience of those who employ them, these constructs must be interpreted historically.

As sociologists we do not attempt to explain the forms and variations in conservative thought, for example, solely by reference to the [ideal] conservative *Weltanschauung*. On the contrary, we seek to derive them firstly from the composition of the groups and strata which express themselves in that mode of thought. And, secondly, we seek to explain the impulse and the direction of development of conservative thought through the structural situation and the changes it undergoes within a larger, historically conditioned whole (such as Germany, for instance) and through the constantly varying problems raised by the changing structure.[28]

As each of these steps (and their interdependence) has already been discussed at some length, it is necessary only to emphasize their general consequence: that what is imputed to a social group by the sociology of knowledge is a common *means* of expression, not a common expressive content.

The more sophisticated critics of Mannheim's use of imputation concede this point but question the propriety of attempting to identify any such entity as a 'context of meaning', as something other than the content of the expressions being interpreted. What

[28] IAU, pp. 307-9 (IUU, pp. 264-5).

reality can such a construct have? 'Far from being a reconstruction of reality,' writes Child, 'this ideal type or integrated totality would seem to exist solely in the mind of the investigator.' But if this is the case, what sense can there be to talk of 'imputing' it to individuals or groups?[29] The force of this objection is not eliminated by pointing out that it overstates the dilemma in two respects. First, the imputed construct is not confined to the mind of the singular investigator, since Mannheim requires that the criteria of its construction be explicit and subject to intersubjective verification by others.[30] And second, the imputed construct is not excluded in an absolute sense from the mind of the subject since, as we have seen, it is at least possible to see one's own conceptual assumptions by a self-reflective act of awareness 'after the fact'.[31] Still, Child is correct to point out (as our earlier discussion emphasized repeatedly) that, on Mannheim's account, the conceptual context of thought does not 'exist in the mind' (as a conscious content) of the person who employs it—and to whom it is imputed.

The question, then, is whether it can be legitimate to impute to someone a position in reference to a structure of meanings even if he cannot be said to be consciously aware of occupying such a position, or even capable of characterizing it. Can a position which is not 'in the mind' of a subject be none the less imputed to him? If it is true, as the preceding argument about the nature of communicative experience sought to demonstrate, that successful expression requires not only a determinate content but also a determinate context and that the latter can never itself be the intended object of expression, then the answer to this question is a rather simple 'yes'. What seems counter-intuitive about such a suggestion turns out, on reflection, to be a fairly familiar feature of what may be called practical knowledge; i.e. we are often in a position of 'knowing how' without 'knowing that'. We have already mentioned the most striking example of this situation: the capacity to apply often extremely complex rules of language successfully without knowing those rules. But the condition is a more general one. A construct such as Weber's 'protestant ethic' just cannot be said to exist 'solely in the mind of the investigator'. If we impute such a construct to the expressions of, say, Josiah

---

[29] Child, 1941, p. 206 and *passim*.
[30] e.g. IAU, p. 308 (IUU, pp. 264–5).
[31] FKM, p. 23 (WAW, p. 109); IAU, pp. 75–83 (IUU, pp. 69–75) and *passim*.

Wedgwood, we have made a statement about 'reality', fully subject to various kinds of intersubjectively accessible evidence, in spite of the fact that the construct itself might be entirely unrecognized or even incomprehensible to Wedgwood himself. The same is true when we speak of such things as the French character, the classical style, the Victorian sensibility, or the liberal view of the polity. Whether participants in the social process become aware of such constructs depends largely upon whether they are challenged, in their activities, by a group holding a conflicting set of assumptions. When, on the other hand, a particular 'conceptual apparatus is the same for all the members of a group, the presuppositions (i.e. the possible social and intellectual values), which underlie the individual concepts, never become perceptible'.[32] But whether or not an actor is aware of the historical particularity of his context or even is capable of grasping it with self-reflective clarity does not affect the legitimacy, indeed the indispensability, of the concept as a tool for the reconstruction of expressed meanings.

To defend the legitimacy of imputation as part of any interpretative method is not, of course, to defend any particular imputation or to suggest that the procedure is straightforward or free of dangers. The attempt to characterize the conceptual context of other subjects is a necessary part of interpretation precisely because if it is not done, we are likely to impose our own presuppositions upon them. This purpose is entirely contradicted if the procedure of imputation becomes a licence for fanciful, unhistorical, dogmatic, or arbitrarily 'original' schemes of interpretation, in which the conceptual framework imputed to others is limited only by the inventive imagination of the investigator. In attributing meaning, whether to an expressive object or to a socio-historical context, the interpreter always has the responsibility to listen: to be guided by 'what is there'.

An accurate reading of the interpretative method of the sociology of knowledge requires also that the conventional criticism of Mannheim's view of the role of intellectuals be revised. Probably no aspect of his thought has received more comment or less sympathy than Mannheim's use of Alfred Weber's notion of a 'socially unattached intelligentsia'.[33] According to the common view, Mannheim tries to escape his self-imposed dilemma (that

[32] IAU, p. 102 (IUU, p. 90).
[33] See IAU, pp. 153–64 (IUU, pp. 134–43).

thought is dependent on social location) by arbitrarily elevating one particular group (of which he naturally happens to be a member) above and outside of the historical process, where it may think freely and truthfully, unencumbered by the constraints of *Seinsverbundenheit* which bind other mortals.[34] The naïvety of such a 'solution' has stimulated a great many clever remarks at Mannheim's expense. Tonsor remarks that 'one of the greatest of Mannheim's achievements' was his ability to combine 'Marxist eschatological certitude with the egocentricity and ambition of the intellectual'. Horowitz complains that 'Mannheim's intellectual is a man who steadily rinses his brain with ideas, but never knows enough to wash his hands with soap'. And Merton concludes that such 'efforts to rescue oneself from an extreme relativism parallel Munchhausen's feat of extricating himself from a swamp by pulling on his whiskers'.[35]

To see what Mannheim's claims for a *freischwebende Intelligenz* really entail it is necessary both to pay attention to what he says and to recognize the relation of these remarks to his argument as a whole. His view of the capacities of the intelligentsia does not come, as so many writers have made it appear, out of an arbitrary and presumptuous professional self-confidence, and in no way does he exempt this group from the conditions which he associates with the historical character of thought in general. For Mannheim, as we have seen, thought is located in shared social experience in the sense that it is formulated and expressed in terms of a context of meaning that is given in that experience. This is a condition of knowledge for everyone: no observer can claim, as a prerogative of his status as a scientist, priest, savant, or anything else, to stand above or outside of the historical process and to look down upon the human subjects of his investigation from the transcendent perspective of a god. On the other hand, Mannheim does not deny but strongly affirms the ability of men to understand one another, even if they do not share the same social location. The method of the sociology of knowledge is designed to serve this very purpose. It counsels us to perform the 'first preparatory step' of attempting to grasp the context of meaning employed by another, so that we can be in a position to understand

---

[34] This reading is so prevalent that references can only be arbitrarily chosen: see Aron, 1964, p. 61; Brecht, 1959, p. 300; Hartung, 1970, pp. 701–2; Merton, 1957, pp. 506–8; Schelting, 1934, pp. 161–7; Speier, 1970, p. 276; Stark, 1958, pp. 300–6.

[35] Tonsor, 1968, p. 625; Horowitz, 1961, p. 76 (he makes essentially the same remark in 1960, p. 183); Merton, 1957, p. 507.

his thought and thus engage in an authentic discussion rather than 'talk past' him. Mannheim considers it established that this 'first step' can, in principle, be taken and executed successfully. The question, then, is who is most likely to do so? Which social position is most favourably placed for such a task? And his answer is that among different social groups it is the intelligentsia which is most likely to take it, first because intellectuals are more likely to have the occasion, the inducement, to take it, and second, because they are more likely to have the resources to carry it out effectively.

To see why intellectuals are more likely than members of other social groups to undertake the effort of cross-contextual understanding it is only necessary to consider those conditions in which whatever is distinctive about their life activity is carried out. Because they are not directly engaged in the productive process, intellectuals carry out their work in comparative (this word must always be stressed) independence of the different institutional domains that define and structure the activities of other members of society; their lives can be said to be comparatively self-directed, and free of the kind of organizational constraints which elsewhere impose synchronization of individual acts, integrated modes of operation, formalized structures of authority, etc. On the other hand, the intellectual does not work in isolation from the community of intellectuals: on the contrary, his activity depends critically upon the interaction made possible by the transmission of ideas—criticism, reinforcement, commentary, collaboration. This situation of independence without isolation maximizes the likelihood that the intellectual in the normal course of his work will be forced to make an effort to achieve cross-contextual understanding relatively frequently. The community of which he is a part and to which his activities must be oriented is dispersed, relatively free of institutional co-ordination or direction, and composed of members who have been recruited from many different backgrounds and social positions. (Mannheim puts particular emphasis on this last point.) In addition, at least a considerable part of the intellectual's activity is oriented toward members of other *periods* as well as other societies and other social classes; the community of co-workers with whom common terms of reference must be established is not only often distant in a spatial sense but may also be distant historically as well. For these reasons, the problem of cross-contextual understanding is 'built in' to the normal activities of the intellectual in a sense in which it is not in the activities of most other social groups. The intelligentsia, to a greater degree than other types of social location (such as family, church, factory, civic association, administrative office, etc.) finds the experience of bridging conceptual gaps a natural, normal, and necessary part of its social activity.[36]

The advantageous position of the intelligentsia is determined, in the second place, by its special resources for extending understanding across contexts of meaning. The 'first preparatory step' of grasping the meaning of an alien frame of reference is a step which *can only be performed intellectually*. We can only grasp the context of another's expression by a conscious, self-reflective act of 'documentary interpretation'. We cannot possibly hope to come to share this context by sharing the experience in which it is given. We cannot decide to relive our life as an Elizabethan actor in order to understand Shakespeare. We cannot decide to expand our horizon of understanding by becoming, for instance, an Asian peasant (the most that we might achieve is to become, say, a 'middle-aged Western professor who has decided to become an Asian peasant' which is, of course, not at all the same thing). We can only understand an other by the imperfect but still not entirely hopeless method of using our intellectual resources to loosen the limitations of immediate experience and to attempt (intellectually rather than experientially) to gain access to the meaning given in the experiences of others. Unless this kind of effort is carried out first, attempts to acquire 'objective' knowledge will forever succumb to a self-absolutizing parochialism.

The advantage of the intellectual, therefore, is to be found not in any magical or privileged feature of his existential position, but in the relatively rich resources which are available to such a position for looking beyond it. Education, Mannheim says, can serve as a 'replica' of other social experiences and thus of other ways of

---

[36] It must be emphasized that by *freischwebende Intelligenz* Mannheim means to refer to the class of socially unattached intellectuals—*not* to claim that all intellectuals are socially unattached. 'The more intellectuals became party functionaries,' he notes, 'the more they lost the virtue of receptivity and elasticity which they had brought with them from their previous labile situation' (IAU, p. 38). The same comment applies to intellectuals who have become the salaried 'functionaries' of business, government, or even universities. To the extent that the intellectual vocation of the sort Mannheim saw practised in his student days in Budapest was already anachronistic, his argument can be convicted of undue optimism. This is *not*, however, the *naïvety* with which he is charged by most of his critics.

looking at the world. This 'simulation' subjects the intellectual to a wider range of experience; he is exposed to

the influence of opposing tendencies in social reality, while the person who is not oriented toward the whole through his education, but rather participates directly in the social process of production, merely tends to absorb the *Weltanschauung* of that particular group and to act exclusively under the influence of the conditions imposed by his immediate social situation.[37]

But to maintain that it is only as intellectuals that we have 'the *capacity* to acquire a broader point of view'[38] is not in any way whatever to imply that intellectuals automatically or necessarily have a broader point of view, much less the truth. Merton's claim that 'Mannheim finds a structural warranty of the validity of social thought' in the position of the *freischwebende Intelligenz*[39] is without foundation; Schelting's suggestion that Mannheim thinks 'the fact that a conception comes out of the brain of a socially unbound intellectual is the guarantee of its validity'[40] is an outrageous inaccuracy. That the intellectual's position in no way provides a 'structural warrant' for the validity of his views is apparent not only from the general character of Mannheim's argument but from his various specific and quite unambiguous remarks on the subject.

First, it is evident in his repeated observation, throughout his empirical investigations, of intellectual currents of thought that are clearly socially attached and can make no claim to general validity. His essay on conservatism, for instance, concentrates primarily on the positions of intellectuals, and contains not the slightest suggestion that their position was any kind of guarantee of validity. In *Ideology and Utopia* itself, he makes it clear that no structural warrant of validity can attach itself to the position of the intelligentsia by making the explicit distinction between intellectuals who attach themselves to the perspective of a particular social location and those who engage in the 'scrutiny of their own social moorings'. To say that the intellectual has the ability to scrutinize and so potentially to overcome his social moorings is obviously not to deny but to affirm that he has such moorings. Thus the resources of the intellectual provide him certain 'opportunities' *(Chancen)*—opportunities which Mannheim be-

[37] IAU, p. 156 (IUU, p. 136).
[38] IAU, p. 161 (IUU, p. 140); italics added.
[39] Merton, 1957; he makes the same comment in 1972, p. 29.
[40] Schelting, 1936, p. 673 (in the original, the entire passage is in italics); essentially the same comment appeared in his 1934, p. 166.

lieves he has a responsibility to exploit—but in no way do they provide him with any guarantees.[41]

This reading is confirmed by a more extended essay on the intelligentsia which Mannheim (according to his editors) wrote shortly before coming to England in the early thirties, but which was published only after his death.[42] By virtue of his training, he writes here, the intellectual

is *equipped* to envisage the problems of his time in more than a single perspective, although from case to case he may act as a partisan and align himself with a class. His acquired equipment makes him potentially more labile than others. He can more easily change his point of view and he is less rigidly committed to one side of the contest, for he is capable of experiencing concomitantly several conflicting approaches to the same thing.

Referring to criticism of his treatment of the intelligentsia in *Ideology and Utopia,* Mannheim emphasizes his use of the word 'relatively' in respect to the detached position of that group, and concludes:

After this reminder, it should not be expected that the critics will again conveniently simplify my thesis to the easily refutable proposition that the intelligentsia is an exalted stratum above all classes or that it is privy to revelations. In regard to the latter my claim was merely that certain types of intellectuals have a maximum opportunity to test and employ the socially available vistas and to experience their inconsistencies.[43]

Mannheim's faith in the intellectuals is, then, a faith in the powers of the intellect to overcome the limitations of this or that personal experience as a ground of knowledge, to expand the self by engaging in authentic communication with others, to aspire to a more comprehensive view of our shared human condition by virtue of the communicative ability to gain access to contexts of thought other than the one into which we are born. His argument is not that to be an intellectual is a sufficient condition for overcoming the limitations of a given social location, but that the exercise of intellectual resources is a necessary condition for making the attempt to do so. What Wolff has properly called Mannheim's 'passion for thinking'[44] may have led him to an

[41] IAU, pp. 158, 161 (IUU, pp. 138, 140).
[42] ESC, part 2. There is some question, regarding this text, of the degree to which it is influenced by its editors who, according to an editorial note, 'had to rethink the original text without distorting the author's intentions' (p. vi.). Since the original manuscripts have been withheld (see Wolff, 1971, pp. lxxxvii–lxxxviii), we are forced to rely on their judgement as to whether or not they succeeded in this aim.
[43] ECS, pp. 105, 106.
[44] Wolff, 1971, p. lxvii.

unduly hopeful estimation of the powers of intersubjective communication, but such a mistake is a very long way from the espousal of a 'priesthood of scientists [which] would actually wield power'.[45]

---

[45] Tonsor, 1968, p. 625.

6. The Sociology of Knowledge and Social Theory

WHAT, IF any, are the consequences of the sociology of knowledge for the construction of social theory? What are the grounds for supposing that a hermeneutic method, concerned with the interpretation of ideas, can make any substantial contribution to our understanding of social or political behaviour? Such questions do not permit compact answers, but to appreciate the significance of Mannheim's enterprise it is necessary to consider at least some of its implications for social science practice and its relation to some of the main debates that have occupied social theory during the last fifty years. Without suggesting that his work resolves such issues, or even that he deals with all of the aspects of such debates in any deliberate way (Mannheim was unquestionably no system-builder), I want to sketch the case, which is adumbrated in his writings, for considering the hermeneutic sociology of knowledge a central part of any social science method, and to place this case in relation to the vigorous and controversy-ridden literature that continues to our own day.

I

If the sociology of knowledge is to be employed as an interpretative method, one might be tempted to conclude that it is not, after all, of *any* major relevance to the construction of social theory. This view, which assimilates the sociology of knowledge to intellectual history, has been widely accepted. Stark, for instance, subtitles his book on the subject 'An Essay in Aid of a Deeper Understanding of the History of Ideas', and frequently suggests that there is an equivalence between 'historian of ideas' and 'sociologist of knowledge'.[1] Many have stressed the preoccupation of Mannheim (and the European proponents of this method in general) with 'the intellectual elite who formulate knowledge and

[1] Stark, 1958, p. 142.

disseminate it' rather than with popular belief and opinion.[2] Berger and Luckmann conclude their brief survey of the literature by remarking: 'This has made one fact very clear. Apart from the epistemological concern of some sociologists of knowledge, the empirical focus of attention has been almost exclusively on the sphere of ideas, that is, of theoretical thought.' This, in their view, is not a good thing; for 'the problem of "ideas", including the special problem of ideology, constitutes only part of the larger problem of the sociology of knowledge, and not a central part at that'.[3]

But Mannheim is far less vulnerable to such a critique than they suppose. It is true, certainly, that his analysis is in large part devoted to 'theoretical thought', and much of the argument and most of the examples of the preceding chapters of this study have been concerned with the application of this approach to the history of political ideas. (Berger and Luckmann, of course, concede that this is a legitimate *part* of the sociology of knowledge.) It is also true, and this represents the main contribution of the Berger and Luckmann volume, that a sociology of knowledge which restricts itself entirely to this dimension is excluded from the questions which are most significant to social theory. The 'knowledge' which is most important to social life is not to be found in theoretical constructs of professional thinkers but in the common-sense 'pre-theoretical' constructs of everyday life. (Mannheim was, of course, acutely aware of the degree to which the latter might reflect the former; as Keynes once observed, 'Practical men, who believe themselves to be quite exempt from any intellectual influences, are usually the slaves of some defunct economist. Madmen in authority, who hear voices in the air, are distilling their frenzy from some academic scribbler of a few years back.'[4]) It is such 'commonsense "knowledge" then', they write, 'that constitutes the fabric of meanings without which no society could exist' and it is for this reason that sociology of knowledge must concern itself with what they call 'the social construction of reality'.[5]

Such an argument, however, is not at all foreign to Mannheim, who expresses a continuous and persistent concern with the

    [2] Fuse, 1967, p. 250.
    [3] Berger and Luckmann, 1967, pp. 12–13, 14; cf. Berger, 1970, p. 377.
    [4] Keynes, 1936, p. 383.
    [5] Berger and Luckmann, 1967, p. 15.

problem of taking theoretical account of the 'pre-theoretical' forms of experience. Such was a major concern in his early essay on *Weltanschauung*.

To 'reflect' these forms and what is in-formed by them, without violating their individual character, to 'translate' them into theory, or at any rate to 'encompass' them by logical forms, that is the purpose of theoretical inquiry, a process which points back to pre-theoretical initial stages, at the level of everyday experience.[6]

In his 1924 manuscript 'A Sociological Theory of Culture and its Knowability', Mannheim identifies the object of the cultural sciences as the 'conjunctive sphere' of thought, 'the sphere of "real life"', of the irrational, emotional life of communities, of the everyday substratum underneath the formal, contractual, societal veneer'.[7] And in turning to the sociology of knowledge, we find no restriction of focus. In the essay on competition, for example, he remarks that 'within this concept of existentially-determined thought [*seinsverbundenen Denken*] are included historical thought (the way in which man interprets history, and the way in which he presents it to others), political thought, thought in the cultural and social sciences, and also ordinary everyday thought'.[8] Of these, only the third is unequivocally in the realm of 'theoretical thought' (as Berger and Luckmann put it); the first and second are partially and the last entirely in their larger category 'common-sense knowledge'. It is difficult to see, especially after following Mannheim's discussion later in the same essay of patterns of 'public interpretation of reality' why the later writers should consider 'far-reaching redefinition' of the field necessary to accommodate their conception of the 'social construction of reality'.

The decisive evidence, however, against restricting Mannheim's methods to the interpretation of theoretical ideas is to be found in *Ideology and Utopia,* the arguments of which consistently subordinate Mannheim's interests as an intellectual historian to his interests as a social and political theorist. The very first page, as we saw earlier, emphasizes the book's concern with thought as 'it really functions in public life', and goes on to criticize philosophers for their preoccupation with 'exact modes of knowing' which are not at all sufficient for understanding the thought of 'living

[6] FKM, pp. 14–15 (WAW, p. 99).
[7] Kettler, 1967, pp. 422–3.
[8] ESK, p. 193 (WAW, p. 569).

human beings who are seeking to comprehend and to mould their world'. Therefore, he maintains, 'It is the most essential task of this book to work out a suitable method for the description and analysis of this type of thought and its changes, and to formulate those problems connected with it which will both do justice to its unique character and prepare the way for its critical understanding'.[9] The purpose of *Ideology and Utopia,* these first pages state explicitly, is to analyse the function of thought in social action. In doing this, Mannheim's sociology of knowledge is designed (no less than Berger and Luckmann's) to 'furnish a foundation for the social sciences'[10] and not merely to aid in the 'deeper understanding of the history of ideas'.

Now the merit of this claim clearly depends on the legitimacy of applying an interpretative method to the investigation of social action in general, and not merely to verbal acts of communication of the kind discussed earlier. In other words, the sociology of knowledge can be considered something more than a tool of the intellectual historian only on the supposition that the sciences of men are themselves hermeneutical. And this is, in fact, the main consequence of Mannheim's arguments against behaviourism: a formal, external description of behaviour is necessarily incomplete because 'a human situation is characterizable only when one has also taken into account those conceptions which the participants have of it'.[11] We must, in other words, refer to the 'intentional' character of an action just as we must refer to the 'intentional' character of a text if we are to be able to understand what it means. But is it appropriate to treat these two objects, the act and the text, according to the same method?

Although discussion to this point has focused on the problem of interpreting a written text, I have rather casually referred to speaking and acting, as well as writing, as meaning-conveying gestures. Both speaking and writing are, of course, forms of action, but it is clear that there are attributes which distinguish them from non-linguistic forms of activity, as well as from one another. A spoken utterance, for instance, conforms much more strictly to the dialogic model required for interpretation than does the written

---

[9] IAU, pp. 1–2; cf. p. 71 (IUU, p. 65): 'the history of thought is not confined to book alone, but gets its chief meaning from the experiences of everyday life, and even the main changes in the evaluations of different spheres of reality as they appear in philosophy eventually go back to the shifting values of the everyday world'.

[10] Mannheim, IAU, p. 5.

[11] IAU, pp. 44.

text. The speaker can draw upon a more complex variety of contextual resources (gestures, facial expressions, timing, etc.), he can orient his expression to a far more precisely defined audience, he can adjust and refine his expression on the basis of the 'feedback' information that he receives from this audience. On the other hand, the permanence, the objectified separation from its source, the openness of its audience which constitute the distinctive qualities of the written text, make necessary a much greater care and precision of expression than is required in conversation. (There appears to be not so much a sharp difference of kind here, as a gradation of forms of expressive experience: a formal lecture is much closer to a written text than is normal conversation; an informal note or a private letter is much closer to conversation than is a published treatise.) In a real sense, communication by means of a written text is more difficult to achieve than communication by means of a spoken utterance, although the benefits associated with this medium (its greater range, its greater permanence, its greater opportunity for rigour) may justify the effort. Whatever the differences between these forms, however, they can both be considered legitimate objects for the interpretative methods that have been defended here. Both an utterance and a text have a determinate content, an intended meaning. Both an utterance and a text are the products of an act undertaken in order to make it possible for some other to understand that content (i.e. they are both expressions). Both an utterance and a text manage to accomplish that objective only by means of reference to a socially constituted context of intersubjective meanings.

But what about other forms of action? Although spoken utterances and written texts are important parts of the subject matter of disciplines such as sociology, economics, or politics, they are clearly not the only or the most important objects of such fields. Actions such as competing, obeying, voting, enacting, buying, selling provide the stuff of which the social sciences are made; if the methods of the sociology of knowledge are not applicable to them, then Mannheim's claim to 'furnish a foundation for the social sciences' is surely specious. And the argument for confining the applicability of the sociology of knowledge to the history of ideas has an immediate plausibility. Actions such as those mentioned are distinguishable from speaking and writing precisely because they are not expressions: the communication of some meaning content is not the ostensive purpose of such actions, or, if their accomplishment may require some act of speaking or writing, it is still analytically separable from a different and separate purpose of the undertaking as a whole. (It is true that there is a class of gestures which can be taken as expressive in the full sense of the word, even though they do not involve either speaking or writing—for instance, the policeman's raising of his hand to 'express' his order to stop. Physical signs of this sort, however, are plainly not sufficient to justify the claims of the sociology of knowledge as a social science.) Does it make sense, then, to hold that an interpretative method is applicable to social actions as well as to utterances and texts?

We have seen that an intentional act of verbal expression requires (a) that the expression have a determinate content of intended meaning, (b) that the agent intend by his action to bring it about that this meaning be understandable by others, and (c) that to accomplish this he employ a shared context of intersubjective meanings. To what extent can we say that non-verbal (or non-expressive) social actions conform to this model? The first requirement would seem to be pertinent by virtue of the decision to characterize an instance of human behaviour as 'social action' in the first place. As we saw earlier (in chapter 3), to adequately identify an event as self-monitored behaviour it is necessary to be able to give an 'intentional description' of it, which is to say that we must be able to grasp what it is that the agent understands himself to be doing. Like a text, an action can thus be said to have a determinate content of meaning, the identification of which is necessary in order to specify just what kind of an action it is. (An action may also, of course, have any number of other 'objective' meanings—i.e. meanings determined by the framework of the observer—but this feature does not distinguish it from a text or an utterance.) The second requirement appears at first to be less relevant. An interest in being understood is attached to the notion of 'expression' in a more immediate and emphatic way than it is to many social actions. To the question 'why did you write that book?' the answer is likely (though, as we have seen, not necessarily) to be, at least in part, 'because I wanted to communicate something'. This would be a most unlikely answer, however, to the question 'why did you buy that book?' or 'why did you agree to that contract?' But this difference does not greatly affect the issue. In buying or contracting I may not be particularly concerned with communicating my intended meaning, but I none the less must do so if the action is to be accomplished successfully.

The bookseller must understand the meaning of my action in putting money on the counter, he must, in fact, correctly identify the 'intentional description' of that action, if the transaction is to occur. The third requirement (which is logically connected to the second) is clearly applicable to the successful accomplishment of social actions. If I expect my act to 'count' as a performance with a certain kind of social meaning, I must respect the rules and conventions that make it possible for others to recognize it as such. The fact that, in writing a name on a piece of paper and sending this to the Town Hall I intend to express my preference for a candidate for the office of mayor obviously does not mean that I have 'voted'.

It appears, then, that there is at least a *prima facie* case for deciding that social action in general, and not the acts of speaking and writing alone, require the use of an interpretative method of inquiry. And if this is the case, the concern of the sociology of knowledge with the identification of socio-historical contexts of meaning can be considered an important constituent of any adequate social theory. This is, of course, Mannheim's position: 'A situation is constituted as such when it is defined in the same way for the members of the group,' he maintains, and 'it is only by means of this meaning-giving, evaluating definition that events produce a situation where activity and counteractivity are distinguishable, and the totality of events are articulated into a process'.[12] In order to clarify what such a claim entails it may be helpful to consider an example, which is borrowed from Taylor's important essay on 'Interpretation and the Sciences of Man'.[13]

Negotiation is a commonplace activity in contemporary industrial societies. We can, without difficulty, recognize a variety of circumstances in which this concept provides an appropriate characterization of social 'reality': discussion between union and management representatives regarding a wage contract, a party conference over the passage of a piece of legislation, the bargaining between customer and salesperson in a market, etc. Once any one of these situations is identified as an instance of 'negotiation', furthermore, we are able also to give an appropriate description of any of a variety of states or acts which are understood to be implied by the activity: making (or withdrawing) an offer, negotiating in

---

[12] Mannheim, IAU, p. 21.
[13] Taylor, 1971, pp. 22–4 and *passim*. (I have adapted Taylor's account to serve my own purposes.)

good (or bad) faith, breaking off (or concluding) negotiation, etc. Now in understanding or explaining any such event, on Mannheim's account, the three different levels of meaning must be acknowledged. First, the observer notices any number of 'objective' events: someone enters or leaves the room, certain words are uttered, a document is signed, etc. The meaning of these events, at this level, is determined by the observer's framework of relevance: he may fit the events into his own notion of the meaning of negotiation, or he may be interested in quite another system of relevance—say the measurement of changing states of muscular tension. If these physical events are to be understood as social events however, as action rather than mere behaviour, the observer's description must be consistent with the actors' own understanding of what they are doing. For the action of leaving the room to count as 'breaking off negotiations', there must be reason to believe that the actor himself intended such a meaning (in the sense described earlier) in performing the act. Evidence to the contrary changes the appropriate description of the act. If, for example, we learn that a customer signs a contract in ignorance of the obligations he thereby undertakes, we will be forced to characterize the event differently; perhaps the activity previously supposed to be 'negotiation' is in fact 'fraud'.

But even the behaviourist will acknowledge, in some fashion, the relevance of this intentional dimension of the meaning of an act. (In just what fashion, and how adequately, is a question to which we shall have to return.) The interesting questions are raised by the third level of interpretation: the 'documentary' reference of the act, or its socially constituted context of intersubjective meaning. For the practice of negotiation presupposes what Mannheim, in the passage just cited, calls the common 'definition of the situation' by means of which 'activity and counteractivity are distinguishable'. As Taylor puts it with respect to the present example: 'That the practice of negotiation allows us to distinguish bargaining in good or bad faith, or entering into or breaking off negotiations, presupposes that our acts and situation have a certain description for us, e.g., that we are distinct parties entering into willed relations.'[14] But the shared meanings (involving personal autonomy, the competition of interests, norms of good faith and rationality, etc.) which make negotiation possible are not common to all groups or all societies. Taylor refers

[14] Taylor, 1971, p. 24.

to the organizing force of consensus in the social life of traditional villages in Japan and elsewhere, such that the idea of bargaining and the practices associated with it have no reality. It is not just that we 'know' or 'believe in' something that the members of such a village do not; the difference concerns the presence or absence of contextual meanings such that knowledge or belief of this kind is possible. 'The meanings and norms implicit in these practices are not just in the minds of the actors', he points out, 'but are out there in the practices themselves, practices which cannot be conceived as a set of individual actions, but which are essentially modes of social relation, of mutual action.'[15]

The act of negotiation, therefore, requires not merely that an actor engage in some form of behaviour, intending some meaning, but also that he share a socially constituted context of meaning that establishes the possibility of such action in the first place. It is worth stressing again (as Taylor does) that what must be shared is not any particular collection of beliefs or attitudes but a 'set of common terms of reference': at issue is not whether the parties to negotiation agree with one another, but whether they have a common understanding of what they are doing. Thus we can expect that those who are negotiating will bring with them any number of different objectives, interests, approaches, etc.

But what they do not bring into the negotiations is the set of ideas and norms constitutive of negotiation themselves. These must be the common property of the society before there can be any question of anyone entering into negotiation or not. Hence they are not subjective meanings, the property of one or some individuals, but rather intersubjective meanings, which are constitutive of the social matrix in which individuals find themselves and act.[16]

Although Taylor's argument offers a very different path from the one followed by Mannheim (whom he never mentions), his position both illustrates and confirms the major claims of the sociology of knowledge. He concludes that the meaning of an act is no more a self-evident 'given' than the meaning of an utterance; that to recover it requires that 'the meaning for agents of their own and others' action, and of the social relations in which they stand' be interpreted in terms of the intersubjective meanings which constitute that social reality; and that because these intersubjective meanings are historically specific, thought must be compre-

---

hended (as Mannheim puts it) 'in the concrete setting of an historical-social situation'.[17] It is this circumstance that mandates, for Taylor as for Mannheim, that the sciences of man be hermeneutical.

II

Mannheim was not, of course, original in propounding an interpretative social science. Max Weber's sociology represents the first really significant effort to fashion a method for the social studies that would do justice to the meaningful character of human behaviour without relinquishing the aim of giving a scientifically credible explanation of it. Weber's attempt to bridge the gap between the traditions of idealism and positivism is expressed concisely in the famous definition of sociology that opens *Wirtschaft und Gesellschaft:* 'a science which attempts the interpretive understanding of social action in order thereby to arrive at a causal explanation of its course and effects'.[18] In contrast to the individualizing focus of the historian, he continues, the social scientist 'seeks to formulate type concepts and generalized uniformities of empirical process', but whatever is lost by such abstraction is offset by the conceptual precision that can be 'obtained by striving for the highest possible degree of adequacy on the level of meaning'.[19] Weber's position stands squarely in the centre of the major modern debates about the method of the social sciences. 'Interpretive understanding' and 'causal explanation' are treated not as alternatives but as necessary complements to one another. The social sciences are neither 'ideographic' nor 'nomothetic' but require aspects of both a generalizing and a particularizing procedure of investigation.[20] The principles he upholds admit neither historicism nor naturalism, idealism nor materialism, holism nor psychologism, as one-sided alternatives.[21] One need not, I think, underestimate the

[17] Ibid., pp. 17, 32, 40; IAU, p. 3.
[18] Weber, 1964, p. 88. 'In "action" is included all human behaviour when and in so far as the acting individual attaches a subjective meaning to it' (same page).
[19] Ibid., pp. 109–10. 'We apply the term "adequacy on the level of meaning" to the subjective interpretation of a coherent course of conduct when and in so far as, according to our habitual modes of thought and feeling, its component parts taken in their mutual relation are recognized to constitute a "typical" complex of meaning. It is more common to say "correct" ' (p. 99).
[20] Cf. Weber, 1963, pp. 382–7.
[21] Cf. Parsons' introduction to Weber, 1964, pp. 8–9; Weber, 1958, p. 183; Runciman, 1972, p. 11.

magnitude of Weber's accomplishment to suggest that his dominating presence in twentieth-century social theory owes something to his ability to sustain a multi-front war in which nearly all combatants can find him, at least part of the time, a powerful ally. It is the centrality and influence of Weber's position which makes it an advantageous point of departure from which to survey the place of interpretative method in contemporary social science.

It would be incorrect, of course, to imply that Weber's methodology can be taken as a standard of orthodoxy or (to use the recently fashionable terminology of Kuhn) a paradigm, providing 'model problems and solutions to [the] community of practitioners'[22] engaged in investigation of society. For one thing, it is a widely acknowledged fact (lamented by some, a source of satisfaction to others) that no such paradigm and hence no singular 'community of practitioners' exists in the social sciences. Second, Weber's position itself is not entirely unambiguous. His methodological writings never attained a systematic final formulation, and the closest approximation to such a statement (the opening sections of *Wirtschaft und Gesellschaft*) is sufficiently sketchy to permit a variety of constructions of the position that Weber would have developed had he lived (and had the will) to complete it.[23] Finally, Weber's interpretative method has not lacked criticism, either from those who find that his treatment of the problem of meaning yields too much to the positivist case, or not enough.[24]

The important point, however, is that Weber's methodology has provided a point of reference to which most of the discussion of his successors can be related. The self-understanding of social science, as articulated in the debates, the manifestos, the working assumptions of its practitioners over the past two or three decades can with considerable justification be considered a response to, an interpretation of, or an extrapolation from, the position developed in his essays on method and (implicitly) in his substantive

---

[22] Kuhn, 1970, p. viii.

[23] Beyond differences in interpretation, commentators differ as to whether Weber's methodological writings constitute (as Runciman, 1972, p. 8, puts it) 'a more or less coherent whole' or (as Rex, 1971, argues) a succession of distinguishable sociological methods.

[24] In the first group the most influential writings have probably been those of Schutz (especially 1967) and from another direction, Winch, 1958; representative of the second line of critique are Abel, 1953; Nagel, 1963; and Lazarsfeld and Oberschall, 1965.

empirical research. The dominant 'objectivist' developments in the social theory of mid-century can trace a lineage to Weber, but so can the less influential 'subjectivist' movements which continually reappear to criticize them.[25] Consequently, an attempt to estimate the significance of interpretative method (and in particular, of course, Mannheim's sociology of knowledge) for contemporary social theory can most usefully begin by examining the nature of the answers that have been put to questions posed by Weber. Three such questions, implicit in Weber's characterization of interpretative sociology cited above, are particularly important to this purpose. First, how does the observer identify the 'subjective meaning' which an actor attaches to his act? Second, what is the relationship between understanding and explaining an act so identified? Third, what is the relationship between the 'subjective meaning' of the actor and the concepts and theory constructed by the observer?

(1) Weber's answer to the first question, according to one writer, 'is really quite simple: We perceive the meaning of an action in the same way as we perceive the meaning of a word or a sentence'.[26] Now if the argument developed earlier has any merit, Munch is wrong to suppose that the way we perceive the meaning of a word or a sentence is at all simple. As a description of Weber's treatment of the problem, however, his observation is perfectly correct: in the act of *Verstehen* I am able to infer an actor's subjective meaning from his behaviour in the same way in which I can infer his meaning from the physical sounds or marks of his words. Both possibilities presuppose a common 'language', and Weber makes it clear that 'the basis for certainty' in understanding

[25] The choice of labels to affix to characteristic tendencies or styles of thought is always most unsatisfactory. Few would deny that a fairly sharp contrast of assumptions and approach is discernible in the methods of social scientists, yet it is impossible to identify the alternatives by name without at once burdening the characterization with spurious associations, connotations, and a wholly misleading appearance of precision and unanimity. Earlier (above, pp. 108 ff.) I made use of Miller's contrast 'historicist/positivist', but for a number of reasons these terms are more satisfactorily applied to the milieu of Weber and Mannheim in the Europe of the first decades of the century than they are to our own. The contrast I wish to draw on here (and develop in the following discussion) is, of course, closely related to Miller's, as also to Easton's 'traditionalist/behaviouralist' (1953), Morgenbesser's 'social scientific naturalist/anti-social scientific naturalist' (1966), Runciman's 'intuitionist/positivist' (1971), and von Wright's 'aristotelian/galilean' (1971). It seems to me, however, that 'subjectivist/objectivist' have a slight advantage in terms of the issues I wish to emphasize, as well as a helpful vagueness of historical association; cf. Gewirth, 1954.

[26] Munch, 1957, p. 28.

depends upon the degree of precision made available by the relevant language: thus the understanding of rational activity has 'the highest degree of verifiable certainty', empathetic or appreciative understanding has less, and (where the actions of another depart radically from our own experience and values) 'sometimes we must simply accept them as given data'.[27] Weber's distinction between *aktuelles Verstehen* and *erklärendes Verstehen* acknowledges the point that an identification of subjective meaning is not necessarily an identification of motive; it is possible to see what an actor is *doing* by direct observation, but to determine what he is doing it *for* requires a further grasp of the 'complex of meaning' in which the act occurs.[28] Thus, for the observer to grasp the subjective meaning of an act is considerably less problematic to Weber than his commentators have made it out to be. Neither psychological intuition nor sociological investigation is a necessary part of the act of *Verstehen:* in so far as a 'language' is shared, the subjective meaning of an act is simply there to be grasped, as the meaning of a sentence lies open to anyone who knows how to read.

Objectivist social science treats the problem of identifying subjective meaning as in part spurious to scientific investigation, in part no different from the problem of identifying any kind of empirical data relevant to knowledge. In as far as 'understanding' consists in 'the application of personal experience to observed behaviour', it cannot be used 'as a scientific tool of analysis'; at best, such non-verifiable 'insight' can serve as a useful heuristic technique 'helpful in setting up hypotheses, even though it cannot be used to test them'.[29] In as far, on the other hand, as subjective meaning is relevant to social scientific knowledge (and none but a rather extreme form of psychological behavourism would claim otherwise) it can only be admitted as a unit of empirical information which can be identified with intersubjective certainty. Both intentions and motives, in other words, can be treated (and, as far as scientific knowledge is concerned, can *only* be treated) as 'brute data'—data which can be identified without any interpretative reference to strata of meaning which 'stand behind' the fact. A rigorous social science, on this view, takes cognizance of the subjective meaning attached to physical behaviour

by taking the meanings involved in action as facts about the agent, his beliefs,

---

[27] Weber, 1964, p. 91.
[28] Ibid., pp. 94–6.
[29] Abel, 1953, pp. 684–5.

his affective reactions, his 'values', as the term is frequently used. For it can be thought verifiable in the brute data sense that men will agree to subscribe or not to a certain form of words (expressing a belief, say); or express positive or negative reaction to certain events, or symbols; or agree or not with the proposition that some act is right or wrong. We can thus get at meanings as just another form of brute data by the techniques of the opinion survey and content analysis.[30]

This manner of dealing with the subjective meaning attached by an actor to his behaviour is readily familiar to anyone with even a cursory familiarity with the behavioural literature—especially in politics and sociology.

To Weber's heirs in the subjectivist tradition, on the other hand, his treatment of the problem of identifying subjective meaning requires correction in a sense precisely opposite to the complaints of the objectivist. Schutz, for instance, argues that Weber has taken insufficient precautions to assure that an act's motive as given to the observer is in fact the same motive as given to the actor.[31] In Weber's account, he maintains, both the actor's subjective feeling about the complex of meaning in which his behaviour is placed and what the observer supposes that complex to be are misleadingly combined in the concept of motive. Consequently Weber is himself guilty of treating action as 'a discrete unified datum with which one can operate immediately, without further inquiry as to the principle of its unity'.[32] Schutz seeks to correct this defect with a complex phenomenological analysis of the structure of a motive, marking in particular the temporal distinction between its 'future-directed' and 'past-directed' senses.[33] We need not pursue his analysis in any detail; the point of importance is that Schutz, and the phenomenological school of sociology which he inspired, have developed an elaborate case for concluding that Weber's error lay not in going beyond the 'brute data' identification of subjective meaning to interpretative understanding, but in not going far enough in this direction.

The same conclusion is reached by a different route by Winch, who argues that the problem of identifying subjective meaning is

---

[30] Taylor, 1971, p. 19.

[31] Neither Schutz nor Weber adequately distinguishes between the 'intentional description' of an action and its motives (although Schutz recognizes difficulties in Weber's account; see 1967, pp. 25–7). If our earlier account of intended content is correct, however, Schutz's criticism applies as much to *aktuelles Verstehen* as to *erklärendes Verstehen*.

[32] Schutz, 1967, pp. 86–7.

[33] Ibid., pp. 86–96.

not, as Weber's objectivist critics would have it, primarily an *empirical* problem, but a *conceptual* problem. Thus Weber himself was wrong to suggest[34] that *'Verstehen* is something which is logically incomplete and needs supplementing by a different method altogether, namely the collection of statistics'. Brute data of the latter sort, in Winch's view, are neither more nor less relevant to successful identification of the meaning of an action than is statistical information about the likely occurrences of words in a language relevant to understanding what a speaker of that language is saying. '"Understanding", in situations like this, is grasping the *point* or *meaning* of what is being done or said. This is a notion far removed from the world of statistics and causal laws: it is closer to the realm of discourse and to the internal relations that link the parts of a realm of discourse.'[35] It is for this reason that Winch is led to conclude that many of the most important theoretical issues raised by the social sciences (among them the question of what constitutes social behaviour) are properly settled by the conceptual elucidation of philosophy rather than by the empirical research of science.[36]

These examples suffice to indicate the dimensions of the debate about the importance which Weber attached to the identification of subjective meaning. The mainstream of objectivist social science, finding the issue to be something of a pseudo-problem as far as scientific theory is concerned, takes the view that he attached altogether too much importance to it; the scattered and far from cohesive group defending a subjectivist approach continue to maintain that he attached not enough.

(2) Weber's definition of the science of sociology makes very evident his departure from the view of Dilthey and the Historical School that interpretative understanding and causal explanation are independent and opposed methods, appropriate to distinctive subject matters. On the contrary, to have knowledge of social action, according to Weber, it is necessary *both* to grasp its subjective meaning and to give a causal account of its occurrence such that 'according to established generalizations from experience, there is a probability that it will always actually occur in the same way'. An interpretation of behaviour that fails to provide the

---

[34] Cf. Weber, 1964, pp. 96–100.
[35] Winch, 1958, pp. 113, 115.
[36] Ibid., pp. 17–18 and *passim*. Needless to say, this conclusion has met with not a little resistance. See, in particular, his exchange with Louch, 1963; Winch, 1964.

confirmation of 'causal adequacy' is necessarily incomplete; likewise, even a highly precise estimation of the probability of a behavioural event's occurrence cannot be considered sociological comprehension if 'adequacy at the level of meaning' is lacking.[37] Since a complete explanation requires that the interpretation of the motive of an act *(erklärendes Verstehen)* be causally adequate, it seems reasonable to suppose that Weber regards motives as causes of behaviour. This point, which I do not find altogether clear in his writings, acquires considerable significance in the dispute as it has developed since Weber on this question of the relationship of understanding to explanation.

To put the matter briefly (and, as this is probably the most complex and widely discussed issue of the philosophy of social science, it is probably impossible to put briefly), the dominant objectivist approach to social science treats the problem of explanation in accordance with the guide-lines set forth in the neo-positivist literature of philosophy of science. The objective of explanation, as a classic document of this literature puts it, is 'to answer the question "why?" rather than only the question "what?" '; to go, in other words, beyond the mere description of a phenomenon, the 'explanandum', to its 'explanans'. Explanation is achieved when we manage to correctly deduce a sentence describing the phenomenon to be explained (the explanandum) from other sentences specifying antecedent conditions and general laws (the explanans). This model, it is explicitly argued, applies fully as much to the explanation of human action as to any other phenomenon of science.[38]

Once explanation is identified in this way, as a causal relation between events[39] in terms of at least one general law, the nature of the connection between understanding (in Weber's sense) and explanation of action becomes perfectly straightforward. Shorn of any metaphysical trappings, understanding is an act of *description* which specifies (in brute data identifiable terms) the event to be explained, or a condition necessary to explain something else. To identify the subjective meaning of an action, therefore, is not to explain anything, since 'merely to redescribe a phenomenon is not in any way to account for it'.[40] If, on the other hand, this act of

[37] Weber, 1964, pp. 99–100.
[38] Hempel and Oppenheim, 1953, pp. 319, 321, 326–31.
[39] Strictly speaking, this should be 'sentences describing events'.
[40] Ayer, 1969, p. 16.

understanding is extended to the recovery of the actor's motives for performing the action, then it merely amounts to a redescription of certain of the 'initial conditions from which we seek to derive his performance of the action by means of a causal law'.[41] This defence of the naturalist thesis that social action requires the same kind of causal explanation as another event can be regarded as a presupposition of the working methods of objectivist social science.[42]

The subjectivist approach to social action has been fortified, however, by a wide-ranging literature in the philosophy of action which defends the proposition that a distinctive model of explanation is appropriate to an intentional act. Thus, post-Wittgensteinian emphasis on the non-contingency of the relation between motive and act has led to the conclusion that explanation in terms of motive is a wholly non-causal attempt to 'make sense' of an action;[43] explanation has been judged to involve the elucidation of the social convention or 'rule' in accord with which the action is undertaken;[44] the language of motive is held to imply an explanation in terms of appraisal or justification, called 'moral explanation';[45] impressive efforts have been made to revive and justify teleological explanation as appropriate to social action;[46] and it has been argued that even if the naturalists are justified in treating motives as causes, 'illocutionary redescriptions' in terms of intentions are genuinely explanatory yet manifestly non-causal.[47] These writers (and the others that could be added to the list) can scarcely be considered to take a single view of the problem, and both their arguments and their substantive conclusions vary considerably. What they share, however, is not merely an unwillingness to accept the authority of the objectivist model of causal explanation as binding upon the social sciences, but a conviction that the objectivist account has failed to grasp the real nature of the problem. By refusing to treat understanding as other than a matter of the identification of brute data, the objectivists have always begged the question of meaning: for this tradition, as

---

[41] Ibid., p. 23.
[42] Weber's position is assimilated to this model by Runciman, 1972, pp. 19–20; for a discussion of its impact on objectivist social science, see Gunnel, 1968.
[43] Melden, 1961.
[44] Winch, 1958.
[45] Louch, 1969.
[46] Taylor, 1964, 1967a, 1967b, 1970; Wright, 1971.
[47] Skinner, 1971, 1972b.

Apel puts it, ' "understanding" was evaluated right from the start on the basis of how much it could contribute to the objective explanation of facts; and thus it was no wonder that it was found to be only of "heuristic" value as a "prescientific" method'.[48] It is possible, then, to make two general points about the contemporary debate over the relationship of understanding to explanation in the social sciences.

First, this cannot properly be considered a debate between proponents of 'understanding' and proponents of 'explanation', as the battle lines of the older dispute between historicism and positivism were drawn. What is at stake is rather the sense that is to be assigned to both terms, and the nature of the relationship that is recognized between them. Wright makes this point in the context of his defence of the teleological explanation of action:

> understanding what something is in the sense of *is like* should not be confused with understanding what something is in the sense of *means* or *signifies*. The first is a characteristic preliminary of causal, the second of teleological explanation. It is therefore misleading to say that understanding *versus* explanation marks the difference between two types of scientific intelligibility. But one could say that the intentional or nonintentional character of their objects marks the difference between two types of understanding and explanation.[49]

The second point, which follows from this, is that the way in which we determine to understand an action implicates the type of explanation which we can then appropriately offer for it. To treat an action as a brute data identifiable event is to commit one's self to explaining it (if at all) in terms of other, similarly identified events, prior in time, which can be said to have caused it to occur. To understand it, on the other hand, in terms of the intentional project of the actor is to require an explanatory account that elucidates what he *means* to do (including his reasons, goals, plans, etc., and the context of meaning in terms of which they are formulated). It is true, of course, that we can without contradiction describe human behaviour in both objective and subjective terms; in everyday life we treat others both as objects and as agents, and we explain what they do (and even what we do) both in terms of causal antecedents and purposeful projects of action. The subjectivist need not deny the legitimacy of the former; what

48 Apel, 1967, p. 21.
49 Wright, 1971, p. 135.

he does reject is any claim that would reduce the second (more significant) dimension of social life into the first.

(3) This leads us to the third general question posed earlier, that which concerns the nature of concept and theory formation in the social sciences. Weber's view, we recall, is that the necessarily abstract concepts of sociology can be none the less rendered precise 'by striving for the highest possible degree of adequacy on the level of meaning'.[50] It is customary to contrast Weber's position on this matter with Durkheim's famous injunction to 'consider social facts as things'.[51] Objectivity, according to Durkheim's rules, is made possible by reference to the 'permanent forms' of social life rather than to the subjective vagaries of the diverse applications made of them.

I consider extremely fruitful this idea that social life should be explained, not by the notions of those who participate in it, but by more profound causes which are unperceived by consciousness, and I think also that these causes are to be sought mainly in the manner according to which the associated individuals are grouped. Only in this way, it seems, can history become a science, and sociology itself exist.[52]

At first sight, Weber's requirement of *Sinnadäquanz* would appear to stand in total contrast to the method espoused by Durkheim. But the manner in which Weber develops and employs his sociological constructs in the pages that follow the methodological introduction suggests that his own attention to 'the notions of those who participate' in social life can be given both an objectivist and a subjectivist gloss.

Weber's theoretical constructs are ideal types which delineate the structure of social relationships. But as constructs of science, they are subject to his postulate of *Wertfreiheit,* which means that they are formulated in terms which translate the evaluative content of the (ideal typical) actor's own understanding of his social world into value-neutral 'reports' on such belief. The consequence of this approach to concept construction is well-illustrated by his treatment of the notion of a 'legitimate order' which he defines as 'an order which enjoys the prestige of being considered binding': not, it is important to note, an order which *is*

---

[50] Sinnadäquanz. Weber, 1964, p. 110.
[51] Durkheim, 1964, p. 14.
[52] From an 1897 review by Durkheim, cited in Winch, 1958, pp. 23–4; cf. the discussion of objectivity in Durkheim, 1964, pp. 44–6.

binding, but an order which *is considered* binding.[53] For the purpose
of making the concept empirical, it is formulated not in terms of
the (necessarily normative) characteristics of legitimacy—such as
conformity with law, rule, or right—but rather in terms of the fact
of the *belief* that some such characteristics are present, a fact that
can be validated by reference to the presence or absence of
appropriate forms of conduct. Weber himself makes this point
quite emphatically: 'naturally,' he writes, 'the legitimacy of a
system of authority may be treated sociologically only as the
probability that to a relevant degree the appropriate attitudes will
exist, and the corresponding practical conduct ensue'. [54] Now it is
clear that the requirement of 'causal adequacy' is suitably
discharged here, but it is not at all clear that this empirical
definition (and Weber's entire treatment of the problem to which
it refers) can be reconciled with the requirement of 'adequacy on
the level of meaning'. From the standpoint of a project of action,
such a concept of legitimacy becomes incomprehensible: one
cannot even pose the (surely rather important) question 'is this
government legitimate?' for it has been assimilated into the
question 'is this government considered legitimate?' In effect, for
the ideal typical actor (from his standpoint) to 'consider the
government legitimate' is for him to 'consider that he considers the
government legitimate'. By dissolving 'legitimacy into acceptance
or acquiescence', Schaar points out, this analysis renders 'opaque
whole classes of basic and recurrent political phenomena': for
example, the decision to disobey on the grounds of the illegitimacy
of a command, the decision to disobey irrespective of the
legitimacy of a command, etc.[55]

Whatever the merits of the procedure Weber recommends, it is
evident that it corresponds to the prevailing assumptions of
objectivist social science concerning concept formation.[56] Attention is placed not on the critical elucidation of the concepts by
which men and women experience the social world, but rather on
the development of an observational language with which the
scientist can distance himself from that world; 'this has meant the

[53] Weber, 1964, p. 125. Several discussions of this concept elaborate the point that
concerns me here: Schaar, 1970, pp. 282–90; MacIntyre, 1971, pp. 277–9; Taylor, 1971,
pp. 35–40; Pitkin, 1972, pp. 280–6.
[54] Weber, 1964, p. 326.
[55] Schaar, 1970, p. 284.
[56] Each of the writers just cited gives evidence for this with references to the treatment
of 'legitimacy' in contemporary political science.

invention of new, technical concepts, the attempt to confine work to those concepts which seem "realistic" or "factual", the use of "operational definitions," and the attempt to redefine familiar concepts in such a way as to make them realistic, factual, or scientific'.[57] It is important to notice that the approach to conceptualization that I am characterizing as objectivist is not limited to the work of those who aspire to the construction of highly abstract, formal, general, theory (of the variety proposed, for example, by Easton) but also applies to the empirically-oriented wing of the behavioural movement. Thus Kalleberg is mistaken, I believe, in supposing that reference to attitude studies and participation studies supports the conclusion that 'the methodological principle that the concepts of the political scientist must be meaningful to the actor as well as to the observer is a principle that is exemplified in contemporary behavioural research'.[58] The sense of 'meaningful to the actor' which is relevant to the subjectivist case is not met by reference to brute data identifiable evidence of attitudes and beliefs.[59]

But what is the subjectivist case? Surely it would not make much sense to argue that the scientist can see no more than can those he studies, that the observer is confined, in his interpretation of the world, to the categories of thought employed by the observed in *their* interpretation of the world. Schutz, who devoted most of his work to various aspects of this problem of giving scientific account of the 'life-world',[60] construes Weber's criterion of *Sinnadäquanz* as follows: 'Correctly understood, the postulate of subjective interpretation...means merely that we always *can*

---

[57] Pitkin, 1972, pp. 274–5. One might think that this is a losing battle, since the concepts of 'science' so quickly filter into the language of everyday conduct as, for example, the jargon of systems theory has done in the last ten years. It is especially amusing (and perhaps alarming) to find non-evaluative, observational language accepted and employed quite readily by the subjects it presumably is intended to describe. Thus, it becomes increasingly common to respond to the speech of a public official not with an evaluation of its content but with an estimation of its impact; opinion research polls inquire of the public not 'do you believe in the government?' but 'do you believe the government has a credibility gap?'; the press reports to its readers that a political official 'achieved a great deal of verisimilitude'; etc.
[58] Kalleberg, 1972, p. 55.
[59] Criticism of the principles of concept formation employed by objectivists in political science has become increasingly common; some differing examples may be found in Gunnel, 1968; Wolin, 1969; Gunther and Reshaur, 1971; Taylor, 1971; Tribe, 1972.
[60] The concept of the *Lebenswelt*, derived from Husserl's late writings, plays a primary role in the thinking of those who have sought to exploit the sociological implications of phenomenology; cf. Schutz, 1966, pp. 116–32.

—and for certain purposes *must*—refer to the activities of the subjects within the social world and their interpretation by the actors in terms of systems of projects, available means, motives, relevances, and so on.'[61] Schutz repeatedly emphasizes that what is 'given' in the social world is not merely data to be interpreted, but interpretations of data: that is, the actors we study 'have preselected and preinterpreted this world by a series of common-sense constructs of the reality of daily life, and it is these thought objects which determine their behaviour...' Thus the constructs we employ, as social scientists, to explain that behaviour must be 'constructs of the second degree, namely constructs of the constructs made by the actors on the social scene'.[62] They refer not to observations of brute data but to interpretations of the meaning constructs given in experience. Failure to refer in this way to 'the meaning structure of the social world' deprives social theory of any claim to realism:

The safeguarding of the subjective point of view is the only but sufficient guarantee that the world of social reality will not be replaced by a fictional non-existing world constructed by the scientific observer....

Only this methodological principle gives us the necessary guarantee that we are dealing in fact with the real social life-world of us all, which, even as an object of theoretical research, remains a system of reciprocal social relations, all of them built up by mutual subjective interpretations of the actors within it.[63]

The fact that Schutz argues empirically, from the standpoint of fidelity to reality, is significant. The insistence of subjectivists that the theoretical explanation of behaviour refer to the interpretation of projects of action and the self-understanding of actors appears at first to be merely a reversion to the 'pre-scientific' tradition in which the study of society was one part history, one part moral philosophy. There is, of course, considerable justification for applying the label 'traditionalist' to this approach. But contemporary critics of the objectivist principles of concept formation argue with increasing confidence that it is behaviourism itself that has been guilty of failing to meet the fundamental responsibility of science toward the 'facts'. Thus a recent effort to give a unified theoretical account of social behaviour considers its 'most radical proposal' to be 'that we should treat people, for scientific purposes,

61 Schutz, 1962, p. 35.
62 Ibid., p. 6.
63 Schutz, 1964, pp. 8, 16.

as if they were human beings'. The objectivist strategy of treating people, for scientific purposes, as if their activity as agents could be reduced to behavioural elements that are brute data identifiable renders the most significant areas of social life incomprehensible, indeed invisible according to Harré and Secord, who support this argument with a wealth of reference to the empirical studies of recent social psychology. 'Rule-following, convention-obeying, meaning-giving, or any other form of self-monitoring by the individual involved', they conclude, 'is fatal to the idea that the heart of an explanation lies in the causal story.'[64]

The purpose of the subjectivist critique is not to insist that the concepts and theory of social science should be congruent with the self-understanding of actors; social science, very properly, aspires to a more comprehensive, a more consistent, a more critical, a more far-sighted perspective on social experience than that which is given immediately in that experience. Even the objectification of essentially subjective phenomena may, on occasion, be legitimate and enlightening as a means of helping one to see the too-familiar in a fresh way. The point, however, as Apel puts it, is 'to let "objectification" serve "disobjectification", i.e. that condition in which man is freed by knowledge to act responsibly'; and the success of this attempt can only 'be judged according to whether the "objects" of the theory can become "subjects" who can incorporate that theory into their own language and self-understanding'.[65] Objectification itself can never be the primary —much less the final—goal of social science. Its concepts and theory must refer fundamentally to subjective meaning, because it is subjective meaning which constitutes the reality we seek to comprehend. Gunnell (and others) have pointed out that the activity of the social scientist is really less to be compared with that of the natural scientist than with that of the historian or philosopher of science.

Both the philosopher of science and the social scientist are concerned with the illumination of second order realms. For the philosopher of science to understand, explain and evaluate the theory and practice of science raises no questions of intuition, introspectionism, or imaginative reliving on the one hand and demands no deductive causal explanations on the other. To ask for a general theory of social action and to endeavor to construct definitive analytical frameworks and constructs for describing and explaining the social

---

[64] Harré and Secord, 1972, pp. 87, 168.
[65] Apel, 1967, p. 57; cf. his discussion of psycho-analysis as an example of 'objectification' in the service of 'disobjectification', pp. 25–7.

world would be as logically queer as asking for a general causal and predictive theory of scientific activity.[66]

Of course the parallel is not exact, but it is closer to the mark than the one which would treat human beings as if they were physical objects. And this, according to the subjectivist argument, is precisely the consequence of a social science which regards its evidence as a matter of brute data rather than readings of meanings.

III

These few remarks on some of the unresolved issues of contemporary social theory can do them little justice; they do, however, provide a frame of reference into which the question of Mannheim's contemporary relevance can be placed. If it is correct to suppose that the alternatives of objectivism and subjectivism place before any contemporary practitioner of social science certain real and highly consequential options, then it follows that the sociology of knowledge deserves far more serious attention than it has received. Assuming that my earlier characterization of it was correct, it would appear that Mannheim's method of socio-logical interpretation constitutes a critique of the objectivist posi-tion which adds an important new dimension to the subjectivist case. At the same time, it delineates a field for empirical investigation that invites fresh attention to a number of areas that have, in recent years, been dominated by objectivist methods.

In reducing social action to elements of brute data, objectivism adopts a strategy for dealing with meaning that bears considerable resemblance to the approach which earlier I identified with the proponents of the doctrine of textual autonomy. Faced with a datum which, by virtue of being meaningful, refers beyond itself to a context of intersubjective meanings, the objectivist (as Taylor has put it) 'reconstructs reality in line with certain categorical principles'. That is, the mediate reference of the act or text is ruled out of court on the grounds of being subjective (non-verifiable) and the meaning of the datum is defined in terms of the system of relevance employed by the observer. Just as verbal meaning is judged to be confined, in this way, to what the words *say* (rather

---

[66] Gunnell, 1968, p. 183. Winch makes the same point when he remarks that the social scientist's 'understanding of social phenomena is more like the engineer's understand-ing of his colleagues' activities than it is like the engineer's understanding of the mechanical systems which he studies' (1958, p. 88); cf. also Schutz, 1962, pp. 53–4.

than to what the author intended), so the meaning of social action is confined, according to the supposed rules of scientific method, to what is brute data identifiable.

Thus any description of reality in terms of meanings which is open to interpretive question is only allowed into this scientific discourse if it is placed, as it were, in quotes and attributed to individuals as their opinion, belief, attitude. That this opinion, belief, etc. is held is thought of as a brute datum, since it is redefined as the respondent's giving a certain answer to the questionnaire.[67]

In both cases, interpretative reference to the context of meaning which 'stands behind' the overt act is deliberately excluded, at the cost of precluding authentic understanding. Mannheim's rejection of the attempt to divorce meaning from its context thus corresponds fully to the subjectivist critique of behavioural methods in social science.

But the literature of subjectivism, while clear-sighted about the need for interpretative reference to the meaning context of an act, is notably vague about the procedures of investigation that might serve, if not in the strict sense to *validate* an interpretation, at least to render it maximally plausible and to provide some basis for the resolution of disputes respecting the authentic characterization of an action should they arise. Obviously this problem does not arise as long as the observer and the subjects being observed share a common context of intersubjective meanings; hence the great appeal, in the earlier literature of historicist subjectivism, of the 'methods' of intuition, empathy, subjective insight, etc. But this type of answer, as objectivists have always been quick to point out, wholly begs the question of how a community of observers who do not share the same intuitions can come to any kind of objective agreement as to what shall count as knowledge. The main threat to the subjectivist position is that in the quest for authentic knowledge the legitimate scientific ideal of intersubjectivity be surrendered altogether. This, of course, has been the most common complaint levelled against the exponents of the subjectivist position that I have cited. It is held, for instance, that Schutz's 'emphasis upon subjective meaning divorced from verificatory procedures of a broadly scientific sort loses much of what was essential to Weber's approach.... Thus one danger is that phenomenology might trivialize sociology and never establish that kind of explanatory purchase on empirical reality which

[67] Taylor, 1971, p. 21.

Weber so notably achieved.'[68] Winch's position has repeatedly been charged with entailing that inter-cultural understanding is impossible and that the criticism of a belief or practice is meaningless.[69] In part such criticisms represent a demand for a kind of verificatory procedure that is simply inapplicable to a hermeneutic method (a point to which I shall return in the next chapter). But in part they represent a quite legitimate complaint that the subjectivists have not carried their argument sufficiently far.

For we have already seen that the interpretation of the meaning context presupposed by the author of an act is saved from being a private, inner affair of the psyche by virtue of the fact that it is constituted socially. As Schutz himself points out, 'all knowledge taken for granted has a highly socialized structure, that is, it is assumed to be taken for granted not only by *me* but by *us*, by *"everyone"* (meaning "every one who belongs to us"). This socialized structure gives this kind of knowledge an objective and anonymous character.'[70] For this reason, doubt about the accuracy of an interpretation of meaning of one 'who does not belong to us' need never (and therefore must never) be left to personal intuition; an imputation of meaning can never be defended by a mere 'that's how it seems to me', for the norm of intersubjectivity is an obligation which any claim to knowledge must recognize and respect. But it can be met, where the validity of interpretation is at stake, by turning investigation to the social relations which constitute that shared context of intersubjective meanings in the first place. This is not, of course, an easy task. As we have seen, such investigation moves in a 'hermeneutic circle'; the observer must guard continually against the automatic tendency to impose his own context of meaning upon those whom he wishes to understand; we can never reach a point at which we can say with assurance, 'the case is proven, the proffered interpretation *est demonstrandum*'. But we are far from being in a position of simply trading hunches. Thus it is proper to argue that the subjectivist position is never complete, and cannot be complete, without the sociology of knowledge.

Recent defenders of the subjectivist tradition continually seem to come to Mannheim's door, but rarely do they pass through it.

[68] Rex, 1971, p. 26.
[69] Cf. especially Gellner, 1973, ch. 2–4; Jarvie, 1972, ch. 2; Silvers, 1967.
[70] Schutz, 1962, p. 75.

In part, this may be due to the power of the conventional misrepresentation of his method as implying the reduction of 'knowledge' to 'facts'—a reading that would make the sociology of knowledge the very opposite of an interpretative method. Schutz, for example, when on occasion he refers to the method, does so in such a fashion.[71] Winch, though he speaks continually of the fact that the concepts by which one comes to understand action are socially established, never mentions the sociology of knowledge. Nor does Taylor, though he advocates the investigation of 'just what these [social] practices and institutions are, what the meanings are which they require and hence sustain'[72]—i.e. precisely the programme set forth by Mannheim's method. If my argument has any merit at all, therefore, it suggests that a renewal of interest in the sociology of knowledge would have useful consequences for social theory.

[71] Schutz, 1964, p. 121.
[72] Taylor, 1971, p. 29.

7. Can The Sociology of Knowledge Be Critical?

DURING THE 1960s, another round in the seemingly perennial dispute over the nature and method of the social sciences was stimulated by a conference of the German Sociological Association in Tübingen at which Popper and Adorno presented papers on the logic of the social sciences. This *Positivismusstreit*[1] echoed many of the themes of the turn-of-the-century *Methodenstreit* that had provided the background for Mannheim's thought, and like the earlier debate, the dispute at Tübingen concerned underlying moral and political differences as well as logical and epistemological ones. Indeed, the distance between the defenders of a 'critical rationalism' and a 'critical theory' was even more substantial than a first glance (at least at the initial contributions of Popper and Adorno) might make it appear; as Dahrendorf pointed out in his summary of the discussion, it 'provided a series of amusing instances of similarities in the formulations of the symposiasts behind which profound differences in the matters discussed were hidden'.[2]

None the less, there is a sense in which the attachment of critical rationalist and critical theorist to the common term 'critical' does express a genuinely shared concern, and oddly enough (or perhaps, considering the general complexion of the critical literature on Mannheim noted earlier, not so oddly) this can be seen most vividly in their common hostility toward the sociology of knowledge. Twenty-five years before the Tübingen conference, Adorno had lamented what he called the 'innocuous scepticism' of Mannheim's position, which 'calls everything into question and criticizes nothing'.[3] And about the same time, Popper had argued,

---

[1] This label is problematic in that Popper, no less than Adorno, repudiates the 'positivist' position; it is clear that the concept of 'positivism' was itself a point about which the participants in the debate reached no common understanding. For clarification, see Frisby's fine introduction to the English edition of the main papers of the dispute: Adorno, *et al.,* 1976, pp. x–xv.

[2] Ibid., p. 124.

[3] Adorno, 1967, p. 37.

as part of his critique of 'historicism', that Mannheim's doctrine was 'based on the naïve view that objectivity depends on the psychology of the individual scientist' and that, in consequence, it 'overlooks the fact that it is the public character of science and of its institutions which imposes a mental discipline upon the individual scientist and which preserves the objectivity of science and its tradition of critically discussing new ideas'.[4] When, in commenting upon the 1961 dispute, Popper calls attention to this earlier criticism of Mannheim, he adds: 'objectivity is based, in brief, upon *mutual rational criticism,* upon the critical approach, the critical tradition'.[5] Common to both positions, then, is the conviction that the sociology of knowledge dissolves the capacity for criticism. The gap between Adorno and Popper remains an enormous one, of course, for the kind of critique being advanced is essentially political in one case, epistemological in the other. Even so, the quality which is found alarming about the sociology of knowledge, and which represents the main object of attack of virtually all of its critics, can be expressed in a single charge: by insisting upon the *Seinsverbundenheit* of all thought, Mannheim undermines the possibility of grounding any position at all; the sociology of knowledge destroys *any* standards to which critique might appeal and it therefore leads inevitably to an indiscriminate and thoroughly passive acceptance of anything at all. The spectre of relativism, of a debilitating scepticism, has been noticed throughout the foregoing discussion, and I believe that the essential reasons for clearing Mannheim of this charge have already been presented. None the less, the question is of sufficient importance, and it has exerted so pervasive an influence among Mannheim's readers, that it seems essential to try to address it head on: is the sociology of knowledge capable of making the distinction between what is true and what is false?

Although Mannheim's suggestion that it is 'possible to present the sociology of knowledge as an empirical theory of the actual relations of knowledge to the social situation without raising any epistemological problems' is unduly optimistic, and although he himself recognizes that such a separation represents an 'artificial isolation' of the problem since the actual relations of knowledge to society 'transcend bare fact, and call for further epistemological

[4] Popper, 1961, pp. 155–6.
[5] Adorno, *et al.,* 1976, p. 293.

reflection',[6] still it is the case that we can consider the question from two different sides: viz., 'are there epistemological considerations that establish decisive arguments against the sociology of knowledge?' and 'does the sociology of knowledge have any consequences for epistemology?'. We shall consider these in turn, before taking up the different (but I think ultimately related) question: 'is the sociology of knowledge consistent with the emancipatory interest implicit in a critical theory of the social order?'.

I

One thing at least is certain. Mannheim did not believe that his position entailed irrationalism, mysticism, or destructive scepticism; on the contrary, he counted his labours as a continual struggle against whatever would imprison thought in an isolated and private subjectivity. His expressed hope for the sociology of knowledge was 'to overcome the vague, ill-considered, and sterile form of relativism with regard to scientific knowledge which is increasingly prevalent to-day'.[7] He repeatedly protested against any inclination, in the name of the sociology of knowledge, to repudiate the ideal of objectivity.

Nothing could be more pointless, and incorrect, than to argue as follows: Since every form of historical and political thought is based to a certain degree upon metatheoretical assumptions, it follows that we cannot put our trust in any idea or any form of thought, and hence it is a matter of indifference what theoretical arguments are employed in a given case. Hence each one of us ought to rely upon his instinct, upon his personal and private intuitions, or upon his own private interests, whichever of these will suit him best. If we did this each one of us, no matter how partisan his view, could hold it in good conscience and even feel quite smug about it. To defend our analysis against the attempt to use it for such propagandistic purposes, let it be said that there exists a fundamental difference between, on the one hand, a blind partisanship and the irrationalism which arises out of mere mental indolence, which sees in intellectual activity no more than arbitrary personal judgments and propaganda, and on the other the type of inquiry which is seriously concerned with an objective analysis, and which, after eliminating all conscious evaluation, becomes aware of an irreducible residue of evaluation inherent in the structure of all thought.[8]

If Mannheim's position is to be rejected on epistemological grounds, it is necessary to show that he convicts himself in spite of

---

[6] IAU, p. 286 (IUU, p. 245).
[7] IAU, p. 264 (IUU, p. 227).
[8] IAU, p. 100n. (IUU, pp. 87–8).

his good intentions. Such a challenge might be put in any one of three different (though interrelated) claims: that the propositions of the sociology of knowledge are not intersubjectively transmissible, that they preclude any appraisal of truth claims, and that they are self-refuting.

(1) The requirement that knowledge be public rather than private has generally been regarded as the hallmark of scientific method. The distinctive virtue of *scientia transmissibilis,* as Brecht has argued, is that 'it supplies a type of knowledge that can be transmitted from *any* person who has such knowledge to *any* other person who does not have it but who can grasp the meaning of the symbols (words, signs) used in communication and perform the operations, if any, described in these communications'.[9] The procedures of investigation that are mandated by this ideal, however, are far from unproblematic. Under the influence of positivist standards of admissibility, Brecht and other representatives of the objectivist tradition take the view that 'what is transferred are only basic data (reports) and strictly analytical reasoning (as in mathematics)'[10] with the consequence that the domain of scientific knowledge proper (Brecht's S_1) is confined to facts that are brute data identifiable and to the inferences which the rules of logic make possible on the basis of these facts. Mannheim, as we have seen, denies that social reality (or at least, the more important part of social reality) is susceptible to 'scientific explanation' understood in these terms. But he does not renounce the ideal of intersubjective transmissibility; on the contrary, it is precisely in the pursuit of this ideal that the sociology of knowledge investigates the obstacles to cross-contextual understanding. The force of the challenge of *scientia transmissibilis,* therefore, depends entirely upon a judgement about the kind of intersubjective certainty that is attainable in social investigation, and about the procedures best suited to maximize it. Here Mannheim's position coincides with a comment made by Taylor: 'The point about science is to strive for the degree of certainty of which the domain under study is capable, not to apply an inappropriate model just because such a model would give more satisfactory results *if* it applied.'[11]

Underlying the objectivist espousal of *scientia transmissibilis* is the

9 Brecht, 1959, p. 114.
10 Ibid., p. 280.
11 Taylor, 1973, p. 65.

supposition that only evidence which is directly given to observation can be reliably shared: the scientist must be able to say 'these are the facts—look', and other properly trained observers must then be able to look, and to confirm or disconfirm the reality of that evidence.[12] The evidence of meaning, as we have seen, is not accessible in this way. Because it is presented mediately, it is not simply 'there' for all to see, but must be established by means of the procedures of interpretation. This does not imply, however, that such evidence is indeterminate or arbitrary. Failure to achieve an intersubjective consensus about the evidence of meaning is *never* resolved by saying 'well, that's *your* interpretation; this is *my* interpretation'. The procedures for identifying expressive and documentary meaning may require probabilistic judgements, and they are certainly subject to revision, refinement, and reformulation, but the process of interpretation is always and necessarily grounded in an appeal to evidence which is public and intersubjectively transmissible.

What Mannheim rejects is not the norm of intersubjective transmissibility, but rather the claim to be able to dispense with the interpretative process altogether by adopting the 'universal framework' of Science in the monolithic, ahistorical, formalized model recommended by many of his contemporaries. The passages in *Ideology and Utopia* which are sometimes cited to show that he repudiated the norm of intersubjective transmissibility almost always turn out to be directed not against this norm, but against the conception of knowledge in terms 'of a purely contemplative consciousness-as-such' which would exclude, on epistemological grounds, all forms of knowledge which become accessible only by means of the 'detour' of interpretation.

It may be said for formal knowledge that it is essentially accessible to all and that its content is unaffected by the individual subject and his historical-social affiliations. But, on the other hand, it is certain that there is a wide range of subject matter which is accessible only either to certain subjects, or in certain historical periods, and which becomes apparent through the social purposes of individuals.[13]

Taken by itself, the first phrase of the second sentence of this passage might seem to signal the most abject surrender to

---

[12] Even the 'objective' evidence of the natural sciences is far more problematic in this respect than many proponents of objectivism (and indeed, Mannheim himself) would seem to realize; cf. Hanson, 1958, on this.

[13] IAU, p. 169 (IUU, pp. 147–8).

epistemological subjectivism, but as the last phrase already hints, and as the larger context of his argument (a critique of 'the intellectualistic conception of science, underlying positivism'[14]) shows clearly, Mannheim's point is that much of the subject matter of the *Geisteswissenschaften,* and especially, of political studies, is only *directly* accessible to certain subjects or in certain historical periods, and that for this reason a method of science which repudiates historical understanding and refuses to undertake the kind of interpretative inquiry that might make a foreign context of meaning accessible, can *never* have access to such knowledge. Thus he concludes this section:

It may well be that our intellectualism will repeatedly stimulate in us the longing for a point of view beyond time and history—for a 'consciousness as such' out of which there arise insights independent of particular perspectives, and capable of formulation into general laws which are eternally valid. But this objective cannot be attained without doing violence to the subject matter. If we seek a science of that which is in the process of becoming, of practice and for practice, we can realize it only by discovering a new framework in which this kind of knowledge can find adequate expression.[15]

Such a framework is, of course, the interpretative framework proposed in the sociology of knowledge. Intersubjectivity is attained not by reducing all thought to the categories of our science, but by expanding the horizons of our science to comprehend all thought. The objectivity of our knowledge is not something which can be warranted in initial metatheoretical assumptions (the authority of Science) but must be won in the process of inquiry itself. 'In so far as different observers are immersed in the same system,' Mannheim points out in the encyclopedia article, 'they will, on the basis of the identity of their conceptual and categorical apparatus and through the common universe of discourse thereby created, arrive at similar results, and be in a position to eradicate as an error everything that deviates from this unanimity.' On the other hand, he continues,

when observers have different perspectives, 'objectivity' is attainable only in a more roundabout fashion. In such a case, what has been correctly but differently perceived by the two perspectives must be understood in the light of the differences in structure of these varied modes of perception. An effort must be made to find a formula for translating the results of one into those of the other and to discover a common denominator for these varying perspectivistic insights. Once such a common denominator has been found, it

---

[14] IAU, pp. 166–7 (IUU, p. 146).
[15] IAU, p. 171 (IUU, p. 150).

is possible to separate the necessary differences of the two views from the arbitrarily conceived and mistaken elements, which here too should be considered as errors.[16]

(2) To affirm the possibility of intersubjective communication is to affirm the existence of a common world and hence, of truth. For the *content* of any act of communication refers neither to speaker nor listener, but to a state of affairs: I express *something,* you understand *something,* and therefore the hermeneutic interest in the narrow sense (i.e. that these two 'somethings' be identical) always implies a more comprehensive interest in the validity of that 'something' which is communicated. Strictly speaking, one does not understand another, but rather that something which the other recommends, or proposes, or asserts about a common world. To grasp what he means is to grasp that state of affairs for which his expression makes a claim of validity. If this orientation toward validity is absent, communication itself becomes pointless and unintelligible: if any conceivable state of affairs exists and any conceivable claim about the world is accurate, then it is impossible to communicate 'something' about that world.

In affirming the possibility of intersubjective understanding across different socio-historical contexts of thought, the sociology of knowledge therefore also affirms the possibility of cross-contextual appraisals of the validity of the claims expressed. But it denies that such appraisal can be achieved (any more than understanding can be secured) by the simple and unreflective application of the standards which are 'given' in the observer's location to the content expressed in terms of a foreign framework. The epistemological implications of this view are described by Mannheim as 'relational'. 'Relationism does not signify that there are no criteria of rightness and wrongness in a discussion. It does insist, however, that it lies in the nature of certain assertions that they cannot be formulated absolutely, but only in terms of the perspective of a given situation.'[17] The truth of any proposition can only be considered on the basis of a correct identification of its meaning and this, as we have seen, is possible only in relation to the situational context in terms of which it was formulated. On the other hand, consistency with the terms of reference established in the documentary context of an expression does not warrant the validity of whatever content is so expressed. For one thing (as we

---

[16] IAU, pp. 300–1 (IUU, p. 258).
[17] IAU, p. 283 (IUU, p. 242).

saw earlier), a shared intersubjective context cannot be understood as establishing common opinions and beliefs; persons can
understand one another perfectly and still disagree as to what is
true. Moreover, the structure of the context of thought itself may
serve to obstruct or distort the capacity to make valid judgements
about the reality in which it functions. In the political sphere, the
problem of 'false consciousness' is particularly severe because the
structure of domination generates conceptual frameworks that are
tied to the self-justificatory interests of particular strata and
positions; i.e. those persons whose activities are most influential in
constituting the prevailing context of thought are precisely those
persons whose interests are served by the distortions which it
sponsors.

The appraisal of conflicting claims about reality can be accomplished, then, not by the unilateral assertion of a privileged
viewpoint but by interpretative inquiry aimed at expanding the
contextual framework available to the observer. Objectivity is
possible because cross-contextual communication is possible; by
bringing the very frameworks of thought (including the observer's
own) under critical scrutiny, it is possible to apply shared
standards of truth and appraise them at the same time. Mannheim
believes that it is both futile and disingenuous to hope to resolve
the problem of incommensurable standards (leading to conflicting
truth claims) by an appeal to formal and timeless criteria of Truth.
Instead, what is required is the substantive investigation of the
conflicting partial perspectives and the attempt to establish,
discursively and reflexively, a more comprehensive and more
adequate framework. 'The peculiar one-sidedness of a social
position is always most apparent when this position is seen in
juxtaposition to all the others',[18] he maintains, but such a
transcendent perspective must be accomplished, not assumed, in
the process of inquiry itself. The ultimate ideal of such inquiry is to
be able to appraise claims to truth by standards that are
appropriate to *all* possible social positions. But a universal
perspective of this sort can only stand as the norm toward which
inquiry is oriented. It can never be fully and finally realized
because the historical process itself, and the observer's position
within it, can never be transcended in any complete or definitive
sense. Mannheim's use of the concept of 'totality' is intended to
articulate that norm:

[18] IAU, p. 172 (IUU, p. 151).

Totality in the sense in which we conceive it is not an immediate and eternally valid vision of reality attributable only to a divine eye. It is not a self-contained and stable view. On the contrary, a total view implies both the assimilation and transcendance of the limitations of particular points of view. It represents the continuous process of the expansion of knowledge, and has as its goal not achievement of a super-temporally valid conclusion but the broadest possible extension of our horizon of vision.[19]

(3) A position which makes standards of truth depend, ultimately, upon the consensus that can be reached among participants in the process of inquiry (conceiving this process in the most comprehensive and open-ended way) clearly leaves any number of epistemological options open, and Mannheim emphasizes that the sociology of knowledge does not 'supplant epistemological and noological inquiry'.[20] He insists that the thesis of the *Seinsverbundenheit des Wissens* is not to be construed as a claim about validity since 'we need not regard it as a source of error that all thought is so rooted'.[21] The relevant question, therefore, is not whether the thesis of *Seinsverbundenheit* constitutes an adequate epistemology (since it is not an epistemological thesis at all) but rather whether such a claim undermines any adequate epistemological position: whether, in other words, it necessarily impugns any attempt to appraise validity claims. This is, of course, precisely the argument of the many critics who have charged Mannheim with self-referential inconsistency. Gustav Bergmann, for instance, reasons as follows: 'If this proposition that every rationale is an ideology is itself objectively true, how can he know it? If it is not, why should we pay any attention to it? And what is the value of a social science thus construed?'[22] The merit of this argument (which has been repeated, in different ways, in virtually every critical piece ever written on the sociology of knowledge) depends upon the legitimacy of assimilating the thesis of the *Seinsverbundenheit des Wissens* to the classic logical dilemma posed by a proposition of the form 'What I am now saying is false'. But the logical conundrum entailed in such a formulation has no useful application to the substantive claim about the historicity of thought presented by Mannheim; to argue against him, for instance, on the basis of an assumption of absolutism ('what I am now saying is true') is clearly trivial, for self-referential consistency in such a sense is achieved only by taking as settled, without any

---

[19] IAU, p. 106 (IUU, pp. 92–3).
[20] IAU, p. 287 (IUU, p. 245).
[21] IAU, p. 80 (IUU, p. 73).
[22] Bergmann, 1968, p. 132.

reference to evidence, the very question which Mannheim proposes to investigate. This is an odd way indeed to convict him of 'scepticism'.

If Mannheim's work is to be dismissed out of hand for logical reasons, it must be shown that he does in fact commit the nonsensical mistake of making a claim of falsehood for his own position; it must be shown that he concludes, as one of his critics put it, 'from the diversity of thinking among groups that all thinking is false'.[23] But this is precisely what Mannhiem repeatedly emphasizes he does *not* conclude.[24] Identification and elucidation of the perspective of a thinker, he says, 'as yet tells us nothing about the truth-value of his assertion. It implies only the suspicion that this assertion might represent merely a partial view.'[25] Now such a position may be judged sensible or foolish, but it is plainly not self-refuting. The claims of the sociology of knowledge can be applied reflexively without inconsistency, and in point of fact Mannheim does just this in *Ideology and Utopia* and elsewhere.[26] To affirm the fallibility, the possible one-sidedness of one's position, is not to undermine it but to encourage the adoption of procedures of inquiry that would strengthen it. 'As a matter of fact,' Mannheim suggests, 'if we believe that we already have the truth, we will lose interest in obtaining those very insights which might lead us to an approximate understanding of the situation. It is precisely our uncertainty which brings us a good deal closer to reality than was possible in former periods which had faith in the absolute.'[27] Hence, the recommendation of those who would refuse to investigate the question of the historicity of thought on the ground of the self-referential paradox is both unfounded and unprofitable: by treating a problem of substance as a matter of logical form only, the question of significance is begged entirely. Mannheim believed, in any case, that epistemological considerations were misplaced if they were used to inhibit or obstruct any area of inquiry:

New forms of knowledge, in the last analysis, grow out of the conditions of collective life and do not depend for their emergence upon the prior

---

[23] Dahlke, 1970, p. 83.

[24] Dahlke provides no references for his attribution; for Mannheim's contrary claims see, in addition to the passages cited above, IAU pp. 46, 86, 125, 168, 172, 282, 296 (IUU, pp. 77, 109, 147, 151, 242, 255).

[25] IAU, p. 284 (IUU, p. 243).

[26] See, for instance, IAU, pp. 5–13, 22–3, 32, 189, 244 (IUU, p. 165, 211).

[27] IAU, p. 84 (IUU, p. 76).

demonstration by a theory of knowledge that they are possible; they do not therefore need to be first legitimized by an epistemology.... The revolutions in methodology and epistemology are always sequels and repercussions of the revolutions in the immediate empirical procedures for getting knowledge.[28]

The historical justification for such a view, even in the so-called 'hard' sciences of nature, is considerable. 'Despite twentieth-century claims for the autonomy of philosophical epistemology,' Toulmin has pointed out, 'men like Einstein and Heisenberg have unavoidably trespassed into the theory of knowledge.'[29] The objectives of inquiry in any discipline are ill-served by treating a set of formal principles as authoritative, in an ultimate and irrevocable sense, over the results of the ongoing process of investigation itself.

II

Although the sociology of knowledge must be considered innocent of the crimes against reason with which it has so often been charged, it is certainly the case that such investigations have epistemological consequences—consequences which Mannheim believed were salutary rather than debilitating. Recognition of the historicity of thought, he concluded, forces us to look unfavourably on the attempt to ground science in any ahistorical system of 'supra-temporal logic' or in the static standard of some absolute sphere of 'truth in itself'.[30] To acknowledge our own historical condition is to surrender the illusion that knowledge can be warranted by an appeal to timeless principles of reasoning; 'history is only visible from within history and cannot be interpreted though a "jump" beyond history, in occupying a static standpoint arbitrarily occupied outside history'.[31] Or, as he puts it in the introduction to the English version of *Ideology and Utopia,* 'the absoluteness of thought is not attained by warranting, through a general principle, that one has it or by proceeding to label some particular limited viewpoint (usually one's own) as supra-partisan and authoritative'.[32]

Such a position requires that the problem of objectivity itself be reformulated in historical terms. In espousing his doctrine of

[28] IAU, p. 289 (IUU, p. 248).
[29] Toulmin, 1972, p. 2; cf. Mannheim's comments on this example in IAU, pp. 305–6 (IUU, pp. 262–3).
[30] IAU, pp. 42, 306 (IUU, p. 263).
[31] FKM, p. 97 (WAW, p. 357).
[32] IAU, pp. 42–3.

relationism, Mannheim attempts to establish a satisfactory alternative to what he views as a false choice between epistemological absolutism and epistemological relativism. His point, it should be stressed, is not to find some compromise, some safe middle ground between two extremes, but rather to correct a critical defect common to both: viz. the inability to ground standards of rational appraisal in the discursive procedures of inquiry itself. Both absolutism and relativism accept the assumption that criteria of reliable (objective) knowledge can only be formulated *within* the context of a single, permanent set of formal principles. Once the problem of objectivity has been posed in this way, only two alternatives stand open. (1) Evidence that cannot be made to conform to these criteria is rejected as subjective and on that basis excluded from the realm of reliable knowledge. This means that the 'facts' of social science are drained of their meaning content and reduced to brute data, with the result that the norm of objectivity sanctions the distortion of reality. This is the alternative of absolutism. (2) Evidence of different contexts of thought is taken to imply that the ideal of reliable knowledge is appropriately applied only to the boundaries of one's own framework, governed by one's own principles of understanding. This means that the possibility of objectivity with respect to cross-contextual judgements is relinquished altogether, and any attempt to compare or rationally appraise the 'facts' given by different standpoints is dismissed as untenable. This is the alternative of relativism. But because these 'options' share a common misconception about the nature and source of intellectual authority, each proves in the last analysis to partake of the defects of the other. On the one hand:

There is no more relativistic solution than that of a static philosophy of Reason which acknowledges a transcendence of values 'in themselves', and sees this transcendence guaranteed in the *form* of every concrete judgement, but relegates the material content of the judgement into the sphere of utter relativity—refusing to recognize in the actual historical cosmos of the realizations of value any principle of approximation to the transcendent values as such.[33]

On the other hand, acknowledgement of the historicity of thought 'becomes relativism only when it is linked with the older static ideal of eternal, unperspectivistic truths independent of the

---

[33] ESK, p. 128 (WAW, p. 301); cf. IAU, p. 87 (IUU, pp. 77–8).

subjective experience of the observer, and when it is judged by this alien ideal of absolute truth'.[34]

The assumption that rational procedures of inquiry require appeal to a static system of unchanging principles which establish a formal standard against which all thought must be appraised was very widely agreed to by Mannheim's contemporaries, and has remained one of the most significant shared assumptions of his critics. The grounds for Mannheim's rejection of such an approach to the problem of securing an impartial standpoint have rarely been given serious consideration. The position of a critic such as Dahlke, for instance, who insists that theoretical thinking is made 'valid in its own right' by virtue of its conformity to 'formal principles of reasoning [which] cannot be impeached by anyone, for they are the ground for any and all thinking whatsoever',[35] would be judged by Mannheim an unwarranted presumption of access to 'a superhuman, supertemporal sphere of validity'. Only by means of the investigation of 'the real factual thinking that we carry on in this world (which is the only kind of thinking known to us, and which is independent of this ideal sphere)', he believed, is it possible to find guidance in the adoption of a more adequate standpoint for the exercise of rational judgement.[36] The epistemo-logical legitimacy of such a position can be defended in two ways: by reference to some version of a pragmatist theory of truth, and by reference to the conclusions of historical inquiry into the nature of the scientific enterprise as it has been expressed, not in the formulations of philosophers, but in work of its practitioners. Arguments of both kinds are adumbrated in Mannheim's writings, but neither is presented in any sustained or systematic way. Only the most casual mention of pragmatism occurs in *Ideology and Utopia,* and his later scattered references to the arguments of this tradition suggest that he was unaware of the most significant contribution from this quarter, that of Peirce. As for the epistemological consequences of the history of scientific inquiry, it is obvious that (notwithstanding Mannheim's very keen interest in this line of argument) the most important and revealing research into such questions has been undertaken only in the period since his death. In commenting briefly on each of these areas I have no wish to imply that they settle the problem of the

---

[34] IAU, p. 300 (IUU, p. 258).
[35] Dahlke, 1940, p. 83.
[36] IAU, p. 298 (IUU, p. 256).

epistemological consequences of the sociology of knowledge but only to draw attention to the lines of inquiry which must be further pursued.

To point to the affinities between Mannheim's approach to the problem of objective knowledge and that developed in pragmatism is not at all novel; the connection has been widely recognized and commented upon.[37] But the defence of the methodological legitimacy of the sociology of knowledge on the grounds of a pragmatist theory of knowledge has been inhibited by the fact that pragmatism itself has been widely held to entail the same kind of unacceptable epistemological implications as have been charged to Mannheim. In part this results from the tendency to rely on versions of pragmatist epistemology, such as that to be found in the writings of James, in which the force of Peirce's original position is substantially diminished.[38] But it also reflects the application of the same formalistic criteria of adequacy that have been taken for granted in the positivist critique of Mannheim's method. This is evident, for instance, in the various papers of Hinshaw who argues that pragmatism and the sociology of knowledge are both guilty of having 'hypostatized such features of scientific inquiry as the approximative character of theories and the indefiniteness of empirical constructs into a theory of truth'.[39] Such an error, he believes, is a consequence of having failed to observe the elementary distinction between the problem of factual truth (which is a matter of relating a sign to its referent) and the problem of verification and belief (which is a matter of relating a sign to its user). Neither pragmatism nor the sociology of knowledge can have anything to say about the first problem, which concerns the 'correspondence between descriptive sentences and the facts to which they refer';[40] on the other hand, pragmatic concern with the use of concepts implicates only the question of what is *believed* to be true, never the question of what actually *is* true. We may, of course, never be certain about the latter; but the

---

[37] See, for instance, Wirth's preface to IAU, p. xviii; Merton, 1957, p. 508; Stark, 1958, pp. 326–8; and most significantly, Mills, 1963, pp. 453–68.

[38] Disturbed by what he considered a popularized distortion of his views, Peirce was moved in 1905 to rename his position 'pragmaticism', a term which he hoped to be 'ugly enough to be safe from kidnappers' (Peirce, 1934, 5.414; following convention, this and subsequent references to Peirce's papers will be by volume number and paragraph—not page—of his collected works).

[39] Hinshaw, 1944, p. 83.

[40] Hinshaw, 1948, p. 6.

fact 'that in actual practice one must be content with no more than successful prediction and control does not give licence for the epistemological identification of effectiveness in inquiry with truth'.[41]

Putting aside the difficulties raised by any non-question begging reference to the notion of 'correspondence', we can see that the heart of the problem raised by such an argument concerns the manner in which the notion of 'truth' can possibly function in inquiry. Neither Peirce nor Mannheim ever denies that 'there are Real things, whose characters are entirely independent of our opinions about them' nor that 'any man, if he have sufficient experience and he reason enough about it, will be led to the one True conclusion'.[42] What is denied, however, is that there can be any path to this Truth, or any warrant for it, other than that which emerges from the process of inquiry itself.

You only puzzle yourself by talking of this metaphysical 'truth' and metaphysical 'falsity,' that you know nothing about. All you have any dealings with are your doubts and beliefs, with the course of life that forces new beliefs upon you and gives you power to doubt old beliefs. If your terms 'truth' and 'falsity' are taken in such senses as to be definable in terms of doubt and belief and the course of experience (as for example they would be, if you were to define the 'truth' as that to a belief in which belief would tend if it were to tend indefinitely toward absolute fixity), well and good; in that case, you are only talking about doubt and belief. But if by truth and falsity you mean something not definable in terms of doubt and belief in any way, then you are talking of entities of whose existence you can know nothing, and which Ockham's razor would clean shave off. Your problems would be greatly simplified if, instead of saying that you want to know the 'Truth', you were simply to say that you want to attain a state of belief unassailable by doubt.[43]

To define truth in terms of a stable set of beliefs does not, then, mean the beliefs attendant upon the psychological state of one person but rather the set of beliefs which *would* ultimately be found if inquiry were pushed to its ultimate and indefeasible issue. It is precisely because of the social dimension of inquiry that truth cannot be equated with any personal or subjective state of mind of an individual.

Peirce's position coincides with Mannheim's in rejecting what has been called the 'foundation metaphor' of knowledge: the view

---

[41] Hinshaw, 1944, p. 91.
[42] Peirce, 1934, 5.384.
[43] Ibid., 5.416.

which represents the knower as a 'spectator' who escapes error by maintaining uncompromising fidelity to the principles of an absolute, rock-bottom foundation for all legitimate knowledge.[44] Peirce denies that knowledge does, or must, have any fixed foundation in such a sense. By placing the problem of epistemology in the context of the process of inquiry, he turns attention from the search for foundation principles to the conditions for resolving doubt. This is to acknowledge that

what you cannot in the least help believing is not, justly speaking, wrong belief. In other words, for you it is the absolute truth. True, it is conceivable that what you cannot help believing today, you might find you thoroughly disbelieve tomorrow. But then, there is a certain distinction between things you 'cannot' do, merely in the sense that nothing stimulates you to the great effort and endeavours that would be required, and things you cannot do because in their own nature they are insusceptible to being put into practice. In every stage of your excogitations, there is something of which you can only say, 'I cannot think otherwise', and your experientially based hypothesis is that the impossibility is of the second kind.[45]

The only substantive sense in which we can say 'I hold X to be true' is equivalent to saying 'I am unable to disbelieve X'. But this impossibility may, as the passage just cited points out, be either of two kinds. The first, since it admits the possibility of future doubt, cannot provide us with stable belief. The essence of the scientific method, on Peirce's account, consists of the attempt to exhaust this possibility: to make every conceivable 'effort and endeavour' to disbelieve, so that we maximize the probability that whatever we still 'cannot in the least help believing' is an impossibility of the second kind.[46]

The view of inquiry as a 'perpetual, critical, and self-corrective process', the image of man 'as a craftsman, as an active manipulator advancing new hypotheses, actively testing them, always open to ongoing criticism, and reconstructing himself and his environment', the ideal of a 'critical community of inquirers'[47] —all are themes that emerge again and again in Mannheim's writings. The individual social investigator can establish truth only in terms of a state of belief that permits the successful

[44] Bernstein, 1971, pp. 174–5.
[45] Peirce, 1934, 5.419.
[46] The approach to the problem of truth introduced by Peirce has, of course, been both vulgarized and refined in an extensive literature; see, for an important recent contribution, the work of Rescher, 1973, 1976, especially his distinction between a 'thesis pragmatism' and a 'methodological pragmatism'.
[47] Bernstein, 1971, pp. 313–14.

resolution of historically specific problematic stituations.[48] Any one of these situations is necessarily defined in terms of a particular perspectival position: inquiry must begin somewhere, we cannot question all claims at the same time. But any such 'truth' is vulnerable to the extent that the problematic situation can be redefined in terms of another perspective. Although this vulnerability cannot be removed in an absolute sense (by referring to some perspective-free foundation), it can be continually reduced by the process of inquiry itself: i.e. by methods of investigation that subject one's own perspective to the critique that is implied by the existence of other perspectives, and that endeavour in this way to overcome such limitations upon objectivity as may be brought about by a restricted horizon of vision. The epistemological conclusions that are to be drawn from Mannheim's work conform, then, rather closely to the counsel of Peirce's pragmatism: do not allow the 'quest for certainty' to overwhelm the capacity for doubt because it is the quality of the latter which provides the only test of any significance to the former. To allow any formal principle to block the path of inquiry or to insulate the investigator from challenge, even to his most trusted beliefs, is to weaken the authority of his conclusions. 'If we are to secure and warrant our knowledge claims, we do not do this by searching for absolute foundations or origins, but by cultivating those habits and forms of conduct that further the realization of the critical spirit.'[49]

A conclusion of this kind must also be considered to have been strengthened by the historical evidence, enormously enlarged in the period since Mannheim's death, respecting the procedures and the standards that have proven themselves effective in guiding the *practice* of science, even in the 'model' sciences of nature. By paying closer attention to the history of conceptual change than had an earlier generation of philosophers of science, writers such as Hanson, Kuhn, Toulmin, Lakatos, Feyerabend, have (in different ways) thoroughly called into question the picture of science that had been sponsored by the positivist rules of method accepted by Mannheim's contemporaries. The general conclusion of such work seems to be that most earlier accounts of scientific procedure have

---

[48] IAU, pp. 95–7 (IUU, pp. 83–6).
[49] Bernstein, 1971, p. 314. A more comprehensive perspective from which to consider these comments on Mannheim and Peirce is provided in the writings of Apel and Habermas on pragmatism and the hermeneutical *Geisteswissenschaften:* see esp. Apel, 1967, pp. 15n., 20, and *passim;* Habermas, 1971a, part II.

misrepresented the character even of natural scientific enterprise because 'they have regarded as paradigms of physical inquiry not unsettled, dynamic, research sciences like microphysics, but finished systems, planetary mechanics, optics, electromagnetism and classical thermodynamics'.[50] Such concentration on completed, even idealized systems has been responsible for a serious distortion of perception, for the problem of the rationality of science came to be understood in terms of the way its accomplishments could be justified after the fact rather than in terms of the intellectual procedures by which those theoretical propositions were arrived at in the first place. Careful historical investigation of the scientific enterprise, and especially of those occasions when a set of beliefs or concepts is given up and replaced or revised, reveals that the most hallowed imperatives of the 'reconstructed logic'[51] of Scientific Method are often violated with impunity in its practice; that, indeed, such violation may even be 'reasonable *and absolutely necessary* for the growth of knowledge'.[52]

In spite—or even because—of the fact that the new literature on the history and philosophy of science has proven so challenging and so fashionable, we should resist the temptation to draw sweeping conclusions for the methods of the *Geisteswissenschaften;* the general consequences of these developments remain in considerable dispute, and many of the more radical arguments remain inchoate. None the less, much of what Mannheim's critics have taken for granted in dismissing his claims can no longer, even on their own terms, be so taken. Mannheim never accepted, of course, the authority of the models of procedure used by the physical sciences in legislating methods for the human studies. But the fact that such rules of procedure as his positivist critics found violated by the sociology of knowledge appear to be inadequate even to the practice of the natural sciences surely weakens whatever force such 'imported standards' of adequacy may have been supposed to possess. The more important consequence, however, of the new sophistication in accounts of intellectual development and conceptual change is the encouragement it may provide to accept rather than ridicule Mannheim's challenge to find an alternative to both absolutism and relativism in

[50] Hanson, 1958, p. 1.
[51] This term is from Kaplan, 1964, p. 6.
[52] Feyerabend, 1970, p. 22.

determining standards of rationality and the appropriate procedures of inquiry. Such an attempt is undertaken, for instance, in a most ambitious way in Toulmin's inquiries into *Human Understanding*.[53] In the first of a projected three volumes, he shows that twentieth-century philosophy has indeed treated the epistemological alternatives which Mannheim found so unsatisfactory as if they were the only possible ways of dealing with the problem posed by the diversity of thought. On one hand, he observes, 'the absolutist treats the actual diversity of men's concepts and beliefs as a superficial matter, behind which the philosopher must find fixed and enduring principles of rationality, reflecting the pure, idealized forms of concepts'. On the other hand, the relativist 'abandons the attempt to judge impartially between different cultures or epochs, and treats the notion of "rationality" as having no more than a local, temporary application'. Taking the positions of Frege and Collingwood as representative of such tendencies, Toulmin shows how positions which at first appear to be polar alternatives turn out to share a central and mistaken assumption:

Frege's absolutism and Collingwood's relativism both construe the demand for a universal impartial standpoint of rational judgement as calling for a system of objective or absolute standards of rational criticism. The absolutist asserts that, on a sufficiently abstract, quasi-mathematical level, such standards can still be formulated as 'eternal principles'; while the relativist simply denies that any such standpoint can have any universal validity. And this same common assumption prevents both men from coming to terms with the rationality of conceptual change.

If neither of these alternatives is satisfactory, we are obliged to question the appropriateness of their common supposition that objectivity must be formulated in terms of a *fixed system* of standards: we must 'reject the commitment to logical systematicity which makes absolutism and relativism appear the only alternatives available'. In fact, Toulmin concludes, it was always a mistake to suppose

that the rational ambitions of any historically developing intellectual activity can be understood entirely in terms of the propositional or conceptual systems in which its intellectual content may be expressed at one or another time. Questions of 'rationality' are concerned, precisely, not with the particular intellectual doctrines that a man—or professional group—adopts at any given time, but rather with *the conditions on which, and the manner in which, he*

---

[53] Toulmin, 1972. I should perhaps note that Toulmin's arguments are in no way dependent upon Mannheim's, and make no reference to him.

is prepared to criticize and change those doctrines as time goes on.[54]

Properly construed, the problem of objectivity concerns not the adoption of this or that doctrine but the process of discursive and self-critical inquiry by means of which such conclusions are reached.

The affinity with Mannheim's position is obvious. Recognition of the social 'rootedness' of thought is always treated by him as the occasion for inquiry and not a substitute for it. Once the perspectival character of knowledge is acknowledged, we are in a position to press investigation beyond the limits of any particular conceptual context of meaning to a more inclusive position. The existence of alternative intellectual vantage points always denotes a problematic situation for the sociology of knowledge; inquiry must continually look toward the possibility of establishing a more comprehensive context, from which incongruent categories of understanding (if not differences of opinion) can be overcome.

The impetus to research in the sociology of knowledge may be so guided that it will not absolutize the concept of 'situational determination' [*Seinsverbunden-heit*]; rather, it may be directed in such a fashion that precisely by discovering the element of situational determination [*Seins*verbundenheit] in the views at hand, a first step will be taken towards the solution of the problem of situational determination [*Seins*gebundenheit] itself. As soon as I identify a view which sets itself up as absolute, as representing merely a given angle of vision, I neutralize its partial nature in a certain sense. Most of our earlier discussion of this problem moved quite spontaneously in the direction of the neutralization of situational determination [*Seinsgebundenheit*] by attempting to rise above it. The idea of the continuously broadening basis of knowledge, the idea of the continuous extension of the self and of the integration of various social vantage points into the process of knowledge—observations which are all based on empirical facts—and the idea of an all-embracing ontology which is to be sought for—all move in this direction.[55]

The ideal of objectivity is not to be secured *a priori* by the adoption of a set of principles 'valid in their own right', but by the continuous process of investigation and evaluation of opposing positions, a process which requires not only authentic access to the positions of others (and hence the interpretative reconstruction of their conceptual presuppositions) but also a critical and self-reflective grasp of the position that is one's own.

The problem is not how we might arrive at a non-perspectivistic picture but

---

[54] Ibid., pp. 53, 84. See also pp. 478–503, in which he gives some indication of how he intends to substantiate this position in the promised third volume of the work.
[55] IAU, pp. 301–2 (IUU, p. 259); cf. p. 27, n. 10, above.

how, by juxtaposing the various points of view, each perspective may be recognized as such and thereby a new level of objectivity attained. Thus we come to the point where the false ideal of a detached, impersonal point of view must be replaced by the ideal of an essentially human point of view which is within the limits of a human perspective, constantly striving to enlarge itself.[56]

The suitability of such a standard of objectivity is confirmed by the history of inquiry itself.[57] An it would seem, after all, not naïve but entirely prudent for a scientist to proceed as if he were a man rather than a god; this, above all else, is what Mannheim recommended with the sociology of knowledge.

III

It should be clear that there is nothing defensive or diffident about Mannheim's approach to the problem of objectivity in the human studies. His rejection of any self-absolutizing standards of 'Scientific Method' in favour of the interpretative and self-reflective procedures of the sociology of knowledge expresses neither scepticism nor naïvety but rather a careful and deliberate attempt to ground social knowledge in the discursive process of inquiry itself. The fact that such an effort admits self-referential application is a strength, not a weakness, of his position, for it affirms the critical powers of reason even against the privileged sanctuary of one's own, most cherished, presuppositions. Alvin Gouldner has well described the ideal of rationality on which such a vision of social theory is based:

Rationality is here construed as the capacity to make problematic what had hitherto been treated as given; to bring into reflection what before had only been used; to transform resource into topic; to examine critically the life we lead. This view of rationality situates it in the capacity to think *about* our thinking. Rationality as reflexivity about our own groundings premises an ability to speak about our speech and factors that ground it. Rationality is thus located in metacommunication.[58]

But a standard of reason which questions all standpoints threatens to bring with it a thorough-going political quietism: from what position can the thought and the institutions of the observer's world be criticized and on what grounds can political action be undertaken if no position of privilege, no 'Archimedian point', is to be admitted against the social reality constituting that world?

[56] IAU, pp. 296–7 (IUU, p. 255).
[57] Cf. Diesing, 1972, pp. 160 ff., for a discussion of the concept of objectivity in relation to its uses in contemporary social science.
[58] Gouldner, 1976, p. 49.

How can we both affirm the *Seinsverbundenheit des Wissens* and also affirm the power of thought to stand in judgement of that being, to negate it by delineating the path through which it might be transformed?

Questions of this sort have been the concern of Mannheim's Marxist critics from the beginning. The 'transition from the theory of ideology to the sociology of knowledge' which he defended as the reflexive application and hence full realization of Marxist method was greeted, especially by the defenders of Third International orthodoxy, as the abandonment of any distinction between Marxist science and ideological mystification, between the 'social location' of the proletariat and that of the bourgeoisie, between true consciousness and false. The complacent assumption of many of Mannheim's non-Marxist readers that the sociology of knowledge was designed to turn Marxism against itself was often accepted, on the Marxist side, as confirmation of Mannheim's anti-revolutionary and apologetic intent. To the extent that Marxist criticism of the sociology of knowledge has merely reproduced the strictures against relativism which preoccupied his non-Marxist critics, any further discussion of the issue would be redundant. It is evident, however, that the problem of standards of truth shows a new dimension when considered from the perspective of a critical social theory and an activist interest in an emancipatory politics, and that this dimension is precisely what is lacking in the epistemological concerns of positivism. Thus the most significant Marxist challenges to Mannheim are to be found in the work of those who share his hostility to the positivist programme for an objectivist social science. 'It is certainly true', Marcuse argued in a representative essay, written in the thirties, 'that many philosophical concepts are mere "foggy ideas" arising out of the domination of existence by an uncontrolled economy and, accordingly, are to be explained precisely by the material conditions of life.'

But in its historical forms philosophy also contains insights into human and objective conditions whose truth points beyond previous society and thus cannot be completely reduced to it.... Their truth content, which surmounts their social conditioning, presupposes not an eternal consciousness that transcendentally constitutes the individual consciousness of historical subjects but only those particular historical subjects whose consciousness expresses itself in critical theory. It is only with and for this consciousness that the 'surpassing' content becomes visible in its real truth. The truth that it recognizes in philosophy is not reducible to existing social conditions. This would be the case only in a form of existence where consciousness is no longer separated from being, enabling the rationality of thought to proceed from the rationality of social existence. Until then truth that is more than the truth of what is can be attained and intended only in opposition to established social relations. To this negative condition, at least, it is subject.[59]

The claim that Mannheim's sociology of knowledge is incapable of intending a truth 'that is more than the truth of what is' and indeed (as is brought out more emphatically in the much harsher discussions of Horkheimer, Adorno, and Lukács) that it must be counted a deliberate effort to obstruct and occlude such a critical standard of truth is a claim of many parts, and it is necessary to differentiate between such tendencies toward political accommodation as may be found in Mannheim's own political make-up and those which are endemic to his approach to the sociology of knowledge. It should be obvious that Mannheim's work presents neither a version of nor an alternative to Marxism. His own political stance (a rather cautious mixture of social democratic and liberal predispositions) and his view of Marxism (which, in spite of the benefit of his readings of Lukács, never seems to have grown much beyond the shallow and faintly condescending attitudes expressed in his early lecture) are of little consequence to an evaluation of the critique of political economy or the theory of capitalist development made possible by Marx. Nor can his protestations against the tendency of positivist social science to turn the norm of objectivity into political quietism and his defence of the viewpoint 'which regards knowledge not as passive contemplation but as critical self-examination, and in this sense prepares the road for political action'[60] be taken as sufficient to settle the question which Marcuse (and critics of like persuasion) have raised about his position. The relevant problem (which can only be finally resolved by reference to the consequences at the level of praxis to which such investigations lead) concerns the critical resources of *any* method that affirms a 'general' conception of ideology. The question, in other words, is whether the reflexive standard of reason required by a sociology of knowledge must, of its own weight, collapse rationality into rationalization.

A variety of considerations, which concern Mannheim's hermeneutics, his pragmatism, his concept of totality, may be

---

[59] Marcuse, 1968, pp. 148–9. See also the essays by Marcuse, Horkheimer, and Adorno in Lenk, 1961, pp. 209–17, 236–63; Adorno, 1967, pp. 37–49; Lukács, 1962, pp. 549–56; and the discussion in Jay, 1974, and Meja, 1975.

[60] IAU, p. 191 (IUU, p. 167).

thought to lead to such a conclusion. Thus a hermeneutic method may be held to imply, from the outset, an attitude of uncritical accommodation of opposing and alternative points of view. The ethos which counsels suspension of one's own conceptual context in the interest of grasping the position of others may seem to invite an abdication of all responsibility to judge, and to lead to a complacent acceptance of the maxim which supposes that *tout comprendre c'est tout pardonner*. Mannheim himself draws attention, in his essay on conservatism, to the corrupting consequences (much in evidence in nineteenth-century romanticism) of 'the tendency to interpret, or understand "from within", causally interrelated situations which, by their objective nature, are incapable of such interpretation, and to dignify mean and brutal power relationships by "interpreting" them'.[61] But the interpretative procedures of the sociology of knowledge clearly take a different form altogether. The point of investigating the socio-historical context of meaningful expression is not, as we have seen, to mystify or romanticize what is 'impenetrable' in thought but precisely the opposite: to make undistorted and competent communication possible. This means that the hermeneutic interest, however, essential, is still only a preliminary moment in a larger communicative interest; 'an analysis based on the sociology of knowledge', Mannheim writes, 'is a first preparatory step leading to direct discussion'.[62] To treat this 'preparatory step' as a *substitute* for direct discussion would be to make the entire enterprise senseless. Mannheim's desire to overcome the condition of 'talking past one another' denotes a commitment not to accommodation but to engagement. Separated from comprehension, he insists, critique becomes wholly vacuous. The sociology of knowledge is necessary precisely so that the issue may be joined: it must be employed 'wherever, because of the absence of a common basis of thought, there is no common problem'.[63] The fact that the consideration of alternative viewpoints is necessarily a self-reflective process and that the challenge intended in discourse is reciprocated does not negate but rather confirms the method's critical intent. To gain access to an alternative context of meaning

---

[61] FKM, p. 187n. (WAW, p. 460n.).
[62] IAU, p. 285 (IUU, p. 244).
[63] IAU, p. 281 (IUU, p. 241). The German is stronger than the translation here, speaking of the absence not merely of a common 'problem' but of a common 'thing' (*Sache*).

is to make possible a critical and transcendent relation to the *status quo*. Thus the hermeneutic moment makes critical thought possible because it makes discourse possible; as long as the phenomenon of 'talking past one another' is not overcome, criticism remains imprisoned in a solipsistic self-certainty, and the consequence of this condition (whether it take the form of cynical passivity or of a dogmatic and manipulative activism) cannot but be destructive of a genuinely emancipatory praxis.[64]

In refusing to locate the ground of truth in the perspective given to any attained socio-historical location, even that of the proletariat, Mannheim defends a view which is consistent with the one taken by his Frankfurt cirtics. He is no more willing than Marcuse to delimit the 'true' by what is merely actual. But the standard from which the world as it appears to us can be rejected as 'untrue' is a standard that can only be determined in the discursive process of inquiry itself: it is in this sense, as we have seen, a pragmatic standard of truth. Now in its vulgar form, such an epistemology may itself be thought to undermine any critical competence. 'Pragmatism', Horkheimer wrote in his *Eclipse of Reason,* 'reflects a society that has no time to remember and meditate' and it sponsors a mindless celebration of practical activity in which 'truth is to be desired not for its own sake but in so far as it works best, as it leads us to something that is alien or at least different from truth itself'.[65] When interpreted according to such a framework, the sociology of knowledge appears to sponsor the most abject submission of thought to the power of whatever is historically given; thus, it is alleged,

according to Mannheim, fascism can be 'true,' that is, non-ideological, if it provides a realistic orientation toward life in a fascist country. In Mannheim's theory, existing reality is taken for granted. It is thus considered as a status quo to which people have to conform, regardless of the nature of the given political arrangements.[66]

Yet such an attribution is obviously utter misrepresentation: Mannheim says no such thing and nothing he does say leads to such a conclusion. 'Existing reality', as we have seen, is precisely what Mannheim refuses to take for granted. The pragmatic criterion of validity is an *ultimate* one: it points to the most

---

[64] We only touch here on issues that are explored at length in the recent literature on Critical Theory and Hermeneutics, and in particular in Habermas's critique of Gadamer. Cf. Apel, *et al.,* 1971; Bubner, Cramer, and Wiehl, 1970; Misgeld, 1976.
[65] Horkeimer, 1947, pp. 44–5.
[66] Kruger, 1969, p. 153.

comprehensive outcome of the discursive interaction of opposing perspectives, and it repudiates any attempt (in the name of scientific or in the name of political authority) to abrogate this process. Truth is, certainly, tied to reality but reality itself (as Mannheim never tires of pointing out) must be grasped as a dynamic historical entity which includes not merely whatever the current moment presents as 'given' but also that which stands to be realized, adumbrated in the categories of utopian thought. 'If the proof of the pudding is in the eating,' Horkheimer himself pointed out in his seminal essay on critical theory, 'the eating here is still in the future.'[67]

Here may be found the significance of Mannheim's concern with 'totality'. If the standard of 'truth' is to have the power to point beyond that diminished and distorted presentation of reality which is given to a single socio-historical location of thought, then it must hold forth the promise of a more comprehensive perspective. Rejection of the relativistic doctrine of the incommensurability of alternative historical contexts of meaning implies, as Mannheim puts it, that we 'constantly seek to understand and interpret particular insights from an ever more inclusive context'. The hermeneutic and self-reflective procedures of the sociology of knowledge escape relativism by affirming the standard of a single truth, the framework of a total view, by reference to which the partiality of any single conceptual context can be criticized and transcended. Such a principle of 'totality' is always a norm: it is the ultimate issue of the unrestricted process of inquiry, and thus it must be conceived not as a 'super-temporally valid conclusion' to be secured finally and dogmatically in any fixed set of principles but rather as 'the broadest possible extension of our horizon of vision'.[68] Thus, Mannheim writes, 'nothing really occurs in the sociology of knowledge but that we let also our own location of thought, which has become critical, encounter us in the form of a report on the situation and penetrate contexts with an intention directed toward totality'.[69]

This 'intention directed toward totality' has also been taken, by some of Mannheim's Marxist critics, as indicative of political acquiescence. 'Mannheim's use of the concept of the social totality', Adorno writes, 'serves not so much to emphasize the

---

[67] Horkheimer, 1972, pp. 220–1.
[68] IAU, pp. 105, 106 (IUU, pp. 92–3).
[69] IUU, p. 93 (This is abbreviated somewhat in the English version, IAU, p. 107.)

intricate dependence of men within the totality as to glorify the social process itself as an evening-out of the contradictions in the whole.'[70] On this account, the sociology of knowledge substitutes for truth the standard of a thoroughly idealistic psuedo-harmony of contradictory interests, of the kind that Marx had attacked in his 1843 notebooks on Hegel's doctrine of the state. But Mannheim's insistence on 'synthesis' of opposing contexts of meaning has quite a different significance. It is, in the first place, a 'dynamic synthesis' which represents not an achieved harmony of the present but rather 'a problem which must continually be reformulated and resolved' as the process of critical inquiry advances.[71] And it is, in the second place, a synthesis not of all opposing *ideas* (in a sense which intends to 'overcome' all contradictions by revealing an underlying harmony of interest hidden within every viewpoint) but rather a synthesis of *conceptual contexts.* The standard of a 'total view' implies not that all claims, all interests, all doctrines can be reconciled; it does imply that they can be communicated, compared, criticized, and hence discursively appraised.[72]

Thus the problem of critique at the level of political practice can be seen to reproduce the theoretical problematic discussed earlier. Mannheim's espousal of interpretative and self-reflective investigation of the *Seinsverbundenheit des Wissens,* his defence of pragmatic criteria of adequacy in the appraisal of conflicting standpoints, and his insistence that these criteria anticipate a viewpoint of 'totality' in which a universal community of inquirers have managed to overcome the 'talking past one another' of distorted communication, all have as their goal a democratic science of society, in which the authority of knowledge is won rather than imposed. Such a goal requires, above all, the rejection of any attempt to treat human beings according to the fixed opposition of those regarded as 'subjects' and those treated as 'objects', those who observe and those who are observed, those who act and those

---

[70] Adorno, 1967, p. 38. Cf. the similar critical obervations of Marcuse in Lenk, 1961, p. 212; Kosik, 1967, pp. 35–6.

[71] IAU, p. 151 (IUU, p. 132).

[72] The model of communicative competence (and its epistemological underpinnings) developed in the recent work of Habermas puts Mannheim's problem into a much clearer light; the constructive reconsideration of the sociology of knowledge in relation to this work, however, clearly must await another occasion. See especially Habermas 1971; 1973; 1975, part III; 1976 for an exceedingly interesting investigation of the problem of (as he puts it) a 'universal pragmatics'.

who are acted upon. The sociology of knowledge is a hermeneutic and self-reflective method because it has as its ultimate aim the self-understanding not only of a community of scientists, or of believers, or of countrymen, or of fellow-travellers, but of the human community as a whole.

These brief comments on the critical capacity of the sociology of knowledge only begin, of course, to touch on a series of questions that have received renewed attention in the literature that has appeared, on both sides of the Atlantic, over the past twenty years. The arguments that Mannheim offered (tentatively and not always very coherently) during the twenties often seem to deliver us directly to the doorstep of the most interesting and suggestive contemporary efforts to reappraise and restructure social theory.[73] Thus the questions that have been taken up, in this chapter and in those that have preceded it, must be pursued in the work of Kuhn and Toulmin, MacIntyre and Winch, Hampshire and Taylor, Skinner and Searle, Ricoeur and Gadamer, Apel and Habermas. Such is not the task of a book on Mannheim, but it is one which a rereading of his investigations should encourage.

[73] See the masterful overview of these developments in Bernstein, 1976.

Bibliography of Mannheim's Published Work

I   *Lélek és Kultura*. Programmelôadás a II. szemeszter megnyitása alkalmából tartotta (Benkô, Budapest, 1918).
     'Seele und Kultur', trans. Ernest Manheim, WAW, pp. 66–84.

II   'Besprechung von G. Lukács, *Die Theorie des Romans. Ein geschichtsphilosophischer Versuch über die Formen der grossen Epik*', *Logos* 9 (1920–1): 298–302.
     Reprinted in WAW, pp. 85–90.
     'A Review of Georg Lukács' *Theory of the Novel*', trans. Kurt H. Wolff, *Studies on the Left* 3 (1963): 50–3.
     Reprinted in FKM, pp. 3–7.

III 'Beiträge zur Theorie der Weltanschauungs-Interpretation', *Jahrbuch für Kunstgeschichte* 1 (1921–2): 236–74.
     Reprinted in WAW, pp. 91–154.
     'On the Interpretation of Weltanschauung', trans. Paul Kecskemeti, ESK, pp. 33–83.
     Reprinted in FKM, pp. 8–58.

IV   'Zum Problem einer Klassifikation der Wissenschaften', *Archiv für Sozialwissenschaft und Sozialpolitik* 50 (1922): 230–7.
     Reprinted in WAW, pp. 155–65.

V   *Die Strukturanalyse der Erkenntnistheorie*. Kant-Studien, Ergänzungsheft no. 57, (Reuther und Reichard, Berlin, 1922).
     Reprinted in WAW, pp. 166–245.
     'Structural Analysis of Epistemology', trans. Edith Schwarzschild and Paul Kecskemeti, ESSP, pp. 15–73.

VI   'Historismus', *Archiv für Sozialwissenschaft und Sozialpolitik* 52 (1924): 1–60.
     Reprinted in WAW, pp. 246–307.
     'Historicism', trans. Paul Kecskemeti, ESK, pp. 84–133.

VII 'Das Problem einer Soziologie des Wissens', *Archiv für Sozialwissenschaft und Sozialpolitik* 53 (1925): 577–652.
     Reprinted in WAW, pp. 308–87.
     'The Problem of a Sociology of Knowledge', trans. Paul Kecskemeti, ESK, pp. 134–90.
     Reprinted in FKM, pp. 59–115.

VIII   'Ideologische und soziologische Interpretation der geistigen Gebilde', *Jahrbuch für Soziologie* 2 (1926): 424–40.
Reprinted in WAW, pp. 388–407.
'The Ideological and the Sociological Interpretation of Intellectual Phenomena', trans. Kurt H. Wolff, *Studies on the Left* 3 (1963): 54–66.
Reprinted in FKM, pp. 116–31.

IX   'Das konservative Denken. Soziologische Beiträge zum Werden des politisch-historischen Denkens in Deutschland', *Archiv für Sozialwissenschaft und Sozialpolitik* 57 (1927): 68–142, 470–95.
Reprinted in WAW, pp. 408–508.
'Conservative Thought', trans. Karl Mannheim and Paul Kecskemeti, ESSP, pp. 74–164.
Reprinted in FKM, pp. 132–222.

X   'Das Problem der Generationen', *Kölner Vierteljahrshefte für Soziologie* 7 (1928): 157–85, 309–30.
Reprinted in WAW, pp. 509–65, 703–5.
'The Problem of Generations', trans. Paul Kecskemeti, ESK, pp. 276–322.

XI   'Die Bedeutung der Konkurrenz im Gebiete des Geistigen', *Verhandlungen des sechsten deutschen Soziologentages vom 17. bis 19. September 1928 in Zürich* (Mohr, Tübingen, 1929), pp. 35–83.
Reprinted (with omissions) in WAW, pp. 566–613.
'Competition as a Cultural Phenomenon', trans. Paul Kecskemeti, ESK, pp. 191–229.

XII   'Zur Problematik der Soziologie in Deutschland', *Neue Schweizer Rundschau* 22 (1929): 820–9.
Reprinted in WAW, pp. 614–24.
'Problems of Sociology in Germany', trans. Kurt H. Wolff, FKM, pp. 262–70.

XIII   *Ideologie und Utopie* (Cohen, Bonn, 1929).
Ideology and Utopia, trans. Louis Wirth and Edward Shils [with a new introductory chapter by Mannheim and a translation of XV, below] (Routledge & Kegan Paul, London, and Harcourt, Brace, New York, 1936).
Reprinted in paper edition (Harvest, New York, n.d.).
Detailed table of contents for original German edition, trans. Kurt H. Wolff, FKM, pp. lxii–lxv.
Ideologie und Utopie, 3rd enl. ed. [adds material original to English edition, trans. Heinz Maus] (Schulte-Bulmke, Frankfurt, 1952).

XIV   'Über das Wesen und die Bedeutung des wirtschaftlichen Erfolgsstrebens. Ein Beitrag zur Wirtschaftssoziologie', *Archiv für Sozialwissenschaft und Sozialpolitik* 63 (1930): 449–512.
Reprinted in WAW, pp. 625–87, 705–10.

'On the Nature of Economic Ambition and Its Significance for the Social Education of Man', trans. Paul Kecskemeti, ESK, pp. 230–75.

XV   'Wissenssoziologie', *Handwörterbuch der Soziologie,* ed. Alfred Vier-kandt (Enke, Stuttgart, 1931), pp. 659–80.
          'The Sociology of Knowledge', trans. Louis Wirth and Edward Shils, IAU, ch. 5.

XVI   *Die Gegenwartsaufgaben der Soziologie: ihre Lehrgestalt* (Mohr, Tübingen, 1932).
          Brief excerpts are translated by Kurt H. Wolff in FKM, pp. lxxvii ff.

XVII   'American Sociology. Review of Stuart A. Rice, ed. *Methods in Social Science* (Chicago: University of Chicago Press, 1931)', *American Journal of Sociology* 37 (1932): 273–82.
          Reprinted in ESSP, pp. 185–94.

XVIII   'German Sociology (1918–1933)', *Politica* 1 (1934): 12–33.
          Reprinted in ESSP, pp. 209–28.

XIX   *Rational and Irrational Elements in Contemporary Society* (Oxford University Press, London, 1934).
          Reprinted, in expanded form, in XXI below.

XX   'The Crisis of Culture in the Era of Mass-Democracies and Autarchies', *Sociological Review* 26 (1934): 105–29.
          Reprinted, in expanded form, in XXI, below.

XXI   *Mensch und Gesellschaft im Zeitalter des Umbaus* [includes XIX and XX, above, in expanded form] (Sijthoff, Leiden, 1935).
          Man and Society in an Age of Reconstruction, rev. and enl. by the author, trans. Edward Shils [includes, in addition to the material in the German edition, XXV and XXVI, below, in expanded from] (Routledge & Kegan Paul, London, 1940).
          Short excerpt reprinted in FKM, pp. 347–9.

XXII   'Troeltsch, Ernst', *Encyclopedia of the Social Sciences,* ed. Edwin R. A. Seligman (Macmillan, New York, 1935), vol. 15.

XXIII   'Utopia', *Encyclopedia of the Social Sciences,* ed. Edwin R. A. Seligman (Macmillan, New York, 1935), vol. 15.

XXIV   'The Place of Sociology', *The Social Sciences: Their Relations in Theory and in Teaching* (Le Play House, London, 1936).
          Reprinted in ESSP, pp. 195–208.

XXV   'The Psychological Aspect', *Peaceful Change: An International Problem,* ed. C. A. W. Manning (Macmillan, London, 1937), pp. 101–32.
          Reprinted, in expanded form, in English edition of XXI, above.

XXVI   'Present Trends in the Building of Society', trans. H. Lewis, *Human Affairs,* ed. R. B. Cattell, J. I. Cohen, R. M. W. Travers (Macmillan, London, 1937), pp. 278–300.
Reprinted, in expanded form, in English edition of XXI, above.

XXVII   'The Sociology of Human Valuations: The Psychological and Sociological Approach', *Further Papers on the Social Sciences, Their Relations in Theory and Teaching,* ed. J. E. Dugdale (Le Play House, London, 1937), pp. 171–91.
Reprinted in ESSP, pp. 231–42.

XXVIII   Untitled, *Prager Presse* (28 March 1937).
'Mannheim's Answer to a Newspaper Poll (1937)', trans. Kurt H. Wolff, FKM, pp. cv–cvi.

XXIX   'Zur Diagnose unserer Zeit', *Mass und Wert* 1 (1937): 100–21.
'On the Diagnosis of Our Time', trans. Kurt H. Wolff, FKM, pp. 350–66.

XXX   'Adult Education and the Social Sciences', *Tutor's Bulletin of Adult Education,* 2nd ser. 20 (1938): 27–34.

XXXI   'Mass Education and Group Analysis', *Educating for Democracy,* ed. J. I. Cohen and R. M. W. Travers (Macmillan, London, 1939), pp. 329–64.
Reprinted in XXXIII, below.

XXXII   'Nazi Group Strategy', *The Listener* (19 June 1941): 877–8.
Reprinted in XXXIII, below.

XXXIII   *Diagnosis of Our Time: Wartime Essays of a Sociologist* [includes XXXI and XXXII, above] (Routledge & Kegan Paul, London, 1943).
Chap. 5 reprinted in FKM, pp. 367–84.

XXXIV   'Democratic Planning and the New Science of Society', *This Changing World,* ed. J. R. M. Brumwell (Routledge, London, 1944), pp. 71–82.

XXXV   'The Meaning of Popularisation in a Mass Society', *The Christian News-Letter,* supplement to no. 227 (7 February 1945), pp. 7–12.

XXXVI   'The Function of the Refugee: A Rejoinder', *The New English Weekly* 27 (19 April 1945): 5–6.

XXXVII   'Foreword' to *The Feminine Character: History of an Ideology,* by Viola Klein (Routledge & Kegan Paul, London, 1946), pp. vii–xiv.

XXXVIII   'Preface to the English Edition' of *A Handbook of Sociology,* by W. F. Ogburn (Routledge & Kegan Paul, London, 1947), p. xi.

XXXIX   *Essays on the Sociology of Culture,* ed. and trans. Ernest Manheim and
        Paul Kecskemeti (Routledge & Kegan Paul, London, 1956).
        Part III reprinted in FKM, pp. 271–346.

XL   'The History of the Concept of the State as an Organism', ESSP,
        pp. 165–82.

XLI   'Planned Society and the Problem of Human Personality: A
        Sociological Analysis', ESSP, pp. 253–310.

XLII   'On War-Conditioned Changes in Our Psychic Economy', ESSP,
        pp. 243–51.

XLIII   *Freedom, Power and Democratic Planning,* ed. Ernest K. Bramstead
        and Hans Gerth (Routledge & Kegan Paul, London, 1950).

XLIV   *Systematic Sociology: An Introduction to the Study of Society,* ed. J. S. Erös
        and W. A. C. Stewart (Grove, New York, 1957).

XLV   with W. A. C. Stewart, *An Introduction to the Sociology of Education*
        (Routledge & Kegan Paul, London, 1962).

List of Other Works Cited

ABEL, T. (1953): 'The Operation Called Verstehen', *Readings in the Philosophy of Science*, ed. H. Feigl and M. Brodbeck (Appleton-Century-Crofts, New York), pp. 677–87.

ADORNO, T. W. (1967): *Prisms*, trans. Samuel and Shierry Weber (Neville Spearman, London).

—— et al. (1976): *The Positivist Dispute in German Sociology*, trans. Glyn Adey and David Frisby (Heinemann, London).

ANSCOMBE, G. E. M. (1963): *Intention*, 2nd edn. (Basil Blackwell, Oxford).

APEL, K. O. (1967): *Analytic Philosophy of Language and the Geisteswissenschaften* (D. Reidel, Dordrecht).

—— et al. (1971): *Hermeneutik und Ideologiekritik* (Suhrkamp, Frankfurt).

ARON, R. (1964): *German Sociology*, trans. Mary and Thomas Bottomore (Free Press of Glencoe, New York).

AUSTIN, J. L. (1962): *How To Do Things With Words*, ed. J. O. Urmson (Harvard University Press, Cambridge).

AYER, A. J. (1969): 'Man as a Subject for Science', *Philosophy, Politics and Society*, third series, ed. P. Laslett and W. G. Runciman (Basil Blackwell, Oxford), pp. 6–24.

BELGION, M. (1945): 'The Germanization of Britain', *The New English Weekly* 26 (Feb.): 137–8.

BERGER, P. L. (1970): 'Identity as a Problem in the Sociology of Knowledge', *The Sociology of Knowledge: A Reader*, ed. J. E. Curtis and J. W. Petras (Gerald Duckworth, London), pp. 373–84.

—— and LUCKMANN, T. (1967): *The Social Construction of Reality: A Treatise in the Sociology of Knowledge* (Anchor Books, New York).

BERGMANN, G. (1968): 'Ideology', *Readings in the Philosophy of the Social Sciences*, ed. M. Brodbeck (Macmillan, New York), pp. 123–38.

BERNSTEIN, R. J. (1971): *Praxis and Action: Contemporary Philosophies of Human Activity* (University of Pennsylvania Press, Philadelphia).

—— (1976): *The Restructuring of Social and Political Theory* (Harcourt Brace Jovanovich, New York).

BOTTOMORE, T. B. (1956): 'Some Reflections on the Sociology of Knowledge', *The British Journal of Sociology* 7: 52–8.

BRECHT, A. (1959): *Political Theory* (Princeton University Press, Princeton).

BUBNER, R., CRAMER, K., and WIEHL, R., eds. (1970): *Hermeneutik und Dialektik* (2 vols., J. C. B. Mohr, Tübingen).

CHILD, A. (1941): 'The Problem of Imputation in the Sociology of Knowledge', *Ethics* 51: 200–19.

CIOFFI, F. (1963): 'Intention and Interpretation in Criticism', *Proceedings of the Aristotelian Society*, new series, 64: 85–106.

COLLINGWOOD, R. G. (1970): *An Autobiography* (Oxford University Press, London).

CONNOLLY, W. E. (1967): *Political Science and Ideology* (Atherton Press, New York).

CRICK, B. (1964): *In Defence of Politics*, rev. edn. (Penguin Books, Harmondsworth).

CURTIS, J. E., and PETRAS, J. W. (1970): *The Sociology of Knowledge: A Reader* (Gerald Duckworth, London).

DAHLKE, H. O. (1940): 'The Sociology of Knowledge', *Contemporary Social Theory*, ed. H. E. Barnes, H. Becker, and F. B. Becker (D. Appleton-Century, New York and London).

DE GRÉ, G. (1970): 'The Sociology of Knowledge and the Problem of Truth'. *The Sociology of Knowledge: A Reader* (Gerald Duckworth, London), pp. 661–7.

DIESING, P. (1972): 'Subjectivity and Objectivity in the Social Sciences', *Philosophy of the Social Sciences* 2: 147–65.

DILTHEY, W. (1962): *Pattern and Meaning in History: Thoughts on History and Society*, ed. H. P. Rickman (Harper Torchbook, New York).

DURKHEIM, E. (1964): *The Rules of Sociological Method*, 8th edn., trans. S. A. Solovay and J. H. Mueller (Free Press of Glencoe, New York).

EASTON, D. (1953): *The Political System: An Inquiry into the State of Political Science* (Alfred A. Knopf, New York).

FEYERABEND, P. K. (1970): 'Against Method: Outline of an Anarchist Theory of Knowledge', *Minnesota Studies in the Philosophy of Science: Vol. IV, Analyses of Theories and Methods of Physics and Psychology*, ed. M. Radner and S. Winokur (University of Minnesota Press, Minneapolis), pp. 17–130.

FUSE, TOYOMASA (1967): 'Sociology of Knowledge Revisited: Some Remaining Problems and Prospects', *Sociological Inquiry* 37: 241–53.

GABEL, J. (1974): *Idéologies* (Éditions Anthropos, Paris).

—— (1975): 'Hungarian Marxism', *Telos*, no. 25, pp. 185–91.

GADAMER, H. G. (1975): *Truth and Method* (Seabury Press, New York).

GAY, P. (1970): *Weimar Culture: The Outsider as Insider* (Harper Torchbooks, New York).

GELLNER, E. (1973): *Cause and Meaning in the Social Sciences* (Routledge & Kegan Paul, London).

GEWIRTH, A. (1954): 'Subjectivism and Objectivism in the Social Sciences', *Philosophy of Science* 21: 157–63.

GOMBRICH, E. H. (1969): *Art and Illusion:A study in the Psychology of Pictorial Representation*, 2nd edn. (Princeton University Press, Princeton).

GOULDNER, A. W. (1976): *The Dialectic of Ideology and Technology: The Origins, Grammar, and Future of Ideology* (The Seabury Press, New York).

GRICE, H. P. (1957): 'Meaning', *The Philosophical Review* 66: 377–88.

——(1969): 'Utterer's Meaning and Intentions', *The Philosophical Review* 78: 147–77.

GRÜNWALD, E. (1934): *Das Problem der Soziologie des Wissens: Versuch einer kritischen Darstellung der wissenssoziologischen Theorien* (Wilhelm Braunmüller, Vienna).

GUNNELL, J. G. (1968): 'Social Science and Political Reality: The Problem of Explanation', *Social Research* 35: 159–201.

GUNTHER, M., and RESHAUR, K. (1971): 'Science and Values in Political "Science" ', *Philosophy of the Social Sciences* 1: 113–121.

HABERMAS, J. (1971a): *Knowledge and Human Interests,* trans. J J. Shapiro (Beacon Press, Boston).

——(1971b): *Thoughts on the Foundation of Sociology in the Philosophy of Language: Six Lectures,* trans. J. J. Shapiro (Gauss Lectures, Princeton University).

——(1973): 'Wahrheitstheorien', *Wirklichkeit und Reflexion: Walter Schulz zum 60. Geburtstag* (Neske, Pfullingen), pp. 211–65.

—— (1975): *Legitimation Crisis,* trans. T. McCarthy (Beacon Press, Boston).

—— (1976): 'Was heisst Universalpragmatik?', *Sprachpragmatik und Philosophie,* ed. K. O. Apel (Suhrkamp, Frankfurt), pp. 174–272.

HACKER, A. (1954): *'Capital* and Carbuncles: The "Great Books" Reappraised', *American Political Science Review* 48: 775–86.

HAMPSHIRE, S. (1960): *Thought and Action* (The Viking Press, New York).

HANSON, N. R. (1958): *Patterns of Discovery: An Inquiry into the Conceptual Foundations of Science* (Cambridge University Press, Cambridge).

HARRÉ, R., and SECORD, P. F. (1972): *The Explanation of Social Behaviour* (Basil Blackwell, Oxford).

HARTUNG, F. E. (1970): 'Problems of the Sociology of Knowledge', *The Sociology Of Knowledge: A Reader* (Gerald Duckworth, London), pp. 686–703.

HEMPEL, C. G., and OPPENHEIM, P. (1953): 'The Logic of Explanation', *Readings in the Philosophy of Science,* ed. H. Feigl and M. Brodbeck (Appleton-Century-Crofts, New York), pp. 319–52.

HINSHAW, V. G. Jr. (1944): 'The Pragmatist Theory of Truth', *Philosophy of Science* 11: 82–92.

——— (1948): 'Epistemological Relativism and the Sociology of Knowledge', *Philosophy of Science* 15: 4–10.

HIRSCH, E. D. Jr. (1967): *Validity in Interpretation* (Yale University Press, New Haven and London).

—— (1976): *The Aims of Interpretation* (University of Chicago Press, Chicago).

HORKHEIMER, M. (1947): *Eclipse of Reason* (Oxford University Press, New York).

—— (1972): 'Traditional and Critical Theory', *Critical Theory: Selected Essays,* trans. M. J. O'Connell (The Seabury Press, New York).

HOROWITZ, I. L. (1960): 'Science, Criticism, and the Sociology of Knowledge', *Philosophy and Phenomenological Research* 21: 173–86.

—— (1961): *Philosophy, Science and the Sociology of Knowledge* (Charles C. Thomas, Springfield, Illinois).

—— (1964): 'A Formalization of the Sociology of Knowledge', *Behavioral Science* 9: 45–55.

HUGHES, H. S. (1961): *Consciousness and Society: The Reconstruction of European Social Thought 1890–1930* (Vintage Books, New York).

HUSSERL, E. (1970): *Logical Investigations,* trans. J. N. Findlay (2 vols., Routledge & Kegan Paul, London).

JARVIE, I. C. (1972): *Comcepts and Society* (Routledge & Kegan Paul, London and Boston).

JAY, M. (1973): *The Dialectical Imagination: A History of the Frankfurt School and the Institute of Social Research 1923-1950* (Little, Brown, Boston).

—— (1974): 'The Frankfurt School's Critique of Karl Mannhiem and the Sociology of Knowledge', *Telos*, no. 20, pp. 72–89.

KALLEBERG, A. L. (1972): 'Concept Formation in Normative and Empirical Studies: Toward Reconciliation in Political Theory', *Contemporary Analytical Theory*, ed. D. E. Apter and C. F. Andrain (Prentice-Hall, Englewood Cliffs), pp. 45–63.

KAPLAN, A. (1964): *The Conduct of Inquiry: Methodology for Behavioral Science* (Chandler, San Francisco).

KECSKEMETI, P. (1952): 'Introduction', *Essays on the Sociology of Knowledge by Karl Mannheim* (Routledge & Kegan Paul, London), pp. 1–32.

KETTLER, D. (1967): 'Sociology of Knowledge and Moral Philosophy: The Place of Traditional Problems in the Formation of Mannheim's Thought', *Political Science Quarterly* 82: 399–426.

—— (1971): 'Culture and Revolution: Lukács in the Hungarian Revolutions of 1918/19' *Telos*, no. 10, pp. 35–92.

—— (1976): 'Rhetoric and Social Science: Karl Mannheim Adjusts to the English-Speaking World' (paper prepared for the 1976 meetings of the American Sociological Association; typescript).

KEYNES, J. M. (1936): *The General Theory of Employment Interest and Money* (Macmillan, London).

KOSÍK, (1967): *Die Dialektik des Konkreten*, trans. M. Hoffmann (Suhrkamp, Frankfurt).

KRUGER, M. (1969): 'Sociology of Knowledge and Social Theory', *Berkeley Journal of Sociology* 14: 152–63.

KUHN, T. S. (1970): *The Structure of Scientific Revolutions*, 2nd edn. (University of Chicago Press, Chicago).

LAZARSFELD, P. F., and OBERSCHALL, A. R. (1965): 'Max Weber and Empirical Social Research', *American Sociological Review* 30: 185–98.

LEAVIS, F. R. (1953): 'The Responsible Critic: Or the Function of Criticism at Any Time', *Scrutiny* 19: 162–83.

LENK, K., ed. (1961): *Ideologie: Ideologiekritik und Wissenssoziologie* (Hermann Luchterhand, Neuwied).

LICHTHEIM, G. (1967): *The Concept of Ideology and Other Essays* (Vintage Books, New York).

LOUCH, A. R. (1963): 'The Very Idea of a Social Science', *Inquiry* 6: 273–86.

—— (1969): *Explanation and Human Action* (University of California Press, Berkeley and Los Angeles).

LUKÁCS, G. (1962): *Die Zerstörung der Vernunft* (*George Lukács Werke*, vol. 9), 2nd edn. (Hermann Luchterhand, Neuwied).

MACINTYRE, A. (1971): 'Is Science of Comparative Politics Possible?' *Against the Self-Images of the Age* (Schoken, New York), pp. 260–79.

MACPHERSON, C. B. (1964): *The Political Theory of Possessive Individualism: Hobbes to Locke* (Oxford University Press, London, Oxford, New York).

MAKKREEL, R. A. (1975): *Dilthey: Philosopher of the Human Studies* (Princeton University Press, Princeton).

MAQUET, J. J. (1951): *The Sociology of Knowledge: Its Structure and its Relation to the Philosophy of Knowledge*, trans. J. F. Locke (Beacon Press, Boston).

MARCUSE, H. (1968): *Negations: Essays in Critical Theory*, trans. J. J. Shapiro (Beacon Press, Boston).

MEILAND, J. W. (1970): *The Nature of Intention* (Methuen, London).

MEJA, V. (1975): 'The Sociology of Knowledge and the Critique of Ideology', *Cultural Hermeneutics* 3: 57–68.

MELDEN, A. I. (1961): *Free Action* (Routledge & Kegan Paul, London).

MERTON, R. K. (1957): *Social Theory and Social Structure*, rev. edn. (Free Press of Glencoe, Glencoe).

—— (1972): 'Insiders and Outsiders: A Chapter in the Sociology of Knowledge', *American Journal of Sociology* 78: 9–47.

MÉSZÁROS, I. (1972): *Lukács' Concept of Dialectic* (Merlin Press, London).

MILLER, E. F. (1972): 'Positivism, Historicism, and Political Inquiry', *American Political Science Review* 66: 796–817, 857–73.

MILLS, C. W. (1963): *Power, Politics and People: The Collected Essays of C. Wright Mills*, ed. I. L. Horowitz (Ballantine, New York).

MISGELD, D. (1976): 'Critical Theory and Hermeneutics: The Debate between Habermas and Gadamer', *On Critical Theory*, ed. John O'Neill (Seabury Press, New York), pp. 164–83.

MORGENBESSER, S. (1966): 'Is it a Science?', *Sociological Theory and Philosophical Analysis*, ed. D. Emmet and A. MacIntyre (Macmillan, London), pp. 20–33.

MUNCH, P. A. (1957): 'Empirical Science and Max Weber's *verstehende Soziologie*', *American Sociological Review* 22: 26–32.

NAGEL, E. (1963): 'Problems of Concept and Theory Formation in the Social Sciences', *Philosophy of the Social Sciences: A Reader*, ed. M. Natanson (Random House, New York), pp. 189–209.

NEISSER, H. (1965): *On the Sociology of Knowledge: An Essay* (James H. Heineman, New York).

PARSONS, T. (1936): 'Review of *Max Webers Wissenschaftslehre* by Alexander von Schelting', *American Sociological Review* 1: 675–81.

—— (1961): *Theories of Society: Foundations of Modern Sociological Theory* (Free Press of Glencoe, New York), vol. 2.

—— (1967): 'An Approach to the Sociology of Knowledge', *Sociological Theory and Modern Society* (Free Press, New York), pp. 139–65.

PEIRCE, C. S. (1934): *Collected Papers of Charles Sanders Peirce*, ed. C. Hartshorne and P. Weiss (Harvard University Press, Cambridge).

PITKIN, H. F. (1972): *Wittgenstein and Justice: On the Significance of Ludwig Wittgenstein for Social and Political Thought* (University of California Press, Berkeley, Los Angeles, and London).

POPPER, K. R. (1961): *The Poverty of Historicism* (Routledge & Kegan Paul, London).

—— (1963): *The Open Society and Its Enemies*, 4th edn. (2 vols., Harper Torchbooks, New York).

RADNITZKY, G. (1973): *Contemporary Schools of Metascience*, 3rd edn. (Henry Regnery, Chicago).

REMMLING, G. W. (1967): *Road to Suspicion: A Study of Modern Mentality and the Sociology of Knowledge* (Appleton-Century-Crofts, New York).

—— ed. (1973): *Towards the Sociology of Knowledge: Origin and Development of a Sociological Thought Style* (Humanities Press, New York).

—— (1975): *The Sociology of Karl Mannheim: with a Bibliographical Guide to the Sociology of Knowledge, Ideological Analysis, and Social Planning* (Routledge & Kegan Paul, London).

REMPEL, F. W. (1965): *The Role of Value in Karl Mannheim's Sociology of Knowledge* (Mouton, The Hague).

RESCHER, N. (1973): *The Coherence Theory of Truth* (Oxford University Press, Oxford).

—— (1977): *Methodological Pragmatism* (Basil Blackwell, Oxford).

REX, J. (1971): 'Typology and Objectivity: A Comment on Weber's Four Sociological Methods', *Max Weber and Modern Sociology*, ed. A. Sahay (Routledge & Kegan Paul, London), pp. 17–36.

RINGER, F. K. (1969): *The Decline of the German Mandarins: The German Academic Community, 1890–1933* (Harvard University Press, Cambridge).

RUNCIMAN, W. G. (1971): *Social Science and Political Theory*, 2nd edn. (Cambridge University Press, Cambridge).

—— (1972): *A Critique of Max Weber's Philosophy of Social Science* (Cambridge University Press, Cambridge).

SAHAY, A. (1971): 'The Importance of Weber's Methodology in Sociological Explanation', *Max Weber and Modern Sociology*, ed. A. Sahay (Routledge & Kegan Paul, London), pp. 67–81.

SALOMON, A. (1947): 'Karl Mannheim, 1893–1947', *Social Research* 14: 350–64.

SCHAAR, J. (1970): 'Legitimacy in the Modern State', *Power and Community: Dissenting Essays in Political Science*, ed. P. Green and S. Levinson (Vintage Books, New York), pp. 276–327.

SCHELTING, A. v. (1934): *Max Webers Wissenschaftslehre: Das logische Problem der historischen Kulturerkenntnis; Die Grenzen der Soziologie des Wissens* (J. C. B. Mohr, Tübingen).

—— (1936): 'Review of *Ideologie und Utopie*', *American Sociological Review* 1: 664–74.

SCHIFFER, S. R. (1972): *Meaning* (Clarendon Press, Oxford).

SCHUTZ, A. (1962): *Collected Papers I: The Problem of Social Reality*, ed. M. Natanson (Martinus Nijhoff, The Hague).

—— (1964): *Collected Papers II: Studies in Social Theory*, ed. A. Brodersen (Martinus Nijoff, The Hague).

—— (1966): *Collected Papers III: Studies in Pehnomenological Philosophy*, ed. I. Schutz (Matinus Nijhoff, The Hague).

—— (1967): *The Phenomenology of the Social World*, trans. G. Walsh and F. Lehnert (Northwestern University Press, Evanston).

SEARLE, J. R. (1969): *Speech Acts: An Essay in the Philosophy of Language* (Cambridge University Press, Cambridge).

SILVERS, S. (1967): 'On Our Knowledge of the Social World: A Note on Levinson's "Knowledge and Society"', *Inquiry* 10: 96–7.

SIMMEL, G. (1968): *The Conflict in Modern Culture and Other Essays,* trans. K. P. Etzkorn (Teachers College Press, New York).

—— (1971): *On Individuality and Social Forms: Selected Writings* ed. D. N. Levine (University of Chicago Press, Chicago and London).

SIMONDS, A. P. (1975): 'Mannheim's Sociology of Knowledge as a Hermeneutic Merhod', *Cultural Hermeneutics* 3: 81–104.

SKINNER, Q. (1969): 'Meaning and Understanding in the History of Ideas', *History and Theory* 8: 3–53.

—— (1970): 'Conventions and the Understanding of Speech Acts', *Philosophical Quarterly* 20: 118–38.

—— (1971): 'On Performing and Explaining Linguistic Actions', *Philosophical Quarterly* 21: 1–21.

—— (1972a): 'The Context of Hobbes's Theory of Political Obligation', *Hobbes and Rousseau: A Collection of Critical Essays,* ed. M. Cranston and R. S. Peters (Anchor Books, Garden City, New York), pp. 109–42.

—— (1972b): ' "Social Meaning" and the "Explanation of Social Action" ' in *Philosophy, Politics and Society,* fourth series, ed. P. Laslett, W. G. Runciman, and Q. Skinner (Basil Blackwell, Oxford), pp. 136–57.

—— (1972c): 'Motives, Intentions and the Interpretation of Texts', *New Literary History* 3: 393–408.

—— (1974a): 'The Principles and Practice of Opposition: The Case of Bolingbroke versus Walpole', *Historical Perspectives: Studies in English Thought and Society in Honour of J. H. Plumb,* ed. N. McKendrick (Europa, London), pp. 93–128

—— (1974b): 'Some Recent Problems in the Analysis of Political Thought and Action', *Political Theory* 2: 277–303.

SPEIER, H. (1970): 'The Social Determination of Ideas', *The Sociology of Knowledge: A Reader,* ed. J. E. Curtis and J. W. Petras (Gerald Duckworth, London), pp. 263–81.

STARK, W. (1958): *The Sociology of Knowledge: An Essay in Aid of a Deeper Understanding of the History of Ideas* (Routledge & Kegan Paul, London).

STEINER, G. (1975): *After Babel: Aspects of Language and Translation* (Oxford University Press, New York and London).

STRAWSON, P. F. (1970): *Meaning and Truth: An Inaugural Lecture delivered before the University of Oxford on 5 November 1969* (Clarendon Press, Oxford).

STRUVE, W. (1973): *Elites Against Democracy: Leadership Ideals in Bourgeois Political Thought in Germany, 1890–1933* (Princeton University Press, Princeton).

TAYLOR, C. (1964): *The Explanation of Behaviour* (Routledge & Kegan Paul, London).

—— (1967a): 'Teleological Explanation—A Reply to Denis Noble', *Analysis,* new series, 27: 141–3.

—— (1967b): 'Relations between Cause and Action', *Proceedings of the Seventh Inter-American Congress of Philosophy* (Les Presses de L'Université Laval, Québec), 1: 243–55.

—— (1970): 'The Explanation of Purposive Behaviour', *Explanation in the Behavioural Sciences,* ed. R. Borger and F. Cioffi (Cambridge University Press, Cambridge), pp. 49–79, 89–96.

—— (1971): 'Interpretation and the Sciences of Man', *The Review of Metaphysics* 25: 3–51.

—— (1973): 'Peaceful Coexistence in Psychology', *Social Research* 40: 55–82.

TILLICH, H. (1973): *From Time to Time* (Stein and Day, New York).

TŐKÉS, R. L. (1967): *Belá Kun and the Hungarian Soviet Republic: The Origins and Role of the Communist Party of Hungary in the Revolutions of 1918–1919* (Praeger, New York).

TONSER, S. J. (1968): 'Gnostics, Romantics and Conservatives', *Social Research* 35: 616–34.

TOULMIN, S. (1972): *Human Understanding* (Princeton University Press, Princeton), vol. 1.

TRIBE, L. H. (1972): 'Policy Science: Analysis or Ideology?' *Philosophy and Public Affairs* 2: 66–110.

WAGNER, H. R. (1952): 'Mannheim's Historicism', *Social Research* 19: 300–21.

WALTER, B. (1967): 'The Sociology of Knowledge and the Problem of Objectivity', *Sociological Theory: Inquiries and Paradigms,* ed. L. Gross (Harper & Row, New York), pp. 335–57.

WATKINS, J. W. N. (1956): 'Massification', *Spectator* 197: 258–9.

WEBER, M. (1958): *The Protestant Ethic and the Spirit of Capitalism,* trans. T. Parsons (Charles Scribner's Sons, New York).

—— (1963): '"Objectivity" in Social Science and Social Policy', trans. E. A. Shils and H. A. Finch, *Philosophy of the Social Sciences: A Reader,* ed. M. Natanson (Random House, New York), pp. 355–418.

—— (1964): *The Theory of Social and Economic Organization,* trans. A. M. Henderson and T. Parsons, ed. T. Parsons (Free Press, New York).

WIMSATT, W. K. Jr., and BEARDSLEY, M. C. (1954): 'The Intentional Fallacy', *The Verbal Icon: Studies in the Meaning of Poetry* (University of Kentucky Press, Lexington), pp. 3–18.

WINCH, P. (1958): *The Idea of a Social ScPence and its Relation to Philosophy* (Routledge & Kegan Paul, London).

—— (1964): 'Mr. Louch's Idea of a Social Science', *Inquiry* 7: 202–8.

WITTGENSTEIN, L. (1958): *Philosophical Investigations,* trans. G. E. M. Anscombe (Macmillan, New York).

WOLFF, K. H. (1963): 'Karl Mannheim on Interpretation: Introductory Notes', *Studies on the Left* 3: 45–9.

—— (1971): 'Introduction: A Reading of Karl Mannheim', *From Karl Mannheim* (Oxford University Press, New York), pp. xi–cxxxiii.

—— (1974): *Trying Sociology* (John Wiley, New York).

WOLIN, S. S. (1969): 'Political Theory as a Vocation', *American Political Science Review* 63: 1062–82.

WRIGHT, G. H. v. (1971): *Explanation and Understanding* (Cornell University Press, Ithaca).

Index